W9-ACS-079

The Rationing of Justice

ARNOLD S. TREBACH

RUTGERS UNIVERSITY PRESS New Brunswick, N.J.

The Rationing of Justice

Constitutional Rights and the Criminal Process

Permission to quote has been granted by the following publishers:

From ONE MAN'S FREEDOM by Edward Bennett Williams, copyright ©
1962 by Edward Bennett Williams, reprinted by permission of Atheneum
Publishers.

From "Account of a Field Study in the Rural Area of Representation
of Indigents Accused of the Crime" by Bertram F. Willcox and Edward J.
Bloustein in COLUMBIA LAW REVIEW, copyright 1959.

From NOT GUILTY by Jerome Frank and Barbara Frank, copyright ©
1957 by Barbara Frank, reprinted by permission of Doubleday & Company, Inc.

From CRIME AND SOCIETY by Nathaniel Cantor, copyright © 1939
by Henry Holt & Company.

From "Pleading Guilty for Considerations: A Study of Bargain Justice"
by Donald J. Newman in JOURNAL OF CRIMINAL LAW, CRIMI-
NOLOGY AND POLICE SCIENCE, copyright 1956.

From address by William B. Neeley in DEFENDER SECTION: COL-
LECTION OF PAPERS, copyright © 1956 by National Legal Aid &
Defender Association.

From CRIMINAL PROCEDURE FROM ARREST TO APPEAL by Lester
Orfield, copyright © 1947 by Oceana Publications, Inc., published by
New York University Press.

From COURTS ON TRIAL by Jerome Frank, copyright © 1949, reprinted
by permission of Princeton University Press.

From "Denmark's Ombudsman: The Parliamentary Commissioner for
Civil and Military Government Administration" by Stephen Hurwitz in
WISCONSIN LAW REVIEW, copyright 1961.

For My Parents

Vina and Morris Trebach

A Salute to Emery A. Brownell

Freedom in America has been advanced more by Emery A. Brownell, in his own quiet way, than by many better-known public figures. Emery was the Executive Director of the National Legal Aid and Defender Association—an organization that has provided more concrete support for constitutional rights than is generally realized, and will continue to provide that support in part because of his work.

I first sought Emery's advice regarding legal aid in 1955. He gave it graciously and managed to save me from missteps without making me feel embarrassed at the immense difference in our stores of knowledge on the subject. He continued to provide advice over the years. On the morning of December 18, 1961, he dictated a letter to me about this book and related matters, offering encouragement in his usual manner. His secretary had to sign his name to the letter, for, in the early afternoon, before it was typed, Emery died—excited and interested in the defense of rights until the very end.

So this is a belated salute to a fine man whose death has hurt us all, but especially the "little" people in our society, who were closest to Emery's heart.

Preface

If we are to keep our democracy, there must be
one commandment: Thou shalt not ration justice.

Judge Learned Hand
1953

Learned Hand's commandment is violated daily. Justice is,
in effect, rationed for the person accused of crime—by the
violation of his constitutional rights and by practices that
make his defense either difficult or impossible. This is most
obvious in the lack of provisions for an effective defense
for the indigent defendant, in police invasions of individual
rights, and in the methods used by some prosecutors to obtain guilty pleas.

To show *how* rights are violated and *how often,* I have
described the process of criminal justice, step by step, from
arrest through conviction and appeal.

The information is based upon my observation of proceedings, upon interviews with men convicted of serious
crimes and with judges, lawyers, prosecutors, policemen,
and prison officials. I began with a survey of conditions and
practices in the state of New Jersey—in 1950 rated the highest in the nation for its compliance with the standards of
judicial administration of the American Bar Association.
For comparison I interviewed officials and prisoners in
Philadelphia and in the federal courts.

After my research was completed, my work for the United States Commission on Civil Rights, which took me on investigations to many other American communities, convinced me that, if I have erred in my criticisms of American criminal justice, it has been on the side of understatement.

Law, like war, is much too important to be left entirely to the professionals. Therefore, I have written this book, not only for those active in the administration of justice, but also for the layman and for the lawyer who does not practice in the criminal courts.

The extent of my indebtedness to those who helped me in this study is great. I owe a special debt to Professor William M. Beaney of the Department of Politics of Princeton University. From our many discussions came the idea for this work as well as continuing encouragement and helpful criticism.

My original interest in the problems of the criminal process came from a survey of the civil and criminal legal aid facilities of the state of New Jersey that I made in 1955. This study was undertaken through the Administrative Office of the Courts of New Jersey at the direction of Chief Justice Arthur T. Vanderbilt. Edward M. McConnell, Administrative Director of the Courts, and Mortimer Newman, the Assistant Administrative Director of the Courts, both provided much assistance. The rugged idealism and wide knowledge of Arthur B. Caldwell, Civil Rights Division, Department of Justice, provided a spur in the latter stages of the study.

Of the many judges who took time from their court duties to answer my inquiries, I want to cite especially Judge G. Dixon Speakman of the Superior Court of New

Jersey and Judges Edward Gaulkin, Gerald T. Foley, and Alexander P. Waugh. Among the score of private attorneys who gave much valuable information regarding the criminal courts and the assigned counsel system, Griffith H. Jones, Arthur C. Hensler, Jr,. and Bernard Horwitz were especially helpful. Joseph L. Burtchaell provided helpful advice based upon his many years of investigating for the defense.

I benefited greatly from my work as staff consultant to the Special Committee to Study Defender Systems. This benefit arose not only from the legal research and field studies that I performed while associated with them, but at least as much from many conversations and meetings with the judges, private lawyers, legal aid experts, and public defenders who were members of that unique body. Their diligence and dedication are reflected in *Equal Justice for the Accused*—a valuable report on criminal legal aid in the United States published in 1959.

I also wish to acknowledge the assistance of the following correctional officials: Douglas H. MacNeil, Department of Institutions and Agencies, State of New Jersey; Warden George F. Goodman, New Jersey State Prison; Assistant Superintendent William G. Nagel, New Jersey State Reformatory, Bordentown; James V. Bennett, Director, United States Bureau of Prisons; Warden Charles R. Hagan, United States Penitentiary, Lewisburg, Pennsylvania; Edward J. Hendrick, Department of Public Welfare, City of Philadelphia; and Warden Fred Krueger, Holmesburg Prison, City of Philadelphia. Lawrence Speiser, Director, Washington Office, American Civil Liberties Union, shared with me his insights into the problems of liberty and justice.

To the many prisoners who patiently answered my questions, I must also express my gratitude. It is true that I took none of them away from pressing business appointments. One prisoner who wanted to speak to me replied, upon being asked if he had time to wait, "Mister, that's all I've got." Nevertheless, the courtesy and patience prisoners displayed toward me were encouraging. As has been observed, it is far easier to hate the crime than the criminal.

Professor Louis Dotson of the Department of Sociology at the University of Tennessee was most helpful with technical advice and criticism regarding the use of statistics. Gordon Garrett, a graduate student in political science at the University of Tennessee, spent many long hours coding questionnaires. Another graduate student, Gene Summers of the sociology department, aided in the tabulations of the statistics. Miss Linda Lee, a law student at George Washington University, Washington, D.C., did the final source checking.

Some of the material presented in these pages originally appeared in my articles in the *Rutgers Law Review*—"The Indigent Defendant" (Spring, 1957) and "A Modern Defender System for New Jersey" (Winter, 1957).

My wife, Shirley, and my sons, David and Paul, stood by me with understanding and patience through the years that were spent in the writing of this book.

A.S.T.
December, 1963
Chicago, Illinois

Contents

The Rationing of Justice

1
The Police:
Arrest and Detention

. . . the third degree—that is, the use of physical brutality, or other forms of cruelty, to obtain involuntary confessions or admissions—is widespread. Protracted questioning of prisoners is commonly employed. Threats and methods of intimidation, adjusted to the age or mentality of the victim, are frequently used, either by themselves or in combination with some of the other practices mentioned. Physical brutality, illegal detention, and refusal to allow access of counsel to the prisoner is common. Even where the law requires prompt production of a prisoner before a magistrate, the police not infrequently delay doing so and employ the time in efforts to compel confession. The practice of holding the accused *incommunicado*, unable to get in touch with their family or friends or counsel, is . . . frequent. . . . Brutality and violence in making an arrest also are employed at times, before the prisoner reaches the jail, in order to put him in a frame of mind which makes him more amenable to questioning afterwards. . . . [T]hird-degree practices are not confined to urban communities.[1]

Since these charges were made in the Wickersham Report of June 25, 1931, there have been remarkable strides in police organization and in scientific crime detection. The Supreme Court of the United States has, during the intervening years, raised the constitutional standards by which police officers are bound. In the opinion of many, there also have been changes in the practices actually followed by law officers, so that rights are now more fully observed than in 1931. But can it be said that the distressing paragraph from the Wickersham Report is no longer realistic? My answer is an emphatic No.

Arrests on Suspicion

The process of criminal justice usually starts operating when a policeman takes some action. That action is often an arrest. While on the surface an arrest may seem to be a relatively uncomplicated step, a morass of legal concepts is involved. Frequently the arrest is subject to a subsequent legal attack, either because of an oversight on the part of the officer or because he deliberately chose to violate the law in order to catch a "criminal."

I am convinced that this combination of police confusion about the law and deliberate police violation [2] means that policemen commit more invasions of individual rights than any other group of officials in the United States.[3] The single practice that produces the largest number of police violations is the arrest "on suspicion," or, as it is sometimes called, "for investigation"—in other words, when there is no definite evidence of specific criminal conduct. The law on this point is clear: no arrest without a warrant can be made unless the officer had "probable cause," not some vague general suspicion, to believe that the person had committed a specific crime.[4] For a variety of reasons,[5] the prisoners in the sample I interviewed were not asked about arrests on suspicion. But such arrests are openly reported yearly in the FBI *Uniform Crime Reports.* For example, during 1960 local police agencies reported to the FBI 136,325 arrests on suspicion.[6] But this by no means reveals the full extent of the practice. According to the definition in the *Uniform Crime Reports* of the FBI, an arrest on suspicion is one made "for no specific offense" and in which the suspect is "released without formal charges being placed."[7] Therefore, when the police arrest a person on suspicion (or for vagrancy or a disorderly persons violation—both not uncommon practices) and later hold him for a specific offense, this arrest would not appear in the statistics. Moreover, the figure reported to the FBI came from police agencies in areas representing only 60 per cent of the country's population.[8] So it is probable that, in this free country, the annual number of arrests where no specific charge can then be placed against the detained person, may be several times the 136,325 reported to the FBI.

A study based on figures issued by the Detroit Police Department reported that in the ten years from 1947 through 1956, one out of every three arrests was listed by the police department itself under the category "arrests for investigation."[9] There were 656,808 nontraffic arrests during this period, of which 219,053 were "arrests for investigation."[10]

Sometimes these arrests are carried out by a large force of policemen who descend on a high-crime neighborhood —almost always inhabited by the poor or by racial minorities—and take dozens of people into custody without con-

cern for the rule of probable cause. These dragnet operations frequently are ordered in response to crimes that
shock the conscience of the community, especially the rape
or murder of white women by nonwhite assailants. For
example, during December, 1960, and January, 1961,
Detroit experienced a series of attacks on women in the
streets; some of the culprits were Negroes. Following the
killing of Mrs. Betty James, the police commissioner ordered the return to "old-fashioned methods of police
patrol," [11] which meant that persons on the streets were
stopped on suspicion, searched for weapons or other possibly incriminating evidence, and, in as many as 1,000
cases, arrested. Most of those arrested were innocent of
any crime. Commissioner Hart explained: "This is a desperate situation requiring desperate measures." [12]

A few months later, it was reported that 88 Negroes
were arrested by the police of Odessa, Texas, following
the rape of a nineteen-year-old white girl. The girl claimed
that she was forced to submit to a Negro youth who held
a knife at her throat as she lay in bed with her fifteen-
year-old sister. A United Press International story stated:

> Police went about arresting almost any young Negro
> they found on the street in the Negro section and let the
> white girl look at them in a police lineup. She could not
> identify any as her attacker.
> [Police Chief Jess] Carriker ordered his men Thursday
> to be more selective and to arrest only persons who fit the
> description of the girl's attacker.[13]

These are but a few examples. Yet from them it is clear
that arrests on suspicion present a grave problem in the
United States. Such arrests, either individually or collec-
tively, do present one method of discouraging criminals

and reducing crime. But it must also be observed that they are illegal, that they invade constitutional rights, and that they force many innocent poor people, who find it difficult to obtain a job under any circumstances, to record a non-traffic arrest on any future application for employment.

Further arguments against arrests on suspicion appeared in one of the best studies ever made of the practice. Issued in July, 1962, it was made by a committee of Washington lawyers headed by Charles A. Horsky, later Special Assistant to the President for District of Columbia Affairs. After an intensive analysis of hundreds of arrests on suspicion cases in the District of Columbia, the committee concluded that the advantage gained by policemen through this clearly illegal practice was slight compared to the personal and social costs. Of those persons arrested during the two years 1960 and 1961 by District of Columbia policemen, members of one of the best police departments in the country, only 5.7 per cent were finally charged with a specific crime.[14] In other words, 17 out of every 18 persons arrested under these illegal circumstances were either completely innocent—or the police did not have even the minimal amount of evidence necessary to establish probable cause. The committee's major recommendation was brief and pointed:

> . . . the cost to the community is more than the practice is worth. Legally, the practice cannot be justified. The practice should stop, and stop immediately.[15]

The Board of Commissioners of the District of Columbia followed this recommendation by banning arrests for investigation.

Treatment of Arrested Persons

When a policeman makes an arrest he may use only "necessary force" in order to effect it. Even though the suspect may have just shot down the officer's partner in cold blood, the officer has no authority to use any violence if no resistance is offered to the arrest.[16]

What is the actual extent of police violence during arrest? Millions of arrests are made every year by American policemen. While it is impossible to know how the officer acted in each instance, the evidence suggests that violence is not involved in the overwhelming majority. Some significant reasons for this were suggested in many discussions with prisoners. First, many, if not most, policemen wish to observe the law against unnecessary violence and have no desire to inflict suffering on another. Second, most people have absolutely no inclination to resist when a policeman armed with a death-dealing weapon says, "Come with me." Third, those policemen inclined to be brutal do not usually want unnecessary violence to be observed by others, and arrests are often made in the presence of several people. Fourth, some people surrender to the police upon hearing that they are wanted—and, therefore, the issue of resistance does not even arise. (I was surprised to find that most of the prisoners I interviewed who had committed homicides claimed that they had either called the police or gone to the police station immediately afterwards.) All of these factors tend to work against police violence during arrest. And yet too much police violence occurs during arrest.

Indeed, I would judge that more official violence takes

place at the point of arrest than at any other phase of the entire criminal process. When a policeman makes his initial contact with a person and indicates that he wants to search him or arrest him, a tinderbox situation is sometimes created, especially if the policeman is insulting, callous, or uses racial slurs—rather than attempting to control the situation through a commanding manner and through persuasion. Under those conditions, violence may simply explode, and it is often difficult later to determine who threw the first blow, the policeman or the suspect.

Clearly unnecessary and, therefore, clearly illegal police violence during arrest occurs for a variety of reasons. Some policemen use excessive force to control an arrestee who shows any resistance. A policeman may use only that degree of force necessary to overcome the resistance of a suspect. He cannot then go on to knock the suspect unconscious or to shoot him so that future resistance is prevented. An example of how policemen can go too far in dealing with a resisting arrestee took place in Philadelphia on June 23, 1960, when two police officers attempted to arrest Eugene Hutchins, who had allegedly slashed his wife with a knife during an argument. Hutchins admittedly punched one of the officers on the head. The officer then knocked Hutchins to the ground with his nightstick and handcuffed his hands behind him. While he was lying on the ground and unable to resist, both officers proceeded to beat him with their clubs and a blackjack. In a subsequent hearing before the Philadelphia Police Advisory Board,[17] both officers claimed that they used only necessary force to subdue Hutchins and to effect the arrest. After hearing all of the witnesses, the board concluded that the officers "were guilty of using unnecessary force in making the arrest," and declared:

The Board recognizes and appreciates the problems that confront the police officer when he is placed in the position of having to use force in order to make an arrest, but this does not give the police officers a license to indulge in the use of club and blackjack *past the point of resistance*.[18]

Other officers use violence during arrest—and at other times—when an arrestee shows disrespect for them. In a misguided attempt to maintain their authority or simply because they are insulted and are prepared to use violence to bolster their egos, they resort to the fist, the blackjack, and even the pistol. A study of the police force in an industrial city of 150,000 published in 1953 by sociologist William Westley provided some insight in this respect.[19] Thirty-seven per cent of the officers Westley interviewed stated that they felt violence was justified when a person showed disrespect for the police. But the worst and most frequent complaints of police brutality to enforce respect that I have encountered have come from the South. It would be impossible for me to count the times that I have heard from Negroes the story that they were required to say "Sir" whenever they were speaking to an officer. If the Negro refused to comply, the penalty was often violence.[20]

Another significant cause of unnecessary police violence during arrest is a desire to impose punishment. It cannot be emphasized too much that no matter what the personal feelings of the officers, no matter how heinous the crime of the arrestee, policemen have no authority to impose any punishment. That authority belongs to a judge and a jury. Yet too many police officers disregard this clear separation of powers between the executive and judicial branches of government. Southern policemen are especially prone to punish Negro arrestees who have violated the regional mores and customs of segregation and white supremacy.

Many Southern officers view themselves in their traditional role as the first line of defense to attacks on white supremacy. Punishment to an "uppity nigger" during arrest (although often it occurs later) may be severe, even to the point of instantly imposing a death sentence.[21] But this is by no means a Southern practice alone.

Punishment is also imposed for nonracial reasons on those the police consider to be "tough cases," especially when the offender has injured a fellow officer. Although it rarely happens so that the press may observe, a newspaperman saw such an incident in Detroit on September 10, 1959. Following a fight as a result of which four policemen were sent to the hospital, sixteen-year-old Thaddeus Steel, who had allegedly hit a policeman with a chair during the melee, arrived at the Vernor police station garage in a scout car. Once inside, the officers proceeded to punch and kick Steel even while he was lying on the floor. Police Lieutenant Raymond Glinski spoke for all too many American police officers when he explained to reporters:

> When policemen are sent to the hospital, we don't want to tap the hoodlums who hurt them on the shoulder and send them home. . . . [W]hen it's a question of a policeman going to the hospital or a hood, I think both should go.[22]

Such actions and statements by members of the Detroit Police Department—later to undergo a positive metamorphosis under Police Commissioner George Edwards—led a Detroit newspaperman to write of conversations with Cuban students:

> A student said the Batista police were so sadistic, once the policemen put you in a scout car, you had your judge and jury, trial and punishment before you get out.

My most embarrassing moment came when a student asked me did the police in Detroit beat people. What could I say? [23]

Seizure of Property

Policemen, like the rest of us, want very much to succeed at their jobs. For an officer of the law, milestones on the road to success are arrests that "stick." One of the best methods for making an arrest stick is to find something tangible that is incriminating, for example, something that can be picked up and put on a table in a courtroom. Therefore, either shortly before or shortly after an arrest, the diligent officer will seek out physical evidence of the crime. But as in the case of arrests, there is a complicated set of constitutional provisions and laws that restrict the powers of the constable to search for property and to seize it for evidence. To the consternation of many policemen, these rules are being interpreted more strictly by the courts in recent years, as is illustrated by the following analysis of the historic *Mapp* case.

DOLLREE MAPP "AMENDS" THE CONSTITUTION

On May 23, 1957, according to evidence presented in the Supreme Court of the United States, three police officers arrived at Miss Dollree Mapp's home in Cleveland, Ohio.[24] She refused them admittance upon advice of her attorney, whom she phoned when the policemen appeared. Some three hours later, the police, then numbering seven, broke into the house. Once inside, they refused to allow Miss Mapp's attorney, who soon arrived, to enter the house or to speak with his client. It is doubtful if the officers had a search warrant. Their reason for seeking entry was "information that 'a person' [was] hiding out in the home, who was wanted for questioning in connection with a recent bombing, and that there was a large amount of policy paraphernalia being hidden in the house." [25] Neither that person nor that gambling paraphernalia was found.

During the initial moment of their entry, the police felt that Miss Mapp was "belligerent." Then, the Supreme Court explained:

> Running roughshod over appellant, a policeman "grabbed" her, "twisted [her] hand," and she "yelled [and] pleaded with him" because "it was hurting." Appellant, in handcuffs, was then forcibly taken upstairs to her bedroom where the officers searched a dresser, a chest of drawers, a closet and some suitcases. They also looked into a photo album and through personal papers belonging to the appellant. The search spread to the rest of the second floor, including the child's bedroom, the living room, the kitchen and a dinette. The basement of the building and a trunk found therein were also searched. The obscene materials, for possession of which she was ultimately convicted, were discovered in the course of that widespread search.[26]

The reaction of all too many people will be: "So what? A criminal was caught by methods that don't exactly satisfy the rules of Emily Post. Don't you want criminals caught?"

Reflection suggests, however, that the policemen were doing precisely what James Otis and other American patriots were so disturbed by shortly before the events of 1776. This was a general search like those authorized by the infamous English Writs of Assistance. These officers apparently had no warrant, and had only a suspicion that there was something "criminal" in that house. When they broke into the house, these officers of the law became criminals.

Even so, the case would have had little to distinguish it from many others like it had not Miss Mapp eventually appealed her conviction to the Supreme Court of the United States.

The Court has maintained that the specific principles of the first eight Amendments to the United States Constitution apply directly only to the federal government, including, of course, its police officers.[27] On the other hand, state or local police officers are theoretically controlled only by the less specific "fair trial" guarantees of the Fourteenth Amendment Due Process Clause,[28] which provides: "No State shall . . . deprive any person of life, liberty, or property, without due process of law. . . ." As a result of this double standard the federal Constitution now requires less of local officers than it does of federal police agents. The double standard extends throughout the process of criminal adjudication.

While the local law varies from state to state, two basic concepts control the preliminary stages of a criminal case, including arrest. These are probable cause, as already indicated, and judicial control. The first means that no arrest should be made unless the officer has probable cause to believe that a person has committed a specific crime. In certain circumstances, such as a breach of peace committed in the officer's presence or where the suspect has apparently committed a serious crime (a felony), the officer may arrest without a warrant. Otherwise, he must go before a judge in a first-level court * and inform him that there is a good reason to believe that a specific person has committed a certain crime. Upon being satisfied that probable cause exists, the judge then issues a warrant. This is one form of judicial control. Another is found in the requirement of all states and of the federal government that once an officer arrests a person, he has one duty that should override all other considerations. That duty is to hasten to a local judge, so that the preliminary question of probable cause for arrest and detention may be subjected to judicial scrutiny in a hearing at which the suspect may be heard. As Justice William O. Douglas has pointed out, there is nothing very novel about all of this for, "The requirement of probable cause has roots that are deep in

* While the court systems and the names of the courts vary from state to state, most state court systems have four functional levels. In this book I often refer to the various court levels as first court level, second court level, etc. My definition of the function of each level is as follows. *First court level:* on serious charges beyond its final jurisdiction, to hold preliminary examinations and set bail; but in a great number of cases involving petty offenses and minor state crimes, to issue a "final" judgment; in New Jersey this is the municipal court. *Second court level:* to hold trials on all serious charges and impose sentences; it is the highest court of original criminal jurisdiction; in New Jersey this level is occupied primarily by the county court. *Third court level:* these are intermediate appellate courts that operate as buffers for the highest court by hearing appeals from a limited number of second-level courts; in New Jersey this level is occupied primarily by the appellate division of the superior court. *Fourth court level:* as the highest court in the state, to hear appeals in those cases not disposed of to the satisfaction of the parties in the lower courts; some cases can be taken directly to this court from the second court level; in New Jersey, as in most states, this is called the supreme court. Where a federal question is involved, the parties need not stop here, but may go on to the United States court system, which, however, handles a very small proportion of the criminal cases prosecuted in this country every year—considering both appeals from state courts and original prosecutions in federal trial courts called district courts.

our history." [29] The same is true regarding judicial control of police powers.[30]

The general rules regarding arrest of persons are closely related to those regarding seizure of property. Probable cause also applies to the need for search warrants. And where a warrant naming the specific property to be seized has *not* been issued in advance, the officers may take such property only in the course of a lawful arrest. It is at this point that the rules regarding arrest and the rules regarding search and seizure of property intersect. For if there is probable cause to arrest, then the search and seizure are usually lawful.

Before the *Mapp* decision on June 19, 1961, the Court required, on the one hand, that *federal officers* follow the Fourth Amendment's requirement of arresting only on probable cause and of seizing property only with a warrant or in the course of a lawful arrest. More important, if the property was not secured according to these rules, it was excluded from evidence and any conviction voided.[31] This exclusionary rule, the Court explained,[32] was required to give full effect to the Fourth Amendment, which states:

> The right of the people to be secure in their persons, houses, papers, and effects, against unreasonable searches and seizures, shall not be violated, and no Warrants shall issue, but upon probable cause, supported by Oath or affirmation, and particularly describing the place to be searched, and the persons or things to be seized.

On the other hand, a different rule was applied to *state* officers. In 1949 the Supreme Court had declared that the Fourth Amendment search and seizure provision was such an important right that it was to be considered incorporated in the Due Process Clause of the Fourteenth Amendment and applied thereby to state officers.[33] But in the same case the Court declared that it would not, at that time, impose the exclusionary rule on the state courts as an "essential ingredient of the right." [34]

All of this meant that when a person was convicted in a state court on the basis of evidence seized in clear violation of the Fourth Amendment, it was conceivable that the best he could hope for from the highest court of the land was a declaration that the officers had indeed misbehaved. The evidence was not excluded and the conviction stuck—[35] that is, unless the state had its own exclusionary rule, which many of them did.[36] This resulted in a rather ironical situation for, while the Amendment applied, the "teeth" did not.

The teeth were finally applied when the Supreme Court, in a five-to-four decision, invalidated Dollree Mapp's conviction because it had been based on evidence seized in violation of the Fourth Amendment's requirement for a search warrant. Justice Tom Clark declared for the Court: "Since the Fourth Amendment's right of privacy has been declared enforceable against the States through the Due Process Clause of the Fourteenth, it is enforceable against them by the same sanction of exclusion as is used against the Federal Government." [37] One may express great satisfaction with this ruling as well as with the subsequent statement in the *Mapp* opinion that "There is no war between the Constitution and common sense." [38]

The *Mapp* case, therefore, made it clear that the United States Constitution guarantees to all the right not to be convicted on the basis of property seized in violation of the Fourth Amendment. But that decision did not state that the United States Constitution requires that persons be *arrested* by state officers only according to the venerable rule of probable cause. Indeed, no American decision has been discovered that overruled a conviction solely because of the manner of arrest—as distinguished from an arrest plus seizure of property. Yet, the *Mapp* decision may have some effect on the rules regarding arrest. In many cases the basis for conviction in a state court has been property taken from the suspect or his home. In the future, if the arrest is illegal, it would seem that the seizure would violate the Fourth Amendment, that the property would be excluded from evidence, and that the conviction would be overruled. So while the *Mapp* case does not directly deal with the rules of arrest, it should have a profound effect on those rules since they overlap the rules of search and seizure.

The national attention focused on the *Mapp* and other search and seizure decisions would suggest that illegally seized property is used to obtain a large percentage of convictions. The responses of the 359 prisoners I interviewed suggest a contrary conclusion. Only two per cent of all prisoners claimed that articles used in the prosecution's case were seized without a warrant. And even if all of these claims were true, this would not prove that the articles were seized illegally, since they might have been seized in the course of a lawful arrest. Therefore, the prisoner responses suggest that illegally seized evidence does not figure prominently in the great majority of ordinary criminal prosecutions. This helps to place the problem in its proper quantitative context, but it does not detract from its seriousness.

Wiretapping

In recent years much national attention has also been focused on another questionable police practice used by diligent officers to catch criminals: wiretapping. The extensive practice of wiretapping should be a matter of great concern to all of us. No man's home is really his castle, nor is privacy possible, even in the bedroom, when those who would spy are about. For a wiretap is an exceedingly simple technical matter—I was taught by a detective, who often practiced the art, in five minutes. All that is really needed is a set of earphones, a few pieces of wire, two safety pins to cut into the telephone wires—plus a disregard for personal privacy. This is not to say that wiretapping is a violation of the United States Constitution. In 1928 the Supreme Court declared that the Fourth Amendment prohibited only physical invasions of the home and seizures of physical things.[39] The decision in this case, *Olmstead* v. *United States*, quite properly was followed by widespread criticism. Certainly, the framers of the Amendment did not in 1791 contemplate that wiretapping would be included within its provisions. But they did intend to prohibit invasions of a man's privacy except upon proof of probable cause. Such arguments led to a provision in the Federal Communications Act of 1934 that stated: "no person not being authorized by the sender shall intercept any communication and divulge or publish the existence, contents, substance . . . of such intercepted communication to any person. . . ."[40] This law ranks high on the list of ignored statutes, for it has been consistently violated by police agents at every level of government—

federal, state and local—and by private persons.[41] Congress has frequently been requested by police and prosecution agencies to change the law to legalize wiretapping, but just as frequently Congress has refused.[42] The Supreme Court has tried to give the statute some force,[43] but thus far its effort has not stopped the practice.

Therefore, it should come as a surprise to find that wiretapping plays a negligible part in the investigation of the great majority of such "ordinary" common law crimes as murder, robbery, larceny, and rape. There was almost no wiretap evidence in the many cases I studied in all three jurisdictions—New Jersey, Philadelphia, and the federal courts. And when the prisoners were asked if their telephone wires were tapped by the police, only 1 per cent answered "Yes." [44]

One factor limiting wiretapping is that many prisoners are of the lowest economic classes and simply do not have a telephone or wires that might be tapped—as evidenced by the numerous prisoner replies of "No phone" to the wiretapping question.

These findings are not inconsistent with the conclusion that wiretapping is widespread. Even a brief review of the written material and cases on wiretapping shows that the police now resort to the technique primarily in cases of espionage, national security, prostitution, gambling, and organized crime.[45] The landmark *Olmstead* case of 1928, for example, involved a West Coast gambler. It is apparent that the police do not resort to wiretapping in most "ordinary" cases because it is neither feasible nor helpful. Many crimes are committed on the spur of the moment by lone criminals, who may not be inclined to talk about criminal activity on the telephone, even if they are among that minority who have one. These findings, however, should not downgrade the seriousness of the problem of electronic eavesdropping with all of its awesome variations that go far beyond simple wiretapping. It is conceivable that as police budgets and skills increase, electronic invasions of privacy in even the most minor cases will also increase. Here, indeed, is a somber spectre that is already looming over the horizons of liberty.

Detention

UNNECESSARY DELAY

The legal authority of the police to detain a man, once he is arrested, is limited. In all states, as well as in the federal courts, there is some legal requirement that the police must make every effort to keep to a minimum the time interval between arrest and preliminary examination. The federal rule [46] and the New Jersey rule [47] both require that an arrested person be taken into court for a preliminary examination "without unnecessary delay." Although the rules are worded the same on this key point, there is a difference in judicial interpretation. In the exercise of its general supervisory powers over federal judicial administration, the Supreme Court of the United States has ordered that preliminary hearings occur very soon after arrest, within a matter of hours in most cases. In *Mallory* v. *United States*,[48] the Supreme Court held that a confession obtained by federal policemen from a defendant approximately nine hours after arrest (during which interval no attempt was made to bring the accused to a U.S. Commissioner for a preliminary examination) was inadmissible as evidence. The Court later drove home the point that in the federal courts, it is the fact of illegal detention that makes the confession inadmissible, which means that the issue of the voluntary nature of the confession is of secondary significance.[49]

The interpretation of this rule in New Jersey, and in many other states, offers a striking contrast. Whereas a federal police officer has reason to fear that a detention of nine hours will destroy his case against the defendant, many state police officers may detain a man for nine days and have little worry of a reversal of the conviction. In a 1952 decision the Superior Court of New Jersey stated that while a delay of nine days between arrest and preliminary examination,

> without satisfactory explanation, is a violation of . . . [the court rule], which requires an officer making an arrest to take the arrested person "without unnecessary delay" before the court or magistrate, it does not of itself constitute a denial of due process which would invalidate the conviction.[50]

This decision is consistent with present requirements of the Fourteenth Amendment Due Process Clause, which controls state procedure. For example, in 1952 the Supreme Court of the United States upheld a similar decision of the California Supreme Court. The fact that the officers violated state law by not bringing the suspect into court promptly did not necessarily invalidate the confession or the conviction.[51]

So the rule for arraignment as rapidly as possible exists in New Jersey as it does in other states. But the rule receives support from neither the state nor the United States Supreme Court. This rule, however, is not nearly so important as the realities of the matter. What are the actual police practices regarding detention before preliminary examination? The evidence at hand indicates that many policemen do not hasten to the magistrate once they have arrested a person.

The mere existence of the rule, without a determined effort by executive officials and the judiciary to enforce it, has not been sufficient to overcome a deeply entrenched police practice. In my research not a single instance was found where a municipal court magistrate questioned the police as to why they had not brought a particular suspect into court sooner for a preliminary examination. Although it may be imagined from the rules that the judges would exercise some control over detention, the truth is that the initiative is left to the police. In many instances, only after the police have completed a preliminary investigation and have interrogated the prisoner for the purpose of obtaining a confession is the prisoner brought in for a preliminary examination. Without support from local police officers, from police or other executive officials, from the local magistrates, or from the appellate courts, the legal requirement for a speedy preliminary examination has the effect of a mild admonition. The attitude of many policemen toward this admonition is summed up by the answer allegedly given to one New Jersey prisoner, one of those few aware of his "right" to a speedy preliminary examination, who demanded that he be brought before a magistrate. The policeman replied, "When we are good and ready."

The statistics calculated from the responses of prisoners interviewed in New Jersey indicate that many officers were not "good and ready" until several days had elapsed. The mean average (the simple arithmetical average—the total number of days divided by the number of responses) number of days between arrest and preliminary examination was 6.58 days. Looking at the median average (the point at which half the responses fell above and half below), you see that half the prisoners had their preliminary examinations within four days or under, while the other half did not see a judge until at least four days had passed. The median for the smaller groups of men interviewed in a Philadelphia and in a federal prison was under one day. Actually, the great majority of these men—not merely half—were brought into court within twenty-four hours after arrest. Many of the federal prisoners had their preliminary examination within two to four hours after arrest.[52] Clearly, the statistics suggest that the general practice in federal courts and in Philadelphia courts is to bring the prisoner in soon after arrest for a preliminary examination. The statistics suggest, on the other hand, that in many cases the police of New Jersey do not do so.

Why the difference in the length of detention between New Jersey and the two other jurisdictions studied? One of the most apparent reasons is that the appellate courts of New Jersey have made it clear that they will not reverse a conviction because of lengthy detention, whereas the federal courts have imposed a stringent rule. This is a partial explanation for the difference between New Jersey and the federal courts, but it does not aid in an explanation of the low figure in Philadelphia, where the Pennsylvania courts are as permissive as in New Jersey.[53] There must be some other explanation for the Philadelphia and the federal practices.

A major factor in creating the difference is the standard imposed upon policemen by their superiors. Apparently, in many New Jersey police departments there is no concerted effort by high-ranking officials to urge their men to observe the speedy arraignment rule. And just as apparently, the "word" has been handed down to the federal police and to the Philadelphia police that the rule is to be followed.

There is one other important factor that would account for the low federal figures. Federal police apparently build a case first and then arrest the suspect. There is then no need to wait before bringing the person before a magistrate since there is no doubt that, if challenged, the police can prove "probable cause." There are, of course, compelling reasons why local police, especially in large cities, arrest on suspicion before a solid case is made out: a literally crushing case-load; less expertise in some local departments than in federal agencies; less money for crime-detection equipment; and so on. Moreover, as FBI Director J. Edgar Hoover has pointed out, in contrast to local police forces, the FBI "is primarily an investigative agency, whose arrests in most instances are made after investigation and upon warrant." [54] But these are only reasons; they do not provide justification. And the Philadelphia statistics suggest that large local departments can observe the speedy examination rule if they try.

This is an analysis of only a relatively few cases out of the millions of arrests that are made every year in this country. But it does shed some light on the incidence of lengthy detention throughout the land. If a thorough study were made in every county and city, it would undoubtedly show a checkerboard pattern. In some areas, both urban and rural, the general practice would be speedy preliminary examination. In others, also both urban and rural, the situation would be just the opposite.[55] The reason for the difference in practices is simple. Where the police make an effort to follow the path of civilized procedure, which helps set America apart from police states, and wish to bring an accused in for a speedy preliminary examination, there is nothing that will stop them. In those areas where state or local policemen do not wish to observe the speedy preliminary examination rule, however, present rules of law generally impose no effective penalty for its violation.

INCOMMUNICADO DETENTION

Some state and local police keep arrested persons under incommunicado detention—without visitors and messages —when they feel that contact with persons in the outside world, especially with a defense lawyer, will adversely affect the prosecution. This does not mean that all defendants are denied outside contacts. Some are so utterly friendless that they never request to speak to a relative or a lawyer; others are too despondent and ashamed to ask. Still others are allowed such contact because the police feel that it will not harm their case or because the police wish to treat the prisoner with consideration.

All prisoners interviewed were asked: "Were you allowed to contact anyone outside the jail while in police custody?" Exactly half of the New Jersey prisoners claimed that they had been subjected to some form of incommunicado detention.[56] The prisoners in Philadelphia and in the federal prison reported a much smaller incidence of this practice.[57] The technique of holding a prisoner incommunicado until *after he signed a confession* was also much more prevalent among the New Jersey prisoners than among the others.

Most cases of incommunicado detention, like most abuses in the process of justice, remain hidden from public sight. But on rare occasions, such a case does receive some publicity. On June 30, 1958, the Supreme Court of the

United States decided a case that involved a New Jersey prisoner, Vincent Cicenia.[58] In delivering the opinion of the Court, Justice John Harlan explained that Cicenia had been implicated in a murder. The police of Orange, New Jersey, tried to locate him, but since he was not at home, the officers left word for him to report at the police station. Cicenia sought the advice of a lawyer, Frank A. Palmieri, who suggested that he go to the police. Cicenia went to the station with his father and his brother. The opinion continued:

> Upon arrival at the Orange police station at 9:00 A.M. on December 18 [1947] petitioner was separated from the others and taken by detectives to the Newark police head-quarters. At approximately 2:00 P.M. the same day petitioner's father, brother and Mr. Palmieri, the lawyer, arrived at the Newark station. Mr. Palmieri immediately asked to see the petitioner, but this request was refused by the police. He repeated this request at intervals throughout the afternoon and well into the evening, but without success. During this period, petitioner, who was being questioned intermittently by the police, asked to see his lawyer. These requests were also denied. Lawyer and client were not permitted to confer until 9:30 P.M., by which time petitioner had made and signed a written confession to . . . murder. . . .[59]

According to Mr. Palmieri, his pleas to see his client were bluntly refused, and the police made such remarks as, "We're working on him." [60] (I have heard similar stories many times from New Jersey lawyers and prisoners—and from prisoners arrested by local police outside of New Jersey.)

So for over seven hours, an attorney in an American city attempted to see his client in police custody and was prevented from doing so. The Supreme Court stated that if Vincent Cicenia had been in the custody of federal officers, it would have reversed the conviction because of the requirement for a preliminary examination "without unnecessary delay." [61] But that ruling would have been under the Court's administrative control over the process of federal criminal justice, a control based on the fact that the Supreme Court is not only the supreme interpreter of constitutional law in this country but also the supreme administrative unit in the federal judicial system. When dealing with arrests and prosecutions by federal officials, the Court wears two hats—and what it cannot find by interpretation when wearing its constitutional headgear, it may demand by fiat when wearing the administrative hat. In cases of arrests and prosecutions by local officials, however, the Court wears only one hat, the constitutional authority, and it can usually reverse state convictions only if they violate a provision of the United States Constitution. Because Vincent Cicenia could not convince the Court that his confession had been coerced, the tribunal had to allow that the conviction was not gained in violation of the Due Process Clause of the Fourteenth Amendment.[62] This is another example of the double standard of procedure that plagues American constitutional jurisprudence. At the same time, all three federal courts that dealt with the case expressed their "strong distaste" for the activities of the Newark policemen.[63] But this expression of distaste did not feed the flame of American liberty.

DETENTION AND THE THIRD DEGREE

The foregoing criticism of lengthy detention should not obscure the essential problem. It may be true that police lock up many people, especially minor offenders, hold them for a short time as a form of punishment, and then release them. This practice is illegal and an impairment of constitutional liberty. But this is a study of cases that went the full route. Illegal detention is undoubtedly of serious constitutional concern in these cases also. But the greater evil in this context is the coerced confession. Both practices, illegal detentions and coerced confessions, should be discouraged. But in all the cases examined in this study, lengthy detention without a charge was not particularly damaging to the defense at later stages of the case, however abhorrent it is to Anglo-American legal traditions. The forced extraction of confessions, however, definitely was damaging to the defense. For if a prisoner is merely held by the police for a very long time before preliminary examination, it is still possible for some defense to be made when the man goes on trial. But if the prisoner is subjected to the third degree and forced into a confession during this period, the props underlying the defense are virtually destroyed months before the defendant actually enters the trial courtroom.

But the relationship between illegal detention and the third degree has not been clearly defined. It could be argued, on the one hand, that illegal detention is a necessary condition for the third degree. A report by the Illinois Division of the American Civil Liberties Union on *Secret Detention by the Chicago Police* came to the conclusion that "the practice of Third Degree methods . . . [is] almost always the fruit of lengthy secret detentions." [64] Many individuals have been of the same opinion. A former Assistant United States Attorney made this statement to me:

It may be that the relatively few cases of coerced confessions in the federal courts are due to the higher calibre and professional training of the federal police, i.e., the F.B.I., but I firmly believe that much of the credit must be attributed to the speedy arraignment rule prevailing in the federal courts.

On the other hand, it could be argued that where policemen are really intent on using third degree methods, a speedy preliminary examination rule will not always discourage them. The result may well be that certain officers will start the process of inquisition and attendant brutality sooner and will work at it with greater rapidity and with fiercer zeal. Curbs on the third degree are found in not one but in a variety of factors: stringent rules in the appellate courts; strong control by top police officials; a speedy preliminary examination rule; professionalization of the police; early enjoyment of the right to counsel; and so on. One of these factors alone is not sufficient to achieve the result. More lengthy discussion of reform in this area is reserved for the last chapter. But it is clear that an exclusive causal relationship does not exist between lengthy detention and the third degree—and that the eradication of lengthy detentions will not necessarily eradicate the problem of coerced confessions.

It should now be apparent that police powers are among the most potentially dangerous weapons that society entrusts to any man. The unrestricted use of those powers was one of the principal sources of irritation leading to the American Revolution. As a result, in the United States Constitution, and in all state constitutions, there are limitations on arbitrary arrest and seizure. In part because of such provisions, the power to arrest persons, to detain them, and to seize property has not often been used in this country as an instrument of political oppression. While this represents a major advance for freedom, it is discomforting to realize that these awesome powers have probably been used illegally in nonpolitical criminal cases by American policemen on every day since the Constitution went into effect on June 21, 1788.

2
The Police:
Violence and Coercion

The Breaking Point of Steel

In the *Daily Trentonian* of January 21, 1957, police reporter Emil Slaboda reported the strange story of an innocent man who had confessed a crime to Trenton, New Jersey, policemen. The next day the real culprit was found, and the innocent man was released. Slaboda asked, "Why had he confessed? There just wasn't any answer." But, according to the man who confessed, there was an answer—he had been the victim of a brutal third degree and had been coerced into that confession. His story follows.[1]

The innocent man was a 30-year-old colored man whom I shall call James Jones, although that was not his name. He was married and had one child. His wife was pregnant with a second child when this incident occurred. The second birth was also to be by Caesarean section, which was to involve large medical bills. To offset the expected expense of the coming child, Jones was working hard and steadily and was not spending money on his own entertainment. He had not been in the bar where the assault took place for four months prior to the night of the attack, December 22, 1956.

On the night of January 3, 1956, while Jones was working at his job on the night shift in a Trenton factory, several policemen had walked up to him in the company of a man who pointed at Jones and said: "That's the man." The police informed Jones that he was wanted for a knife attack on his accuser in a bar the previous month. Jones denied ever having seen the man and denied having had any part in the attack. But the police took him into custody and drove him to the First Precinct building on Chancery Lane in Trenton.

The empty courtroom of the municipal court was used as a place of interrogation. Three Trenton police officers were in the room with Jones. One of them brought in a typewriter, set it on a table, and said, "Tell us what happened." Jones denied any knowledge of the crime. Thereupon, the accuser was brought back into the room and again identified Jones. The officers angrily demanded that Jones confess. The officer at the typewriter started to type the statement. The officers supplied the details. Jones still maintained his innocence. At this point, according to the report Jones gave to a private detective who investigated this case—

. . . the big officer slapped him with his open hand. Jones was ordered to stand up and the smaller man who had been at the typewriter stepped behind him. The bigger man struck him in the stomach with his fist and almost immediately he felt a terrific blow from behind under his right ear. It could have been a fist although he had seen a blackjack in the officer's hand. He fell on his left side and was dazed. When he did not immediately arise both the big and the little officers kicked him in the shins, stomach and groin. He was badly hurt and pleaded with them to stop, finally promising that he would sign anything. The little officer went back to the typewriter and completed the typewritten statement by supplying the details aloud to Jones who would agree that the details were true.

He signed his name to the confession. . . . The interrogation lasted for about an hour. . . . It was about 8:30 P.M. when he was taken to a cell. Twenty-five minutes later he was allowed to telephone a neighbor. . . . He spent the night in a cell, alone.

In the municipal court the next morning, Jones told the judge that he was not guilty and that he wanted a lawyer. The judge postponed the hearing for this reason, evidently, and also on the strength of the fact that the victim admitted that he had been drinking on the night of the fight, which meant that his identification of Jones could have been wrong. Later in the day Jones was taken into the office of a captain of the Trenton Police Department. When asked why he wanted a lawyer, Jones repeated his claim of innocence to the captain. When asked why he had signed a confession, Jones remained silent. He was afraid that he would not be released if he told the captain about the beating. At this point, the captain asked a colored detective named Bill to take Jones into another room. "Maybe he will talk to you," the captain said. Jones told Bill that he didn't do it, and that when he was released, he would prove it. When Bill asked why he had signed the confession, Jones replied, "Even steel will break under enough pressure."

The captain was evidently impressed with Jones's story. It was because of the captain's action that any further injustice was prevented. The captain ordered a policeman to go to the bar where the attack occurred and to return to the station with the bartender. He also requested that the victim return to the station. Upon seeing Jones in his cell, the bartender exclaimed immediately: "You've got the wrong man! The man you want is L———, who lives on S——— Street." The police thereupon went out and found L———. When asked if he had cut the victim, L——— replied immediately that he had indeed done so and for a good reason. The victim had inflicted a severe wound on his head first, L——— claimed.

Meanwhile, Jones had been released on bail, and he and his wife went to her mother's home. Shortly after they arrived there, a friend of Mrs. Jones's came to report that the police had called at Jones's home. Immediately, Jones telephoned the police station and was told by an unidentified lieutenant, "You don't have to come in Monday. We now have the right man."

That night, January 4, 1957, James Jones went to a Trenton doctor to be treated for the beating by the police. The doctor's report, which was given to Jones, stated:

[James Jones, Sr.]
Above examined by me today and found to have multiple contusions of the scalp, abdomen, and flank which are quite tender. He also has a traumatic hernia quite tender.
                                              J——— M.F.———, M.D.

The next day Jones went to the law office of an attorney in Mercer County who had been retained by Jones's wife. This was the only time that Jones and the attorney conferred. The attorney opened the conversation by telling Jones that if what his wife had said was true, there was nothing he could do and that Jones could expect to go to prison for a long time, probably a year. Jones exclaimed,

"Don't you know that I was cleared?" The lawyer called the police and received confirmation of this fact. Jones then related the story of the beating. He showed how his body was taped and bandaged. The attorney said that Jones could sue the officers in the civil courts for assault and battery and perhaps recover a few hundred dollars, but that the legal fee would be about half of that amount. For this reason the attorney advised no further action.

Years have passed since the assault and battery was committed. The higher ranking officials of the Trenton Police Department have taken no disciplinary action against the police officers. The Mercer County Prosecutor has not sought a criminal indictment against the officers. The Attorney General of the State of New Jersey has not begun action. The federal government has not initiated prosecution under the Civil Rights Acts. The incident will be forgotten by everyone except the victim.

This case has many of the ingredients of the third degree as it now occurs throughout the country and as it has existed for years: a victim who is of the lower socioeconomic classes, with little power to retaliate; police officers who seek short cuts, including brutality to perform their job and to "get" a man they believe to be clearly guilty; a confession that was signed by the defendant and in his "own words" but that actually was composed by the officers; the fact that not all of the police officers in the precinct were satisfied with the tactics or the results; and, finally, the lack of any punitive action against the officers. Only one element in this case is unusual—the victim who confessed was innocent. Victims of the third degree often are guilty; this fact is used to justify brutality and coercion. But as this case shows, innocent men may be forced to sign confessions.

Interrogation: Essential Tool

The most important tool of police investigation in the great mass of ordinary cases is the personal interview. This has not yet been displaced by more scientific techniques, such as electronic eavesdropping or the matching of fingerprints. On numerous occasions, policemen of all ranks have impressed on me the great importance of simply asking people questions about crimes. This is frequently done to obtain information about the criminal conduct of another person, or to establish the innocence of the individual being questioned. But in almost every criminal case, the time eventually comes when the police must interrogate the criminal suspect himself. The major reason for the interrogation by the police of a man believed guilty is to obtain incriminating information, preferably a full confession in writing. Therefore, police questioning of criminal suspects creates a situation where rights may be threatened—and the defense may be destroyed at the beginning of the case.

Accordingly, statutes and court decisions impose certain minimum standards of conduct on policemen during the interrogation period. The most important limitation is that confessions cannot be coerced from a suspect. This is the most important limitation because it has a modicum of legal strength. The Supreme Court of the United States has declared that, since coercion of confessions is violative of the Due Process Clause of the Fourteenth Amendment, the Court will overrule the conviction of any person whose conviction was based on a coerced confession.[2] But it is always difficult to determine if a person who was interro-

gated by the police and who confessed to them was subjected to coercion; therefore, the Supreme Court is forced
to review the evidence and make its own factual evaluation of this delicate issue. The Court has found that
coercion occurred and has overruled convictions only
where the evidence strongly indicated that the police used
exceedingly shocking methods to obtain confessions. As
of late 1961, the Court had overruled convictions on this
basis in a total of only twenty-two cases.[3]

In my opinion, these cases represent only the smallest
fraction of the total number of convictions that have been
based on coerced confessions since the Supreme Court reversed the first such conviction in 1936.

The Anatomy of Violence and Coercion

COUNSEL AND SILENCE:
PHANTOM RIGHTS

Many people believe that when a man is arrested, he is
snarling, defiant, fully aware of his rights, and has a high-
priced legal mouthpiece who is pounding on the door of
the jail with one hand while waving a writ of habeas corpus in the other. This may be an accurate description of
a small percentage of the people arrested for serious crimes
each year. But more often the arrestee—even if he has
committed a horrible crime—is a rather scared fellow, in
an undefiant mood, with no knowledge of his rights.

When such a person is arrested by the police, and if he
is indigent, there is no legal duty imposed by the United
States Constitution on any court in the land to appoint defense counsel at that time.[4] But the right to hire counsel

is fully operative at any time, one hour before arrest or a few minutes thereafter. Of course, this is a right that is of little help to that great number of arrestees who have no funds. Even when a man has funds to hire an attorney who comes to the police station, it has been shown that the right to hire counsel may have severe limitations on its effectiveness in the period immediately after arrest. The right to have an attorney in the waiting room of a police station is no right at all to a man undergoing police interrogation, as Vincent Cicenia learned from the Newark police in the case described in the first chapter.

The right to remain silent under police questioning could be very significant in such circumstances. In New Jersey this right is inferred from the legal requirement that confessions be made voluntarily.[5] The right to silence may be exercised by any prisoner, rich or poor, with counsel or without; if adhered to, it would significantly affect the defense of the case. But from all of the evidence at hand, both of these rights—the right to hire counsel and the right to remain silent—mean little in reality to most defendants at this stage of the case when the rights are at least as vital as at the trial stage, when they are usually fully observed. Fifty-five per cent of the prisoners I interviewed admitted that they were aware of their right to refrain from telling the police about the alleged offense; but 42 per cent simply didn't know of their right, or thought they had to answer the police questions.[6]

Most policemen apparently have little inclination to advise prisoners, either of their right to remain silent or of their right to hire counsel while in police custody. The prisoners were asked: "Did the police tell you that you did not have to answer any of their questions?" and "Did the police tell you that you could hire an attorney while in their custody?" The responses of the state convict groups were the same on both questions—77 per cent negative. Fewer negative responses were made by the federal prisoners—52 per cent on the silence question, 64 per cent on the counsel question.[7] Constitutional philosophy and the realities of police practices are consistent on these points. American courts take the position that the police are not compelled to inform an arrested person of his rights.[8]

THE RIGHT TO BRUTALITY

During an interview with a prisoner at the New Jersey State Prison, I intimated in a casual way that, of course, it was illegal for policemen to subject anyone to the third degree, with its frequent brutality. In an amazed voice, the man exclaimed, "I thought the police had a *right* to punch you!" It is not difficult to understand why.

The prisoners were asked if they had signed a written confession to the offenses charged. Forty-eight per cent of the total group—174 out of 359—stated that they had done so.[9] The reasons for signing confessions given by these 174 prisoners present fascinating insights not only into the dynamics of interrogation, but also regarding the extent to which various police agencies observe constitutional rights. Following the questions that established whether or not they had signed confessions, the prisoners were asked three questions aimed at discovering the extent of coercion and brutality.

The first of these questions asked why prisoners had confessed.[10] Many prisoners replied that they confessed voluntarily—frequently because they were ashamed of their crimes. But their answers also suggest that a most important reason why arrested persons in New Jersey confess to serious crimes is police violence. Of those who had signed confessions, 22 per cent of the New Jersey prisoners gave police violence—as distinguished from the threat of violence—as their reason. Yet none of the prisoners in Philadelphia and only 5 per cent of those federal prisoners who signed a confession claimed police violence as the reason.

The single most important cause of written confessions among the federal prisoners, according to their own statements, was good police work; 39 per cent of those who had signed confessions gave as their reasons that they were either caught red-handed or the police had a solid case against them. Faced with this, the attitude of many prisoners arrested by federal authorities was: "Why fight? They've got me."

The second question in the brutality and coercion series was: "How were you treated by the police?" [11] The prisoners were directed to select one of three answers. Fifty-four per cent of the New Jersey prisoners who responded to the question claimed the threat of violence or violence by the police. The comparable figure in Philadelphia was 41 per cent (mainly threat of violence). Twenty-two per cent of the federal prisoners made similar claims, but 70 per cent of them checked the category labeled "Treated well, no complaint."

The mere fact that the police threatened violence or actually resorted to violence does not in and of itself, of course, mean that this action was illegal or unconstitutional. For this reason, a third question was asked to make another approach toward understanding third-degree practices. The question read: "If the police threatened violence or actually hit you, did they do so to force you to sign a confession?" [12] Of those New Jersey prisoners who on this question alleged that they had been subjected to violence or the threat of violence, 70 per cent claimed that the reason was to coerce confessions. There were very few such claims by the Philadelphia and federal prisoners.

FEDERAL-STATE COMPARISONS

A comparison of the responses of the prisoners categorized according to the interrogating police agency revealed even more striking contrasts between the practices of New Jersey policemen, on the one hand, and federal policemen, on the other hand.[13] No really significant differences were found among the prisoner responses when they were broken down according to the interrogating police agency within the state of New Jersey.

Perhaps the most significant set of figures produced in this study is that pertaining to the FBI. Of the twenty-four men who had been arrested by the FBI and who answered the pertinent question, not a single one claimed violence or the threat of violence. On the coerced confession question, the answers were equally impressive. No prisoner arrested by the FBI claimed that he had been subjected to violence or its threat in order to induce him to sign a confession. There have been many statements made about the manner in which the FBI generally refrains from violence and coercion in ordinary criminal cases. Yet it is hard to imagine more impressive documentation than the responses of these prisoners. Every one of them could point his finger at the FBI and say that he was put in prison because of the efforts of its agents. Yet not a single prisoner arrested by the FBI claimed violence or the third degree.

The prisoners arrested by the FBI were not entirely

without bitterness or rancor. Some of them indicated that they thought they had been outsmarted by the FBI in ways that they considered unfair. But none of them stated that the FBI ever resorted to anything approaching the third degree. Other federal agencies did not fare as well as the FBI with the prisoners, but their records are immeasurably better than the police in any of the larger cities of New Jersey.[14]

In striking contrast to the 24 FBI prisoner responses were the responses of the 27 prisoners arrested and interrogated by the police of Newark, the largest city in New Jersey. Only 22 per cent stated that they had no complaint and that they were treated well by the police. The rest claimed either the threat of violence or actual violence. Moreover, in 71 per cent of these cases, the reason for violence or its threat was allegedly the coercion of a confession. This set of statistics coincides with the statements made by many prisoners I interviewed at different times and in different prisons. A number of prisoners from both the New Jersey State Prison and from the New Jersey Bordentown Reformatory stated in interviews that they had been subjected to the third degree in Newark and then described methods that were strikingly similar. These methods were also described to me by attorneys who had handled cases in Newark.

A standard technique in Newark, according to many informants,[15] is to force the prisoner to face the wall and drop his trousers, whereupon a rubber hose is applied to the backs of his legs. The hose may also be applied to other parts of the body. One prisoner gave me a picture of himself that showed faint bruise marks on his body; he had, he claimed, been beaten with a rubber hose by the police in Newark. Those reports and claims describing the matter in detail almost invariably stated that the third degree was suffered at the headquarters building of the Newark Police Department.

The figures listed under Jersey City, the second largest city in the state, were based on only eight answers. This is a very small base upon which to make generalizations. Even so, it is noteworthy that none of these men said that they had been treated well. All stated that they had either been subjected to the threat of violence or violence itself; and all from Jersey City who answered the question stated that the reason for this treatment was the coercion of a confession. Oral statements from prisoners who were arrested in Jersey City are similar to those made by prisoners arrested in Newark. Both groups agree that the police in both cities can be "pretty tough" on a noncooperative arrestee. The claims of those prisoners arrested in Paterson, the third largest city in the state, also presented an unfavorable picture of police practices. And the responses of many other New Jersey prisoners indicate that policemen in some smaller cities and towns act like their brethren in the big cities when it comes to brutality and the coercion of confessions.

The difference between the tactics usually employed by federal civilian police agencies and by state and local police, indicated by these statistics, was brought out even more in two rather extraordinary "seminars" held at the Federal Penitentiary in Lewisburg, Pennsylvania, on the morning and afternoon of one day in the summer of 1959. I was at the front of a large room in which approximately 50 prisoners were seated. Their offenses ranged from the making of "a little shine" in the hills of Kentucky to bank robbery and murder. Many of them had been in other prisons and had been arrested by state and local policemen in many parts of the country. Every one of them had been placed in prison this time because of the efforts of federal policemen. So there was no reason for any of them to praise these officers unnecessarily. After administering the written questionnaire to two groups, one group in the morning and the other in the afternoon, I asked the men a series of questions orally. As bitter as these men were about being in prison, and although they disagreed on many issues, they were in clear agreement on one point: it is an exceedingly rare event when a federal policeman beats or in other ways coerces a prisoner into a confession; but it is a common event when a state or local policeman does so.

One young prisoner described an incident that graphically shows this difference in method. He stated that he was arrested in Cincinnati, Ohio, by the local police for car theft. Several policemen then subjected him to a third-degree session during which they "broke my nose and a bone in my chest." However, since the prisoner had taken the car across a state line, the FBI had jurisdiction under the Dyer Act, which makes the transportation of a stolen motor vehicle across a state line a federal offense. Several FBI agents walked into the room while the prisoner was being beaten. According to the prisoner, the FBI agents demanded that the beating stop immediately or they would see to it that the policemen lost their jobs.

Other comments by the federal prisoners, while not so dramatic, drove home this same point. One prisoner, who had been through the criminal process three times before, stated the matter with simple finality: "It is not the custom of U.S. Marshals to use force to obtain a signed confession." Another prisoner with experience in both state and federal courts indicated that, in his opinion, the more favorable treatment by federal police fits into a larger picture. He wrote on his questionnaire:

> There is more justice on the whole in the federal courts than the state courts. You are not threatened with violence, more consideration as human being, food is better, also the living facilities, allowed more contact with your people, before and after an arrest and conviction.

So here we have men arrested by federal police, convicted by the federal courts, and serving long sentences in a federal prison, men who would have every reason to be bitter against everything "federal," taking the position that these agencies operate more fairly than state agencies.

At least a dozen of these discussions were held with groups of prisoners in New Jersey. Most of them had had experience only with New Jersey police. Their vehement remarks about the third degree administered by New Jersey policemen stand out in sharp contrast to the generally favorable remarks made by the federal prisoners regarding federal police agencies. These contrasts lend weight to the claims of the New Jersey prisoners. They also suggest that it is possible to enforce the law without illegal violence and the coercion of confessions.

COUNSEL AND THE THIRD DEGREE

Because police action affecting the rights of defendants is so significant in any realistic analysis of the criminal process, the prisoners' responses on police treatment were broken down even further. Three additional cross-checks were made on both the police violence question and the related coerced confession question. In the first cross-check, the breakdown was on treatment by police according to the type of counsel who represented the prisoner. The results suggest that the fact that a man is represented by a retained counsel, as opposed to an attorney assigned because of indigence, does not affect the type of treatment he receives from the police. No significant differences on the violence and coercion questions appeared in the answers of these two groups.[16]

However, a surprisingly small percentage of those New Jersey prisoners who were not represented by any attorney claimed that they had been subjected to the third degree. While over 40 per cent of the New Jersey prisoners who were represented by an attorney claimed that they had been victims of the third degree, only 20 per cent of the men in the "no counsel" category made such claims. But their lack of counsel and their somewhat better treatment by the police may both have been effects rather than causes —effects of their generally more cooperative, "no contest" attitude. Many men waive counsel and, as part of the same package deal, agree to plead guilty in return for certain considerations offered by the police or the prosecution.[17] In effect, then, the men without counsel may well have been the most cooperative of any in the entire group. Therefore, the reasons for the third degree may not have been present to the same extent as in the case of other men who may have been in more of a fighting mood.

Moreover, attorneys generally do not confer with their clients until some time after arrest. This means, therefore, that when suspects are being interrogated, virtually all of them have one thing in common regarding the factor of counsel—they do not have the guidance of an attorney.

It might be assumed that the police would treat a man of high social standing with greater consideration than a slum-dweller. These figures do not prove or disprove the point. For the "counsel" categories do not reflect differences in class. There were no great financial or social barriers separating the men who had assigned counsel, or who had no attorney, and those who were able to pay a fee. In only a few instances could it be said that men in the retained group were of the middle or upper classes in society. Most of those who paid their counsel gave him only a few hundred dollars. Virtually all of the men interviewed, regardless of the type of counsel they had, were of the lower social classes.

RACE AND THE THIRD DEGREE

The second cross-check on police treatment broke down the responses according to race. The New Jersey prisoner responses indicated that the extent of police violence and the third degree was almost the same within each racial group, with the whites reporting a slight edge on bad treatment.[18] It would seem that there is some slight comfort here. For this suggests that the third degree in New Jersey, as evil as it is, is not often further infected by the virus of racial hate. Absence of racial discrimination among federal policemen on this score is also suggested by the distribution between the racial groups of the few claims of the third degree by federal prisoners.

Less comfort is found among the responses of the Philadelphia prisoners. Only one (9 per cent) of the white prisoners claimed that he had been subjected to violence or its threat for the purpose of the coercion of a confession. On the other hand, 33 per cent of the nonwhite prisoners claimed that the third degree, accompanied by violence or its threat, was used against them by Philadelphia policemen. Of course, the small number of Philadelphia prisoners interviewed requires that only the most cautious of conclusions be drawn. Therefore, all that can be said is that this set of statistics merely suggests the possibility of a discriminatory attitude toward nonwhite arrestees. But the evidence is neither strong nor conclusive on this point.[19]

GUILT AND THE THIRD DEGREE

A third cross-check on the police violence question was made by breaking down the responses of the prisoners according to their claims of guilt or innocence. The guilt or innocence question had three categories: first, claims of complete innocence; second, admission of guilt qualified by "special circumstances"; and, third, admission of guilt with "no sad story." [20] Seventy-six per cent of the men marked the last two categories and thus admitted their guilt. A major question to be answered, therefore, was whether or not the prisoners who claimed innocence were the only men who also claimed violence by the police. If this was the case, it could well be argued that the prisoners were alleging harsh treatment by the police to buttress a false claim of innocence. The results do not support this conclusion.

It is true that there was, on the part of those who claimed innocence, a greater reluctance to admit that they were treated well by the police and a correspondingly greater tendency by these men to claim the threat of violence or violence itself. Yet, there were many claims of violence or its threat among the 180 New Jersey prisoners who admitted their guilt—23 per cent claiming the threat of violence and 28 per cent claiming violence.[21]

If we exclude the claims of violent coercion made by those prisoners who claimed complete innocence, it appears that 27 per cent of all the New Jersey prisoners both admitted their guilt and claimed they had been subjected to violence or the threat of violence by policemen for the purpose of the coercion of confessions. The comparable figure for the smaller Philadelphia group is 10 per cent and for the federal prisoners is 8 per cent.[22]

When a prisoner claims that he was subjected to brutality and the third degree, the usual answer by police officials is, of course, that the prisoner is attempting to prove a spurious claim of innocence. This answer loses its force when a man who now admits his guilt but who claimed innocence when first arrested states that he was subjected to a brutal third degree. It is rare to find such cases, but, protected by the cloak of anonymity, many were uncovered in the sample of prisoners interviewed. And when a man admits a serious crime and at the same time alleges police brutality, there is a ring of truth to both statements. For example, one young man was arrested for a serious offense by the police of Paterson, New Jersey. When first arrested, he maintained that he was innocent, but he admitted full responsibility for the crime on the questionnaire. In response to the question asking why he had signed a written confession, he wrote,

> Because I was beat and not fed. And they had witnesses. And my partner signed first. And they beat me for further information. And I just reached my breaking point. And finally got fed up with the whole thing. And I also thought I would get off.

At the end of his questionnaire, this young man, who had a ninth grade education, wrote:

. . . A lot of guys get beat. And everyone has a breaking [point], or mostly everyone. They should be protected. The guilty as well as the innocent.

These three cross-checks on the violence and the third-degree questions lend support to the conclusion that such police practices are all too common in New Jersey—and that they are not common practices of federal policemen. For the cross-checks showed that it was not only those prisoners who might have had a special sense of bitterness—the indigent, Negroes, and those claiming innocence —who alleged that New Jersey policemen resorted to unfair, uncivilized, and unconstitutional practices.

The Fruits and the Marks of Coercion

Few men can resist giving a statement when they are subjected to police coercion and brutality. As James Jones said, "Even steel will break under enough pressure." Most people are not made of steel. Many are highly nervous, timid, perhaps susceptible to suggestions to such an extent that any action proposed by a figure of authority, as a policeman so definitely is, will be taken as law. To many people, confinement in a closed room with several policemen is an extreme form of coercion. In one case, the New Jersey Supreme Court said: "Although only three actually participated, there were six persons present besides the accused in a small room during most of the interrogation. The substance of the complaint is that the presence of so many police made the appellant nervous and fearful." [23] The court refused to accept this argument. But are there not many people who would be fearful in a like situation? Are there not many people of normal intelligence and emotional stability who would feel forced to give a confession in such a situation, especially when the police threatened, as the defendant claimed they did here, to bring in his mother for questioning unless he confessed?

In many police interrogation rooms no blow need be struck; the man may well know the penalty for resistance. A man in the New Jersey State Prison told me that although he was not assaulted, he had signed a confession, but "it wasn't a true confession. I didn't write it. They just gave it to me to put an X on it. I can write my name, but I was sorta confused." "If you are innocent, why did you even put your X on the statement?" I asked. His reply was: "Those cops were going to beat my head in with a rubber hose unless I did. I can't stand no beating. After I signed, they laughed."

Threats and psychological pressure alone may, of course, result in unconstitutional coercion and, when properly argued up the court ladder, cause the reversal of a conviction. For example, in 1957 the Supreme Court of the United States overturned a conviction on the basis of a coerced confession although the prisoner had not suffered physical violence. But he had been put through nine days of intermittent questioning. The defendant was a Negro of low mentality, convicted and sentenced to death in an Alabama court for burglary and attempted rape of a white woman. Chief Justice Earl Warren, speaking for the majority, stated that "the circumstances of pressure applied against the power of resistance of this petitioner, who cannot be deemed other than weak of will or mind, deprived him of due process of law." [24] Justice Felix Frankfurter showed an acute understanding of the human emotions involved when he said: "For myself, I cannot see the difference, with respect to the 'voluntariness' of a confession, between the subversion of freedom of the will through physical punishment and the sapping of the will appropriately to be inferred from the circumstances of this case. . . ." [25] Three years later, in reversing another conviction that arose in Alabama, Chief Justice Warren made it clear that "the blood of the accused is not the only hallmark of an unconstitutional inquisition." [26]

Even when violence is used, it is frequently difficult afterwards to find the marks that may be used to help establish a claim of coercion. For there is a guiding rule for police violence during questioning that is often followed: the prisoner should be hit where it will not show by the time a defense doctor examines him. A rubber hose on the head or the back of the legs can cause vicious pain, but it probably won't break bones; and the bruises, if any, will usually heal within a week or ten days. The back of a billy club or a fist in the stomach is also considered good practice. It is rare, as happened in the case of James Jones, that a doctor gets to the man so rapidly that a medical certificate can be produced stating that the defendant was suffering from stomach injuries, from a hernia, and from abrasions the day after being "talked to" by the police.

Judge Jerome Frank and Barbara Frank wrote that "we hear of the merits of the rubber hose; it inflicts severe pain but leaves no traces." Apparently there is, among some policemen, a certain amount of pride in a showing of "scientific" knowledge of the various techniques possible to obtain confessions. The Franks reported the following from the memoirs of a police captain: "A sharp, but not heavy blow on the skull, repeated at regular intervals, so that the regularity of the blows arouses anticipation which increases the torture; assuring the suspect that he will not be hurt, then suddenly felling him with a blow from behind with a club or a slab of wood, followed by further sympathy and assurance when the man revives, only to have the same thing happen again, the man never seeing who strikes him. . . ." [27]

Police Power in a Democratic Society

Several arguments could be made in answer to the charge that confessions are being wrung out of men by violence or other forms of the third degree. The first is that if a confession is made involuntarily, the courts will rule it inadmissible, and it will not affect the defense of the case. This is only a partial truth and, to the extent that it is true, it is barely effective from the viewpoint of the defense. Rarely will a trial judge rule that as a matter of law a confession is invalid. If there is any evidence to the effect that the confession was voluntary, it usually then becomes a question of fact for the jury, not the judge. To anyone who has ever sat in court and watched the issue of coercion dealt with, it is apparent that the jury is seldom impressed by the denial. The prosecutor stands before the jury and reads the confession; thereby the gory facts of the crime are paraded in profuse detail and in the defendant's "own words" before the court. A well-dressed police detective in a neat civilian suit states that he is a notary public, that the defendant swore to the veracity of this particular statement, and that he signed it voluntarily. Much later in the case, the defendant, without supporting witnesses, states that he was forced to sign this statement. Here, then, are conflicting statements that are sufficient to make this a question for the jury. And here a legal fiction commences operation. The jury is charged by the judge:

"If you do not believe the defendant gave the statement voluntarily, disregard it." The effect of such an admonition in most cases needs no comment.

A further argument might be that the police are in a difficult business, where both sides "play rough," and that, in certain cases, this is the only way to get a conviction. It is undoubtedly true that at the time of arrest there is always the possibility of violence by the person detained. Policemen may be in danger at this point. But even if it is granted that at arrest some roughness is necessary, where is the danger when three or four policemen are interviewing one man whose arms are handcuffed to a chair?

The related argument—"this is the only way to get a conviction"—is plainly unsound. No one who has any concern for the great Anglo-American legal tradition of fair play and fair trial could suggest that they be put aside to obtain a conviction in a particular case. It is a fundamental principle in our judicial system that if a man, guilty *in fact*, cannot be convicted *legally*, he goes free. There is a higher value at stake here than conviction of the guilty. That value is preservation of the attitude toward individual dignity that is embodied in our law of criminal procedure. Justice Hugo Black of the United States Supreme Court laid down this dictum against the "conviction" position:

> It is undeniable that law enforcement officers could rack up more convictions if they were not "hampered" by the defendant's counsel or the presence of others who might report to the public the manner in which people were being convicted. But the procedural safeguards deemed essential for due process have been imposed deliberately with full knowledge that they will occasionally impede the conviction of persons suspected of crime.[28]

The argument goes much further. The simple truth is that confessions are often wrung out of innocent people.[29] Each such incident is an irremovable stain on the fabric of justice.

I have presented a dark picture of American police methods. It is not intended as an indictment of the tens of thousands of devoted and fair officers who work long hours for low pay at an arduous task. During 1960, approximately 200,000 policemen [30] had to cope with at least 1,861,300 serious offenses,[31] perhaps two or three times that many minor ones and, in addition, performed uncounted acts of mercy and assistance to citizens in distress. Most Americans probably do not realize the danger to which these men are often exposed. American policemen faced at least 9,621 assaults in 1960; [32] 48 officers were killed during that year in the course of their duties.[33] Moreover, many policemen manage to fight crime while staying within the restrictions of the United States Constitution. This is reflected in the statistics. For example, while 46 per cent of all prisoners claimed police violence or its threat, 49 per cent stated that they had been treated well.[34] Certainly, many of these prisoners were treated well because they "cooperated" with the police, but there is no doubt that many of them were not subjected to the third degree or brutality because the policemen respected the law.

All of this does not in the least change the sad facts regarding the practices of many policemen documented in this study. But it does make clear that criticism should be grounded on an understanding of the extremely difficult and dangerous service that we in American society want our policemen to perform.

While admitting the risk that the discussion of police

practices might subject thousands of devoted officers to unjust criticism, there is one basic philosophical position that can be strongly stated without fear of stigmatizing the "good cops" as opposed to the "bad" ones, for it applies to them all: It is essential to a free society, to a democracy, that those who hold power, whether President or policeman, be subjected to constant scrutiny and challenge. This democratic notion does not involve distrust of our country's policemen or its Presidents—simply a distrust of unlimited power. In a free society, policemen are looked upon as friends by most people, but those officers of the law who violate the law should be treated as enemies. To preserve the free society, even the best-intentioned and most humane policeman should never be allowed to escape the feeling that, in the best Anglo-American tradition, stout-hearted yeomanry and lusty-lunged citizenry are looking over his shoulder. And if any policeman feels he can't work under these conditions, then he should turn in his badge and gun.

As enforcers of the law, policemen have a duty to uphold that law, not only by way of enforcement, but also by way of example. When their practices conform with the law, this is nothing more or less than a policeman's duty. But when the enforcers of the law flout it in the process, this is a serious evil, at which the fire of intelligent criticism should be directed.

A brief summary of the first stages of the criminal process shows that the key fact for the defendant is that a large number of cases are won by the police in the first few days. The fact that the defendant later has the protection implicit in review of the charges by a grand jury, the right to counsel, and the right to trial by jury—great rights, the fruit of hundreds of years of a splendid Anglo-American legal development—does not alter the signal fact that "trials" take place in the police station.

And what can be said of the police? No one should criticize a policeman carelessly. His functions are essential to our society. Large numbers of policemen perform their work of crime detection and apprehension well within the borders of the Constitution and fair play. But many others resort to illegal arrests and seizures, violence, illegal detentions, the threat of violence, and the coercion of confessions. When a defense lawyer enters the case, whether it be one day or one month after arrest, he frequently finds that no legal defense is possible. So large numbers of cases are won in American courts not by the prosecutor but by the police who are using unconstitutional and uncivilized methods. This is a serious problem for it strikes at the very foundations of the democratic state.

3
First Judicial Test

Two formal judicial steps occur before the accused is prosecuted for a serious criminal offense. The first of these is the preliminary examination. The second is the grand jury hearing. In both proceedings the stated legal purpose is not to make a final determination of guilt or innocence but rather to make a preliminary finding that there appears to be sufficient evidence to warrant further action by the state.

Preliminary Examination: Function

Like so many features of American criminal justice, the preliminary examination has roots in the legal history of the Continent and of England. In both places the pre-liminary examination was originally used as a prosecution device. The function of the magistrate was to interrogate the defendant in order to obtain evidence of guilt. If such evidence was found, the magistrate had the further function of preserving it until the time of trial. But over the centuries, the preliminary examination slowly evolved into a judicial hearing with the magistrate taking on the disinterested role of a judge. An important factor in the final stages of this development was the growth of professional, full-time police forces. This helped to establish the distinction between the prosecutive function, now wholly in the hands of the police, and the judicial function performed by the judge or magistrate at the first court level.[1]

If the examination is properly conducted, it is a formidable safeguard against harassment of a defendant by a prosecution not based on fact. In performing its present function of determining whether or not probable cause exists to believe that the defendant committed a crime, the preliminary examination is, in theory, a significant judicial check at an early stage in the prosecution:

> The object or purpose of the preliminary examination is to prevent hasty, malicious, improvident, and oppressive prosecutions, to protect the person charged from open and public accusations of crime, to avoid both for the defendant and the public the expense of a public trial, and to save the defendant from the humiliation and anxiety involved in public prosecution, and to discover whether or not there are substantial grounds upon which a prosecution may be based.[2]

The New Jersey rules provide in this regard that,

> . . . if, from the evidence, it appears to the magistrate that there is probable cause to believe that an offense has been committed and that the defendant has committed it, the magistrate shall forthwith bind him over to await final determination of the cause, otherwise, he shall discharge him.[3]

The rule goes on to state that where an indictable offense is charged, the magistrate must give the county prosecutor notice before the defendant is finally discharged. The defendant has the right to cross-examine state witnesses at the preliminary examination. Such an arrangement for preliminary hearings is common in American courts.

The United States Constitution does not require that the accused in federal criminal proceedings be given a preliminary examination. And the Supreme Court of the United States has not interpreted the Due Process Clause of the Fourteenth Amendment as requiring a preliminary examination in state trials.[4] Therefore, the preliminary examination cannot be listed among those great constitutional safeguards explicitly protected by the Supreme Law of the Land. In the federal courts and in most state courts, provision for the preliminary hearing is found in a combination of statutes and court rules. Some states have considered the preliminary examination sufficiently important, however, to provide for a preliminary examination in their constitutions. Regardless of their constitutional status, however, preliminary examinations are actually held in many criminal prosecutions for serious crimes in New Jersey and in other states.

Effectiveness

The rule universally found in the law throughout the country is that the delay between arrest and preliminary examination shall be kept to a minimum. The reasons for placing a premium on a minimal delay between arrest and preliminary examination are many. In the context of this discussion, one of these reasons is most prominent. If the examination is meant to prevent the harassment of the innocent by a needless prosecution, it is certainly desirable that the examination and the termination of the harassment take place as soon as possible. Whatever premium is placed on a speedy preliminary examination, speed is not the proper description in many New Jersey cases— since, as I have already indicated, the mean average between arrest and examination for the New Jersey prisoners I interviewed was 6.5 days, with the median being 4 days.[5]

Delay in bringing prisoners before the local court would be partially compensated for if it could be shown that once the prisoner arrives at this court, the preliminary examination performs an effective function. That function is primarily, of course, to provide a judicial check on the prosecution. Unfortunately, it cannot be said with assurance that this function is effectively served. This is mainly because of a dearth of information, but also because the data that are available do not point in that direction. A good statistical test of the effectiveness of the preliminary examination in New Jersey would be found in an examination of the number of prosecutions dismissed by the local magistrate in these proceedings. Such statistics are not available. They could not be provided by the prisoners interviewed since in every case probable cause had quite obviously been found.

Statistics are available from the crime surveys of the 1920's and the 1930's regarding other states. These studies indicate that from 10 to 50 per cent of the cases brought into court for a preliminary examination were dismissed at this stage for a variety of reasons, including lack of probable cause, failure to prosecute due to failure of witnesses to appear, and the entry of a *nolle prosequi* by the prosecutor.[6] The fact that so many cases are dismissed at the preliminary examination suggests that the preliminary examination is serving a function, that it has some impact on the course of judicial events. But, in fact, the reasons for dismissals are varied, ranging from poor organization on the part of the prosecution (failure of witnesses to appear) to the more significant "lack of probable cause." And some of these same crime surveys were critical of the conduct of preliminary examinations. Prosecutors held a low estimate of their worth. The Missouri Crime Survey concluded that "the courts of preliminary hearing play an unimportant role in the administration of justice." [7] The evidence available regarding New Jersey is consistent with the finding that the role of the preliminary examination is a minor one.

ASSEMBLY LINE JUSTICE

When I visited several New Jersey municipal court sessions in the late 1950's, the proceedings were not impressive. People milled about the courtroom, among the seats for the audience and within the bench enclosure, frequently talking and creating such a disturbance that the prisoner could not hear what the magistrate or the court clerk was saying.

The court rules make express provisions for a lengthy statement by the magistrate to the accused.[8] In each case the magistrate is required to inform the defendant of the nature of the complaint against him; "of his right to obtain counsel or, if indigent, of the privilege of having counsel assigned"; of the right to make an unsworn statement; of the right to remain silent; of the right to a preliminary examination; of the right of indictment by the grand jury and trial by petit jury in cases where indictable offenses are involved; of his right to have the case tried by the magistrate upon waiver of indictment and jury trial in those cases where this is permissible; and that if a statement is made, it may be used against him. This is a formidable discourse, which, according to the rule, must take place in almost every one of the thousands of cases heard by magistrates in New Jersey. It appears, however, that even in many essential particulars, the rule is not observed.

In the proceedings I observed, the clerk read the complaint in a rapid, clipped monotone that barely cut into the sound of the courtroom, and then asked, "How do you plead?" In one case the defendant replied, "Guilty." As the proceedings started to move on rapidly to the next case, a detective standing beside the defendant nudged him, and said something to him in a low voice. Obviously, the defendant had not heard the complaint. The detective, to his credit, informed the defendant that he had just pleaded guilty to a crime that he claimed he had not committed. At this point the prisoner exclaimed, "Guilty to the breaking and entering. Not to stealing the watch!"

The tabulation of the prisoners' responses lends support to the view that most preliminary examinations are hasty proceedings with little real examination of the facts of the case.[9] The majority of the men tried in New Jersey, as well as in the two other jurisdictions involved, stated that the only step they took was to enter a plea. Although there was an opportunity for the prisoners to cross-examine the complaining officer, it appears that this was rarely done. Prisoners usually picked up only slight additional knowledge of the details of the prosecutor's case during the hearing.

A COURT WITHOUT COUNSEL

Most magistrates advise defendants appearing without counsel at the preliminary examination that an adjournment will be granted to allow them time to hire an attorney. According to the prisoners, the defendant in New Jersey is not usually advised by municipal magistrates, as the court rules require, that he has a right to assigned counsel if he is indigent.[10] Support for this statement is found in the responses to a questionnaire I sent to New Jersey magistrates in 1957.[11] Few of the prisoners indicated that a lawyer was actually assigned to them by the judge at the preliminary examination.[12] There is a strong correlation on this point between the responses of the prisoners and the replies of the magistrates to the mailed questionnaires. Out of an estimated 513 indigent defendants who appeared in their courts at preliminary examinations during a twelve-month period, only three assignments of counsel were reported by the magistrates.

Magistrates were also uncertain of their *power* to assign counsel. They were asked, "Does this court have the power to assign counsel to indigent defendants in these cases?" The responses were about evenly divided, with 17 negative and 18 affirmative responses. One magistrate stated:

The assignment of counsel involves:
(a) the power to compel counsel to accept and act under such assignment;
(b) the ability to compensate counsel for so acting.
A magistrate has neither.

The municipal court is run largely without counsel, either for the prosecution or for the defense.[13] The county prosecutors do not have enough assistants to assign daily to the many municipal courts scattered throughout their respective counties. Certain of the county prosecutors have only in recent years—during the late 1950's—initiated the practice of assigning an assistant prosecutor to appear in the municipal courts of the larger cities, as is done in Newark, for example. Defense counsel rarely appear with the accused at preliminary hearings. Because many defendants are indigent, this is not a matter of choice, but of necessity. The New Jersey assigned counsel system, like other assigned counsel systems in the United States, simply does not provide for assignment until a much later stage in the proceedings.

Most of the magistrates who answered the questionnaire felt that a need for counsel at the preliminary examination existed in certain cases. As one municipal judge put it,

Very often a municipal judge must be an original sifter of facts, draw the complaint, sit as judge, as jury, prosecutor, and defense attorney. *No man* is capable of same, yet we are asked daily to perform this task.

The fact that counsel is not assigned to indigents at the preliminary examination is particularly damaging to the defense from the viewpoint of fact-finding. Because there are no funds provided for defense investigation, it would be advantageous for the defense to cross-examine under oath the state witnesses who appear at the preliminary examination. This would be the only opportunity for the defense to obtain advance insight into the prosecution's case. If this opportunity were fully explored, it would be a weight on the defense side of the scales that would partially compensate for the lack of facilities for investigation. Even if defender systems were operating in all American states with professional investigators, the cross-examination of the state's key witness in advance would, in many cases, be vital for the defense. However, few defendants are even aware of their right to cross-examine the state's witnesses, and, as previously indicated, almost none has the audacity to do so. This right could be implemented only if a system of providing counsel at the preliminary examination was adopted.

A study of rural Tompkins County, New York, published in 1959, found practices very much like those uncovered in this study. On the great defense potential of the preliminary examination, Professors Willcox and Bloustein wrote:

> All but one of our [lawyer] consultants with extensive criminal practice repeatedly stressed the crucial importance to the defense of the preliminary hearing. The people's case appears on this examination. Its weaknesses can then be probed and exploited before the trial. The witnesses are more likely to tell the truth at the hearing than at the trial, because the events are fresher in their memories; hence their later wishful recollections, coached or spontaneous, can more easily be exposed at the trial for what they are.[14]

But, the two professors concluded, it is an unrealized potential in Tompkins County:

> The committing magistrate does not ordinarily impress upon the prisoner the importance of the preliminary examination; instead he usually advises him to save time by either waiving it or "getting it over with." This amounts to suggesting that the prisoner either waive the examination altogether or else allow the People to examine their witnesses before he has a chance to get counsel. The committing magistrate looks upon the preliminary hearing as

an unimportant detail, a mere formal step toward the finding of probable cause. The indigent person, who has no
counsel at this stage nor any offer of assigned counsel, is
most unlikely to withstand the combined pressures from
police and magistrate for his waiver of hearing or for a
"quick hearing" without counsel.[15]

In light of these facts, what judicial function does the
preliminary examination serve in the United States? The
best that can be said for it is this: it presents the opportunity for a challenge to the prosecution by a palpably
innocent man and for cross-examination of the state's witnesses to obtain advance information of the prosecution's
case. But this is an opportunity that is rarely used because
of lack of counsel. In the future, many county prosecutors
will probably fill in this gap on the state's side of the case
by assigning assistants to certain municipal courts. Therefore, from the viewpoint of the defense, the adversary
character of the preliminary examination will be dimin-
ished to an even greater extent. This tendency will probably be halted only when counsel for the defense enter
the case as a regular procedure shortly after arrest. With
proper reforms on both the prosecution and defense sides,
the preliminary examination could serve a vital function
in the machinery of justice. But such reforms are not apt
to occur in the near future, except in small doses.

The Special Committee to Study Defender Systems,
which performed a nationwide study of criminal legal aid,
stated in its report, "There is a strong argument that the
time a defendant needs counsel most is immediately after
his arrest and until trial." [16] In a similar vein are the conclusions of the Commission on Legal Aid of the Bar Association of the District of Columbia. Among other things,

the Commission studied preliminary hearings before United States Commissioners. "The need for legal assistance at this stage is manifest," the report stated.[17]

Municipal Court Trials

Although the main concern of this study is the criminal process in the more serious cases destined for the county courts, it must not be forgotten that the municipal courts serve other functions besides holding preliminary examinations for upper court cases. It could legitimately be argued that preliminary examinations are much less significant than the thousands of cases lower courts hear within their final jurisdiction every year. These local courts of inferior criminal jurisdiction handle all city offenses and a large number of indictable crimes upon a waiver of indictment and trial by jury. The great majority of people who come in contact with the criminal courts do so at the municipal court level in New Jersey, as in most states. There are few jury trials, and most cases are disposed of rapidly.

So, while municipal courts are simply check points for serious cases destined for second-level courts, they provide the whole judicial proceeding for the so-called minor cases. Few defendants who have the choice of having their case heard by the county court or the municipal court [18] select the former. When a case of this nature comes before a municipal magistrate, the usual procedure is for the magistrate to tell the defendant that he has a right to indictment and trial by jury or to have the case disposed of "here and now." In most instances, the defendants I observed responded eagerly, "I want you to handle it, Judge." A block of waiver forms is kept at hand by the clerk of courts. Few defendants seem to feel that they will benefit from indictment or trial by jury. Many fear to face the county court on sentence day. After the defendant signs the waiver form, the case is heard immediately by the judge in the usual summary proceeding.

The sentences imposed by the municipal courts rarely exceed one year. Yet, in many instances a sentence imposed by a municipal court may be more severe than that imposed by the county court. If the county court imposes a sentence of one to two years in the state penitentiary, the prisoner may well be released at the expiration of ten months, as the system of parole now operates. On the other hand, a prisoner sentenced to the county jail for one year may spend the entire period there. Because of the volume of business in the local courts, the percentage of sentences of even six months or more is not impressive. However, a survey of the municipal court docket book in Newark revealed that there were 64 sentences of six months or more in the half-year period from April 1, 1955, to September 30, 1955.[19]

But even in these cases, as in the preliminary examinations, few of the defendants appeared with counsel. Of the 64 defendants who received sentences of six months or more in the Newark municipal court, only three appeared with defense counsel. Most defendants appear without counsel because they are indigent and unable to retain an attorney.[20]

Too often in minor cases, defendants plead guilty to save delay and the expense of counsel. Only later do they realize that they are now branded forever with a criminal record—a brand that becomes a bar whenever they seek employment or apply for a loan. This danger is recognized by some members of the judiciary; witness this statement by Judge William B. Neely of Los Angeles:

The need for adequate defense [counsel] penetrates to the municipal court where every day ill-advised people plead guilty to charges simply because the alternative involves weeks and months of preparation and waiting. Police, fellow prisoners, and well-meaning friends perpetuate the myth that a plea of guilty, with its suspended sentence, is easier for a man who can't afford the time and money to clear his name of false charges. Such minor charges can become very important to the same man years later when the record bars him from employment. There is no attempt to discover the circumstances surrounding a conviction—the record stands as mute testimony to a fact. If the record is so unimpeachable then we must provide adequate counsel to bolster that concept. If conviction of a minor crime is going to be a bar to employment, we must protect the naively innocent from himself by bringing to his attention the exact consequences of his plea of guilty.[21]

The counsel problem in municipal courts is compounded by the fact that the magistrates are not clear in these cases, as in preliminary examinations, as to their duty regarding indigent defendants. This was apparent from the responses to the question, "What advice as to the right to counsel is offered by the magistrate to defendants in these cases (those within his final jurisdiction) as a matter of general procedure?" The division of opinion was approximately the same as when this question was asked regarding preliminary examinations. That is, only one-third of the judges gave some indication that they informed the defendant of the right to assigned counsel. The division of opinion regarding the *power* of the court to assign counsel in these cases within the final jurisdiction of the local court also roughly paralleled responses given to the question concerning preliminary examinations. Approximately 50 per cent of the magistrates felt that the municipal court did have this power of appointment.[22] Significantly, certain magistrates who gave affirmative answers to these questions when they related to cases within the final jurisdiction of the court replied in the negative when the question referred to the preliminary examination. Other magistrates took exactly the opposite position. There is little doubt that there is a need for the judiciary at the federal and state level to clear up this misunderstanding and make explicit the duty of local magistrates in regard to indigent defendants. However, a ruling that required counsel to be assigned in municipal court cases would force major changes in the assigned counsel system. In most counties of New Jersey and of other states, the number of assignments to attorneys that would be required for the thousands of indigents who appear in both serious municipal court cases and in preliminary examinations would present a serious burden for the bar.

The Special Committee to Study Defender Systems was of the opinion that this problem is nationwide. "The practical difficulties which the assigned-counsel system encounters in providing representation in the inferior and lower courts of limited criminal jurisdiction are principally caused by the volume of cases handled by those courts and the speed with which these cases are processed." [23] An example cited by the Committee was the Felony Part of the Magistrate's Court in New York County, which is the lowest court of original jurisdiction in the county. In 1955 this court had 14,000 general dispositions; in at least 40 per cent of the cases the defendants were indigent.

"The difficulties inherent in assigning counsel in more than 5,600 cases are obvious." [24] So the pressures of modern life make old institutions, such as the venerable assigned counsel system, obsolescent and demand intelligent adjustments.

4
"Cop Out"

Brainwashing: One Man's Version

The prisoner sitting before me that July day in 1957 said that he had been pressured to "cop out" by brainwashing. I asked him to explain, and he wrote a long letter that gave his interpretation of the events leading up to his plea of guilty.

"Paul Jenkins" said in his letter that he was in his early forties, that he had the equivalent of a twelfth-grade education, and that he held a first-class coastal pilot's license in the merchant marine. In part because of strained marital relations, he had been a chronic alcoholic for several years.

During the summer of 1954 he had not been a resident of New Jersey but had been driving from Florida through New Jersey. He had stopped to rest in a seaside New Jersey county and there had met a woman in a bar. At the end of a three-day drinking bout at her home, Jenkins had allegedly beaten the woman with a hammer or a revolver and had stolen her ring. He did not deny these charges but claimed that he really did not remember what had happened. He admitted that he had seen a broken revolver handle in the woman's home, that he had had the ring in his possession when he had left the house, and that there had been blood on his light gabardine suit when he had arrived at his hotel.

Leaving on the streets the rented car he had been driving, Jenkins had taken a bus to New York City, where he had continued to drink while wandering about the docks and alleys for several weeks. On July 19, 1954, he had turned himself in to the New York City Police Department. On the next day he had been taken to the Tombs Prison, a city house of detention. He had been treated kindly by the guards and fed well as he went through the horrors of the "DT's." He summed up his feelings regarding the Tombs Prison and its custodians with these words: "I saw that the lowest vagrant was considered and what human dignity he had was preserved."

Several days later one of the prison guards had informed Jenkins that an FBI agent wanted an interview. The guard had stated that it was the prisoner's right to refuse and that in his condition he need not be questioned by anyone unless he desired.

I was grateful again for this courtesy, but did see the FBI officer on my own will. The [FBI] officer that interviewed me and questioned me asked me if I wished to give him a statement. I refused because of my condition and state of mind. The FBI [agent] did not insist.

About a day later I was visited by the —— Police [from a New Jersey city] by a detective [named] ——. I was informed again by the guards that I did not have to see these visitors. But I did. Remorse and weeping jags were beginning to be part of my reactions in drying out. The desire to release the pent-up thoughts which were mine, and the self-disgust in my system, was to the advantage of the ——Police [from the New Jersey city] who had me with shaking hands sign waivers and guilt, [waivers of extradition from New York to New Jersey and a full confession of the crime] contrary to what my custodial officers . . . [wished] me to do until I had legal assistance.

On August 24, 1954, Jenkins had been turned over to an officer from the New Jersey county where he had allegedly committed the assault and robbery. He had been transported by automobile to a city jail in that county.

It was a very old and depressive and closely confined jail. I was put into a line-up. . . . After the line-up I was taken to an office where a woman took dictation. I told of what I knew of what happened and as much as I could remember. Detective —— added his own views and comments as to me but did not give any information as to Mrs. —— [the victim]. The statement as I could see was all one sided and for the benefit of conviction. . . . I never read the statement. After it was typed Detective —— came down to the cell and had me sign it and initial it. He said he was in a hurry and the statement had to be taken to the prosecutor's office. *I asked him if I could see a lawyer and sign it before him. He said I would not get a lawyer until I reached court.* (Italics added.)

The next day Jenkins had been taken before a local magistrate for a preliminary examination.

I was not represented by a counsel or anyone to speak on my behalf and I was not offered any or asked if I had counsel. I was sentenced to be confined at the county jail and held in no bail. This was contrary to any of the other courts I had been before, [since] there was no counsel or friend of the court for the accused.

Jenkins had been taken to the county jail on the following day.

The county jail is a three-story building. The count was one hundred and fifty-eight prisoners, male and female. There were about twelve women prisoners in one half of the upper floors. The ground floor was the bull pen and dormitory for working prisoners. The two upper floors were confinement tiers, each holding accommodations for twenty-eight prisoners. I was placed on the second floor in a tier of cells. These cells held four men and a toilet and an inadequate basin for washing. When the cell was closed, these four men could not stand up together. The average space per man was less than seventy-two inches. . . . The toilet and piping were very old and very unsanitary. Soap and paper was doled out stingy and meagerly. There were no sheets and the blankets, unless washed by the inmates, stunk. Those who had towels supplied from home were fortunate. If an inmate did not have a towel, he was not given any.

Outside the cell was a walk five feet wide and sixty feet long. The cell doors were closed during the day. There was no room for exercise. One either just stood or sat month after month. There was no fresh air, recreation, or opportunity to move about. [This] confinement would have killed the same amount of animals as there were prisoners in confined quarters such as this. The requirement of health of the prisoners was ignored. Complaint to the doctor who made occasional appearance was futile. Any appeal fell on deaf ears. In the canteen there was only candy bars for sale, or they sold apples from the county farm for five cents each which were green and not fit to eat. There was never any given to the inmates voluntarily by the county.

Visitors were not allowed to bring packages of food of

any kind. My brother once on a visit offered to buy apples by the bushel for all the inmates, as they were cheap and plentiful. They would not allow this. These apples sold at seventy-five cents a bushel. Four bushel would have given each inmate four apples. I and the rest of the inmates were always hungry until our stomachs shrunk. Then we did not feel too hungry. This process takes several weeks.

Malnutrition was in everyone's face. Infections and rashes broke out on many. And if a person scratched himself the skin was so thin that it bled and would not heal. Others complained that their jaws hurt and that their teeth were becoming loose.

After sixty-five days elapsed and the weekly visit of the prosecutor's office asking if we were ready to sign a *non vult,* I gave in. Any other confinement would be paradise, and I was getting weaker every day, so I signed *non vult* without counsel present to witness this compulsion.

The papers Jenkins had signed, which he referred to as *non vult,* were undoubtedly waivers of indictment, trial by jury, the right to counsel, and a statement that he wished to plead *non vult* or guilty—a *non vult* plea being the equivalent of a guilty plea in the criminal courts. He later related that at the time he had not understood what he was signing. He claimed that he had been told by detectives that if he wanted to plead *non vult* and thereby obtain the mercy of the court and a speedy trial, to "Sign here!"

Two weeks after signing these waiver forms Jenkins had been arraigned in the county court, where he had pleaded guilty. Like many defendants Jenkins claimed that he hardly had known what was happening at the proceedings.

I had no counsel and never was offered any and was sick and in a mental fog as to the proceedings. I did not know what actually happened until I received a portion of the transcript of the proceedings in state prison on a denial of the writ of Habeas Corpus. I was about thirty-five pounds underweight at the time when I appeared at court.

The record of the proceedings at the arraignment, which consumed a scant few minutes, showed that the defendant had been asked if he desired counsel, and had been asked if any secret promises had been made to him. He had answered, "No."

Later, Jenkins claimed that he had merely been made to believe that it would be better for him if he waived trial by jury and entered a non-contesting plea. Jenkins alleged that he had been unsure of the future and unaware of the penalty awaiting him if he had made any objection in open court. Moreover, Jenkins asked, "If the accused had protested against the proceedings, how much more time would he have had to wait for trial? How many more months of confinement would he have had to endure?"

Several weeks later the defendant had been brought in for sentencing. In what he described as a highly nervous and weakened condition, he had stood before the judge. "There was no one to assist me in any appeal before the court and as to my side of the issue." He had received a sentence of two to three years on the robbery charge, and a sentence of five to seven years on the atrocious assault and battery charge, the equivalent of a five to ten year state prison term.

Jenkins had arrived at the State Prison in Trenton on November 27, 1954. At first his stomach had been unable to take the generous meals given to him at that institution. Within a few months, however, his weight had risen to a normal 175 pounds, a gain of 35 pounds from the date of admission. In my July, 1957, interview with him, he stated that I was the only attorney he had spoken to since his first day of confinement in the city jail, on August 24, 1954.

This is one man's version of the cop out process. I have heard many similar claims from other prisoners, some alleging even harsher treatment. Their stories, combined with other information, reveal certain important patterns.

The Cop Out: Anatomy

IMPORTANCE OF COP OUTS

The machinery of criminal justice operates on the assumption that only a small percentage of defendants will avail themselves of their constitutional right to a jury trial. This is the first important pattern in the cop out process.

When the papers on a defendant are sent by the local police to the county prosecutor's office—which occurs in all cases not within the final jurisdiction of the first-level courts—the prosecutor attempts, as a matter of course, to obtain guilty or *non vult* pleas in as many cases as possible: to obtain cop outs. In many instances, there is nothing improper about this action taken by the prosecutor. Since the prosecutor's office in many counties is confronted by a great mass of cases that must somehow be disposed of, the cop out is an administrative necessity.

The saving of time and expense involved in each cop out is vital. If 10 or 20 per cent of the defendants who now plead guilty refused to do so, there would be an enormous burden added to the court structure. A study of

the Essex County courts made for the Special Committee
to Study Defender Systems determined that a significant
factor in the efficient administration of justice in that
county was the high percentage of guilty pleas.[1] Trials
were thus kept to a minimum. In the four years from 1952
through 1955, only 13 per cent of the cases reaching the
Essex County Court were tried.[2]

BAIL OR JAIL?

The criminal court is pre-eminently an institution for the
poor—because most defendants are of the lower economic
classes. Therefore, when a judge in a first-level court sets
bail, which would allow the defendant his freedom pending proceedings in a second-level or county court, it is no
surprise that many men cannot afford to produce bail.
Others are denied the privilege of bail by the judge because of the seriousness of their alleged offense. Sixty-
seven per cent of the prisoners I interviewed had not been
released on bail.[3]

This, then, is another important pattern in the cop out
process: the fact of confinement. The defendant is often
transferred, following the preliminary examination, from
his detention in the city police lockup to another place
of confinement, the county jail. The picture during this
period when the prosecution is most active, therefore, is
very frequently this: The massive machinery of the state
is moving against a person of grade school or high school
education [4] who is frequently frightened, unaware of his
rights, unaware of how to prepare his defense, and unable
to help himself because of confinement in a cell at the
county jail while awaiting arraignment in the county
court.

COUNTY JAIL CONDITIONS

In the county jail, the prisoner is confronted by the cop out machinery. Of course, he has already been questioned by the local police, and may have signed a written confession. But this is not the same as copping out, which is usually handled by the staff of the county prosecutor's office, and involves, in the end, pleading guilty to formal charges that may only be brought by a county-level agency, either the grand jury or the prosecutor.

It is important to inquire into the conditions at these places of detention since a prisoner may spend months there—and since harsh conditions may adversely affect an individual's determination to exercise his constitutional right to fight the case through to a trial by jury. In some of these jails the prisoners are treated with consideration and fed well. Several prisoners told me stories of kind treatment in New Jersey county jails similar to that related by "Paul Jenkins" regarding his experience in New York's Tombs Prison. But most men came forth with critical comments such as those Jenkins made concerning that New Jersey county jail in which he had been confined.

One nineteen-year-old inmate of the Bordentown Reformatory told me, "I'd rather do six months here than the two months I did down there [a New Jersey county jail]. They starve you to death, don't give you no exercise. They should do something about that place." The comment of another prisoner, who was then confined in the New Jersey State Prison was, "Our Constitution states that a man is innocent until proven guilty. The treatment in the county jail indicates that you are guilty until proven innocent." He went on to complain about the low and brutal mentality of some county jail custodians. Still other prisoners claimed that guards frequently beat prisoners in the county jails of certain urban counties.

The problem of bad county jail conditions is widespread. Federal prisoners are often held in county jails, in various areas of the country, while awaiting trial. The comments of these men, when interviewed in the Lewisburg Penitentiary, coincided with the generally low estimate of the New Jersey prisoners, whose comments were confined only to that state. And in 1959 Richard A. McGee of the California Department of Corrections stated in the *National Probation and Parole Association Journal*:

> I am not the first to observe that the county jail—of which there are more than three thousand and which process about four million people a year—is the lowest form of social institution on the American scene.[5]

McGee said that overcrowding was a great problem in these jails. He cited the example of the Los Angeles County Jail, which has a normal capacity of 900; on the day of his visit, it held 3,001 people.

So it is understandable why so many prisoners, looking forward to long years in prison, maintained, in answer to my question, that the conditions at their present places of confinement were much superior to the conditions at the county jails, where they had spent but a few months. Sixty per cent of the prisoners, from all four institutions, stated that they had been treated better in prison than "in the jail where you waited around to enter your final plea (or for your trial)."[6]

Harsh county jail conditions constitute a most important pattern in the cop out process. Whether they were planned to do so or not, these conditions often reduce defiant prisoners to the point of pliability. To the un-counseled and underfed prisoner in a county jail cell, the question often is not whether he has a legal defense to the charges—but, "How can I get out of this cell in a hurry?" For many men, there was only one answer: a cop out. This usually led to the state prison, which seems a ridiculous solution. But to a man confined in a cell with improper food, an occasional beating, and no exercise—and, perhaps, with the heat of summer coming on—the state prison, with its more enlightened personnel, work, and recrea-tion programs, sounds like the Waldorf-Astoria. The fact that, like the Waldorf, the admission price is rather high, often proves no deterrent.

BARGAIN JUSTICE

All cop outs cannot be grouped together. There are two major categories: those involving a bargain or a deal be-tween the prosecution and the defendant, and those in which no bargain is made.

Bargain justice is possible because the prosecutor has almost complete discretion in drafting the formal charges.[7] He can add charges, drop some completely, or reduce others to lesser offenses. For example, the county prose-cutor may add a charge of possession of a deadly weapon to the original charge of robbery, or he may reduce the robbery charges to larceny. And the prosecutor may even set the charges so low that probation, rather than institu-tional confinement, becomes a possibility. So when he feels disposed to bargain, the prosecutor is in an extremely powerful position. Imposition of the sentence still remains an exclusively judicial function, but the prosecutor can chart the course, can set the upper—and suggest the lower

—limits of the sentence by the manner in which he draws the indictment or the accusation.

The plea-inducing machinery is a combination of sound legal advice, intimidation, and misleading information. This machinery is spearheaded in most New Jersey counties by the prosecutor's detectives. But the county probation officers, the county jail wardens, and the assistant prosecutors may also participate in the quest for the cop outs that are the oil of court machinery. Many of these officials often tell prisoners that they can "throw themselves on the mercy of the court" if they plead *non vult;* in other words, they will receive a smaller sentence if they cop out immediately and don't cause trouble by their obstinacy.

In certain respects this is, of course, true. As one New Jersey county court judge admitted to me in an interview, "I tend to give a lighter sentence if the gory evidence is not paraded before me in the courtroom." Furthermore, there is always some consideration tacitly given by the court to the defendant who saves the government the expense of a lengthy trial. Yet, there are questions involved here deserving the attention of an expert defense counsel. Is a trial advisable? Will a plea of guilty in this case actually result in a less severe sentence than a conviction on trial?

Intimidation enters the picture when the defendant is told by the prosecutor's detectives that it will be very bad for him if he goes to trial, not only because of the judicial tendency to sentence more harshly after a conviction by trial, but also because of the fact that the prosecution will throw the book at the defendant. The defendant may be told that if he pleads guilty, several of the charges pending against him will be dropped. And, on the other hand, if he attempts to go to trial, not only will the present charges be retained, but additional charges will be made.

While the prisoners leveled many charges of senseless brutality against county jail guards, not a single one claimed that county detectives or prosecutors used violence or its threat to induce him to cop out. Some men claimed that they had been subjected to such treatment from county detectives earlier in the case to force them to sign confessions. But it appears that such techniques are generally reserved by those officers so inclined for the first days before the preliminary examination. As Paul Jenkins' story shows, more sophisticated but often no less effective methods are used during the cop out process.

In the face of pressure from the prosecution, many men, especially veterans of the criminal courts, still manage to obtain something of value from the opposition—usually a reduction in the number or the severity of the charges—in return for their guilty plea. I consider this a bargained cop out. Thirty per cent of the prisoners indicated that they had discussed the possibility of a deal with the prosecution.[8]

One of the only other studies that has analyzed the cop out process in depth was made by Professor Donald J. Newman in a Midwestern county during the 1950's. Newman called it "Pleading Guilty for Considerations: A Study of Bargain Justice."[9] He examined the cases of a representative group of ninety-seven prisoners. Professor Newman stated:

The most significant general finding of the study was that the majority of the felony convictions in the district studied were not the result of the formal, combative theory of criminal law involving in effect a legal battle between

prosecution and defense, but were compromise convictions, the result of bargaining between defense and prosecution. Such informal conviction processes were observed
in over half of the cases studied.[10]

But the term bargain justice cannot be used to describe
the guilty pleas of all of the prisoners I interviewed. For
while 30 per cent were involved in some bargaining, 76
per cent of the prisoners pleaded guilty or its equivalent.[11]
Many of these men copped out, not because of a valuable
consideration from the county prosecutor, but for other
reasons—some, like Paul Jenkins, because of a combination
of harsh county jail conditions, ignorance of their rights,
and pressure from the prosecution. Others were obsessed
by a sense of their guilt and the horror of their crime. Still
others found that their assigned attorneys exerted pressure on them to plead guilty. When men cop out under
these circumstances, their pleas cannot be considered part
of bargain justice. They fit into a category that may be
termed "no bargain." Since a cop out so often involves the
waiver of all significant rights, including the right to
counsel, one can fairly wonder if the ends of justice are
served when people convict themselves primarily because
they are ignorant and frightened.

FORMALITIES OF THE COP OUT

A cop out is almost always accompanied by important
forms signed by the defendant. The forms usually include
a waiver of indictment by grand jury, waiver of jury trial,
and, at times, waiver of the right to counsel. Sometimes
these forms are fully explained to the defendant by the
county prosecutor or the detectives. However, in some
cases the consequences of signing the documents are not

made completely clear. When the prisoners sign these forms, it is generally assumed that they desire to plead guilty, although the formal plea must be given in open court before the county judge.

Defendants are also asked about assigned counsel through prepared questions on these forms. The standard form in New Jersey reads, "You are entitled to be represented by an attorney. Do you want an attorney assigned to you by the court to represent you in this matter?" In this way certain defendants are informed of their right to assigned counsel much earlier than the arraignment in the county court. It is at the arraignment that formal notice of the assignment privilege is given to the defendant by the county judge in most New Jersey counties. However, if the prisoner writes that he wishes an attorney assigned by the court, it does not mean that a lawyer will be assigned immediately. Frequently, even though he answers this question in the affirmative, the defendant must wait until the arraignment in the county court for the actual assignment of counsel; and he may wait several days to a week after arraignment before conferring with his attorney.

The use of these prepared waiver forms by the prosecution was tested in the New Jersey Superior Court by the Somerset County prosecutor in 1954.[12] The court commended the prosecutor for recording the questions asked the defendant and his answers—for this record seemed to provide concrete evidence that the defendant had waived his rights with full knowledge of the consequences.

It is indeed commendable where the defendant receives a full explanation before executing these waivers. But in many cases, explanations written into the waivers are a formality. They are executed by a defendant who has been

convinced that this is the only way to save himself from
a terribly severe sentence.

The Cop Out: Fairness and Constitutionality

In many cases the best course for the defendant *is* a plea
of guilty. It is quite proper, from this viewpoint, that the
prosecution offers inducements to defendants in return for
a guilty plea—and because society should be saved the
expense of a trial whenever possible. Moreover, many
prosecutors and detectives are completely honest with defendants as to the probable consequences of this action.
Criticism should be made, however, of the conditions
under which many defendants live during this period
when they are making decisions that will affect their future
lives most significantly—and of the unfair methods used
by some prosecution officials to obtain guilty pleas. One
of the tactics that should come in for the greatest censure
is that of promising a specific sentence—usually much
lower than usual—in return for a non-contesting plea; for
while a prosecutor can influence the sentence greatly, he
cannot actually grant a specific term.

One prisoner related under oath at a post-conviction
proceeding that the prosecutor flatly promised him a sentence of seven to ten years if he signed a "special sessions,"
which, in some counties, is the term used for a cop out. In
this case the cop out included a waiver of counsel and trial,
and an agreement to plead guilty. When he did so, the
prisoner was sentenced to a term of twenty-eight to forty
years in the New Jersey State Prison. Since the promise
of a prosecutor regarding sentence—unknown to many
prisoners—has no binding effect, this prisoner had abso-

lutely no recourse. A broken promise regarding sentence, which is the most important thing in the minds of most prisoners, will frequently so embitter a man toward the authorities as to place him totally beyond the rehabilitative efforts of the institution.

Is the cop out process constitutional? The best answer to this question is that the process has never been declared unconstitutional—or illegal. Interestingly, the procedure is almost entirely uncontrolled by the law. Although it is one of the most important phases of the criminal process, its informal aspects receive scant attention from the courts. Only the formal part of the process has received searching judicial attention on the question of its legal propriety. In other words, the proceedings at the arraignment to plea in a second-level court are usually recorded verbatim. This transcript of the judge's words to the accused and his monosyllabic replies may consume three typewritten pages. But if the defendant later complains from his prison cell that he was unfairly induced to cop out, the events at the arraignment, as recorded in the transcript, may be reviewed by an appellate judge— and usually the prisoner's complaints of unfairness are rebutted by the trial judge's recorded explanation of his rights. This was the case with Paul Jenkins.

Even though many prisoners go through this phase without an attorney, this is not considered a violation of the right to counsel.[13] And, while a prisoner who has signed a cop out form may feel he has made an enforceable contract with the court (because of the oral promises made by the prosecution), this is simply not the case. Therefore, many aspects of the cop out process may be unfair and may subvert constitutional rights; but the process, in its negative aspects, has never been declared unconstitutional and probably won't be in the foreseeable future. On the surface, the prisoner has simply pleaded guilty—there is nothing unconstitutional or illegal about that.

The Formal Charge

A second check of a formal nature before trial—the first is the preliminary examination—is indictment by the grand jury.

The historical roots of the grand jury lie in England. Judges under the Norman and Plantagenet kings left their seat at the capital, Westminster, at fixed times of the year and traveled the circuit. In these circumstances the grand jury slowly evolved. Among many reasons for its growth, two seem highly significant. First, the device cut down on the number of spite charges and baseless allegations presented to the judges. Unless the responsible local people sitting on the grand jury indicated that there was some substance to the matter, the judges did not hear it. This allowed the judges to complete their rounds of the distant localities more rapidly, something they earnestly desired. Secondly, the device evolved into an institution that allowed a degree of local control on criminal prosecutions. It was soon asserted that royal judges had no right to hear cases unless approval was granted by the grand jury in the locality where the crime occurred. So the grand jury was embodied in the Magna Carta as a means of protecting the people against unwarranted exercise of the executive power to prosecute criminal charges.[14]

It is this protective aspect of the grand jury that probably accounts for its continuance in American procedure to this day. Americans of the revolutionary era felt so strongly about royal abuses of the power to prosecute that the grand jury was included in the Fifth Amendment. The provision states that "no person shall be held to answer for a capital or otherwise infamous crime, unless on a presentment or indictment of a Grand Jury, except in cases arising in the land or naval forces, or in the Militia, when in actual service or in time of war or public danger." This provision is not entirely clear since it does not define an "infamous crime." The *Federal Rules of Criminal Procedure* (Rule 7 [a]), however, provide that an offense punishable by death must be prosecuted by indictment; but an offense punishable by either hard labor or imprisonment for over a year may be prosecuted by indictment unless the defendant wishes to waive the right, whereupon the case may proceed by information—a simple statement of charges prepared by the prosecutor. All other cases may be prosecuted *either* by indictment or by information.

The Fifth Amendment provision applies only to federal proceedings. In one of the earliest cases dealing with state criminal procedure after the enactment of the Civil War Amendments, the Supreme Court of the United States held that a grand jury indictment, as required in the Fifth Amendment for federal trials, is not required of the states by the Due Process Clause of the Fourteenth Amendment.[15] Nevertheless, the grand jury still persists in state procedure.[16] This is so despite repeated attacks on its usefulness.[17] As an alternative to the grand jury indictment, there has evolved in this country the practice of allowing the prosecutor to prepare the formal charges, in the form of an information or an accusation.

Whatever form the charge takes, the United States Constitution guarantees the right to clear and adequate notice in both federal and state trials. The right in federal cases is based on the Sixth Amendment provision that guarantees to all criminal defendants the right "to be informed of the nature and cause of the accusation." The right in state trials is based on the Fourteenth Amendment Due Process Clause.[18] Professor David Fellman described the right to adequate notice, along with the right to a fair hearing, as the "indispensable, classic minimum requirement of due process."[19] There can be no intelligent disagreement with this statement.

Fortunately, this right is actually realized in most serious criminal cases. None of the hundreds of prisoners interviewed alleged that they had not been given adequate notice of the charges. None of the dozens of defense lawyers contacted claimed that any person they had defended was denied adequate notice.

As previously indicated, there may be a problem in municipal courts, where cases are disposed of so rapidly that prisoners may not fully understand the charges against them.[20] And the problem of vagueness may arise in those cases, not covered in my research, where the defendant is charged not with a garden-variety, common law crime, whose definition is well settled, but with an esoteric, political crime—such as the charge that Owen Lattimore perjured himself by denying under oath that he was a "follower of the Communist line" and that he had been a "promoter of Communist interests."[21] But such cases involving violations of the basic right to clear and adequate notice are not common.

In New Jersey the law provides for both indictments and accusations.[22] The prosecutor may in most cases proceed by way of accusation. In these cases, the major requirement is that the defendant sign a formal waiver of the right to grand jury action.[23] As we have seen, the cop out process includes as one of its essential elements a waiver of indictment.

Prisoners and attorneys offered few insights into the details of grand jury action in New Jersey. In those few cases when the grand jury is called upon to act, prisoners and their counsel are frequently excluded entirely. This is quite within the power of the grand jury since it does not hold adversary hearings. Its only function is to determine if there is a prima facie case—sufficient prosecution evidence to warrant that the case proceed to trial. One general conclusion did emerge, however, from interviews with convicts, defense counsel, prosecutors, and other officials. The grand jury is definitely not serving its traditional function of providing a check on the prosecution. In the great majority of cases, it is entirely bypassed. On the other hand, in those cases that do go to the grand jury—perhaps 20 per cent, although this is merely an estimate—the prosecutor usually can obtain those indictments he desires.

So the two main formal checks on the prosecution before trial—preliminary examination by a magistrate and indictment by the grand jury—have both suffered from the pressures of the twentieth century. Huge case loads have made it impractical to resort to the full use of these devices. The grand jury, in particular, has had its function eroded by the cop out process. From the time of arrest until trial, while the magistrate and the grand jury are at vital intersections with the power to say "stop" and "go," it is really the police and the prosecutor who are directing traffic.

5

The Indigent Defendant
and the Law

Most people accused of crime do not have enough money to hire an attorney. Forty-five per cent of the prisoners I interviewed for this study had been assigned an attorney because of indigence, and fourteen per cent had not been represented by a lawyer because they had waived counsel.[1] A high percentage of the latter group were indigent. In 1961 the National Legal Aid and Defender Association estimated the total national figure of impecunious defendants charged with serious crimes at a minimum of one million annually.[2] Therefore, it is essential to examine the development of the right to counsel for indigent defendants in United States Supreme Court decisions.

1932: Establishment of Indigent's Right
to Assigned Counsel

On March 25, 1931, a number of Negro youths, later to become known as "the Scottsboro boys," allegedly raped

96 THE RATIONING OF JUSTICE

two white girls on an Alabama train. Nine Negroes were arrested later that day, and on March 31 they were indicted for rape, a capital offense in Alabama. All pleaded not guilty. None had money to hire an attorney. When the first case was called on April 6, there was a discussion about representation of the defendants between the judge and attorneys in the courtroom, but the judge did not impose the responsibility for their defense upon any lawyer.[3] Eight of the youths were convicted and sentenced to death.

The case was taken to the United States Supreme Court, and on November 7, 1932, the Court issued its historic decision in *Powell* v. *Alabama,* the first decision by that Court clearly establishing the right of an impecunious defendant to be assigned an attorney. Speaking for the Court, Justice George Sutherland said that the Sixth Amendment counsel provision—"In all criminal prosecutions, the accused shall . . . have the assistance of counsel for his defense"—applied directly only to federal trials. But, he said, certain rights of the original eight amendments to the United States Constitution had been incorporated, by Supreme Court decisions, in the Fourteenth Amendment Due Process Clause and thereby applied to the states. The test for incorporation was whether the right was among the "fundamental principles of liberty and justice which lie at the base of all our civil and political institutions. . . ."[4] Justice Sutherland then stated, "While the question has never been categorically determined by this court . . . the right to the aid of counsel is of this fundamental character."[5] Thus the opinion *suggested* that a broad right to assigned counsel was established by this decision and that the Sixth Amendment counsel provision applied to the states through the Fourteenth.

The Justice also set down this resounding declaration regarding the need of a layman for an attorney:

> Even the intelligent and educated layman has small and sometimes no skill in the science of law. . . . He lacks both the skill and knowledge adequately to prepare his defense, even though he have a perfect one. He requires the guiding hand of counsel at every step in the proceedings against him. Without it, though he be not guilty, he faces the danger of conviction because he does not know how to establish his innocence.[6]

But near the end of his opinion Justice Sutherland said, "All that it is necessary now to decide, as we do decide, is that in a capital case, where the defendant is unable to employ counsel, and is incapable adequately of making his own defense because of ignorance, feeble-mindedness, illiteracy, or the like, it is the duty of the court, whether requested or not, to assign counsel for him as a necessary requisite of due process of law; and that duty is not discharged by an assignment at such a time or under such circumstances as to preclude the giving of effective aid in the preparation and trial of the case."[7]

1938: Assigned Counsel Required in Capital and Non-Capital Federal Cases

Less than six years later, on May 23, 1938, the U.S. Supreme Court issued its decision in *Johnson* v. *Zerbst.*[8] The facts presented two significant differences when compared to *Powell*—the defendants in *Johnson* had been convicted of a non-capital offense, counterfeiting, and the trial had taken place in a federal trial court. Regarding the defendant's need for a defense attorney, Justice Hugo Black quoted Justice Sutherland's declaration in *Powell* and laid down this rigid rule for federal trials:

> The Sixth Amendment withholds from federal courts, in all criminal proceedings, the power and authority to deprive an accused of his life or liberty unless he has or waives the assistance of counsel.[9]

On this basis, the defendants' convictions were reversed, and it was clearly established that judges had a duty to offer assigned counsel to impecunious criminal defendants in federal trials. This rule applied whether the defendant was charged with a capital or non-capital crime.

1942 Setback: Assigned Counsel Required in State Trials Only for Capital or Unusual Non-Capital Cases

Had the *Powell* and *Johnson* cases established the right of indigent defendants to assigned counsel in *state non-capital* cases? In 1942 the U.S. Supreme Court considered that question in *Betts* v. *Brady*.[10] Betts had been indicted in a Maryland court for robbery, a non-capital offense. He was forty-three years old, of ordinary intelligence, and, since he had been convicted of a crime previously, "was not wholly unfamiliar with criminal procedure." [11] At his arraignment, he had told the judge that he was without money to hire a lawyer and had asked that an attorney be assigned to him. The judge had refused to do so because it was the practice in Carroll County, Maryland, to appoint counsel only in cases of murder and rape. Betts did not waive his right to counsel; he pleaded not guilty and pre-

sented his own defense at the trial. He was found guilty
and was sentenced to eight years in prison.

On June 1, 1942, the U.S. Supreme Court issued its decision in this case. Justice Owen Roberts, who wrote the
majority opinion, reviewed the history of the right to
counsel in this country and its current status in the various
states. His reading of history led him to conclude that "in
the great majority of the States, it has been the considered
judgment of the people, their representatives and their
courts that appointment of counsel is not a fundamental
right, essential to a fair trial." [12] Therefore, the Court refused to rule, as the defendant had argued, that the Sixth
Amendment counsel provision, which had been rigidly
interpreted in the *Johnson* case, was so essential as to be
incorporated in the Fourteenth Amendment Due Process
Clause and applied to the states. Justice Roberts set down
the following test for judging whether a defendant's right
to a fair trial had been denied by lack of counsel in a state
non-capital case: "Asserted denial is to be tested by an appraisal of the totality of facts in a given case. That which
may, in one setting, constitute a denial of fundamental
fairness, shocking to the universal sense of justice, may, in
other circumstances, and in the light of other considerations, fall short of such denial." [13]

Justice Black, joined by Justices William O. Douglas and
Frank Murphy, wrote the dissent. He built his argument
on two alternate grounds. First, he said that the conviction should be reversed because the Fourteenth Amendment made the Sixth Amendment counsel provision applicable to the states.[14] Thus, he said, the rule should be
the same in both federal and state trials—and if the *Betts*
conviction had taken place in a federal court, the Supreme
Court would have reversed it because of the *Johnson* doc-

trine. But since a majority of the Court had never accepted that incorporation argument, Justice Black offered a second reason for reversal. He said that "under the prevailing view of due process, as reflected in the opinion just announced," [15] the conviction could not stand because:

A practice cannot be reconciled with "common and fundamental ideas of fairness and right," which subjects innocent men to increased dangers of conviction merely because of their poverty.[16]

Nevertheless, for twenty-one years the *Betts* decision was the law of the land. This decision meant that *federal* trial judges were required by the United States Constitution to offer the assignment of counsel to impecunious defendants, but that *state* judges were not so required except in capital cases or in unusual non-capital cases. As a result, a defendant tried in a federal court could be assured of legal assistance, but a defendant across the street in a state court might be tried and sentenced to life imprisonment without a defense advocate. Significantly, relatively few cases in this country involve capital charges or a federal trial; the overwhelming majority are non-capital state prosecutions.

Many states, by law or court rule, provided for the appointment of counsel in non-capital cases, but when for some reason a judge failed to assign counsel in a non-capital trial, state appellate courts frequently resorted to the *Betts* decision for an answer to the convict's complaint —and held that lack of counsel would not always invalidate a conviction unless it could be shown that the defendant thereby was denied a fair trial. The law and court decisions in New Jersey during the period when the *Betts* rule prevailed provided a good example of the unsatisfactory results of that decision. A court rule provided that judges in trial courts should advise the defendant of the right to counsel and should assign an attorney to him, if indigent.[17] But when a trial judge did not advise a poor defendant of this privilege of legal assistance, that omission was ruled fatal to the conviction "only when, upon an evaluation of all the facts in a given situation, it appear[ed] that prejudice resulted from such failure." [18] In other words, judges *should have* followed the rule but did not always *have* to!

There was much criticism of the *Betts* decision by lawyers and legal scholars. The Supreme Court itself slowly chipped away at the decision, for in every case presented to the Court after a 1950 decision, it reversed the convictions of men tried without counsel in state non-capital cases—on the grounds that the special circumstances required by the *Betts* case had existed.[19] But the Court did continue to give lip service to the *Betts* doctrine and refused to rule in clear terms that counsel was required in state non-capital cases.

1963 Breakthrough: Assigned Counsel Required in Non-Capital State Cases Involving Serious Crimes

If, by the early 1960's, the U.S. Supreme Court was seeking an occasion to overrule *Betts*, the case of Clarence Earl Gideon was tailor-made. Like Betts, Gideon had been accused of a non-capital offense in a state court. He was of mature years, of ordinary intelligence, and had had experience in the criminal courts. In the Florida trial court, he had stated that he was without funds to hire an attorney and had asked the judge to assign counsel to him. The judge had refused to do so, explaining that the laws of

Florida provided for an appointment only in capital cases. Gideon did not waive his right to counsel; he persisted in his not guilty plea and conducted his own defense at the trial. He was found guilty and was sentenced to five years in prison.

After his conviction and imprisonment, Gideon contested the legality of his conviction by preparing a handwritten petition that eventually reached the highest court in the land. The Court assigned Abe Fortas, a Washington attorney respected for his work in constitutional rights cases, to argue the matter for Mr. Gideon. Both sides were asked by the Court to discuss the question: "Should this Court's holding in *Betts* v. *Brady* . . . be reconsidered?" [20] Twenty-two states filed briefs supporting the argument that *Betts* should be overruled and that counsel should be required for the indigent in state non-capital cases. Abe Krash, Mr. Fortas' co-counsel, subsequently declared, "I know of no parallel for this extraordinary action—a request by nearly half the states that the Supreme Court impose a constitutional requirement upon the states in the field of criminal justice." [21]

Justice Black, who had written the opinion in *Johnson* v. *Zerbst* and the dissent in *Betts*, wrote the opinion of the Court in *Gideon* v. *Wainwright* issued on March 18, 1963. This was a moment of triumph for Justice Black and his principles. His opinion hinged on the issue discussed in *Betts*—whether the Sixth Amendment counsel provision was so fundamental as to be incorporated in the Fourteenth and applied to the states. He concluded:

> The Court in *Betts* v. *Brady* departed from the sound wisdom upon which the Court's holding in *Powell* v. *Alabama* rested. Florida, supported by two other States, has asked

that *Betts* v. *Brady* be left intact. Twenty-two States . . . argue that *Betts* was "an anachronism when handed down" and that it should now be overruled. We agree.[22]

There were three concurring opinions, no dissents. In this manner the broad language of *Powell* v. *Alabama,* as well as the broadest phase of Justice Black's dissent in *Betts,* became the supreme law of the land. The Sixth Amendment counsel requirement was thus applied to the states via the Fourteenth Amendment, and state courts were directed to assign counsel to indigents accused of non-capital crimes, at least those of a serious nature. A landmark in the progress of human freedom, the opinion of the Court is reproduced in Appendix C of this book.

The most immediate impact of the decision was on Mr. Gideon. Since his conviction had been reversed, Florida decided to retry him—with counsel assigned by the court. His attorney, W. Fred Turner, demonstrated the value of a defense advocate. Skilled cross-examination cast doubt on the story of the prosecution's eyewitness. The defense attorney also found a new witness who further weakened that testimony. After a trial that lasted almost a full day, the jury deliberated for one hour and five minutes and rendered a verdict of not guilty. Mr. Gideon, freed after nearly two years in prison, cried. He became something of a folk hero to some American lawyers, for whom Abe Krash spoke when he said:

> The Supreme Court's decision is a monument to the human spirit. It is a testament to the courage and tenacity of Clarence Earl Gideon. A relatively uneducated man, untrained in the law, in prison and without friends or money, he persisted in his conviction that every man charged with a crime in this country is entitled to a lawyer who will

speak in his behalf. Gideon stood up and told the trial judge in the Bay County, Florida, courthouse: "The United States Supreme Court says I am entitled to be represented by Counsel." All nine justices of the United States Supreme Court subsequently held that he was absolutely right . . .[23]

The *Gideon* decision settled beyond dispute that indigent defendants accused of serious crimes must be offered the assignment of counsel. The decision applies to virtually all those offenses categorized by the various states as felonies.

Among the questions not directly dealt with by the *Gideon* case were: In what other kinds of cases does the right to assigned counsel apply? During what phases of a case must counsel be present?

Right to Assigned Counsel: Non-Felonies

The *Gideon* opinion contained these words:

Governments, both state and federal, quite properly spend vast sums of money to establish machinery to try defendants accused of crime. Lawyers to prosecute are everywhere deemed essential to protect the public's interest in an orderly society. Similarly, there are few defendants charged with crime, few indeed, who fail to hire the best lawyers they can get to prepare and present their defenses. That government hires lawyers to prosecute and defendants who have the money hire lawyers to defend are the strongest indications of the widespread belief that lawyers in criminal courts are necessities, not luxuries.[24]

This statement applies to both felonies and non-felonies. To any man facing a criminal prosecution—in any case where his liberty is in jeopardy—a lawyer is a necessity, not a luxury. Indeed, there were no limiting words—similar to those in *Powell*—in the opinion of the Court in *Gideon*. Only Justice John Harlan's concurring opinion contained some indication of the decision's outer limits. He said that the decision applied "to offenses which, as the one involved here, carry the possibility of a substantial prison sentence. (Whether the rule should extend to *all* criminal cases need not now be decided.)" [25] Neither the Court's opinion nor that of Justice Harlan settled the question as to whether counsel was required in misdemeanor cases or in petty offenses—or in juvenile court proceedings.

Assigned Counsel: When Required?

Gideon made it obvious that counsel must be present at the trial. But proceedings before trial and after conviction are also critical to a defendant's life or liberty. Other recent U.S. Supreme Court decisions give some clues as to the time at which counsel must be assigned to the indigent defendant.

BEFORE TRIAL: PRELIMINARY EXAMINATION AND ARRAIGNMENT IN CAPITAL CASES

In the 1961 case of *Hamilton* v. *Alabama*,[26] the defendant had not been represented by counsel at arraignment following indictment, but an attorney had appeared at his trial. Hamilton was convicted and sentenced to death. The Supreme Court reversed the conviction because Hamilton was not represented by counsel at the arraignment. The high tribunal declared: "Arraignment under Alabama law is a critical stage in a criminal proceeding." [27] Certain pleas and motions, the Court said, had to be made at that hearing, or the opportunity to make them would be lost. The Court then laid down this rule:

> When one pleads to a capital charge without benefit of counsel, we do not stop to determine whether prejudice resulted. . . . Only the presence of counsel could have enabled this accused to know all the defenses available to him and to plead intelligently.[28]

Thus, for the first time the Supreme Court dealt directly with the question of the point at which counsel should be assigned and thus determined that the accused in a capital case must be represented by counsel at the arraignment.

In April, 1963, a few weeks after the *Gideon* decision, the Supreme Court issued its decision in *White* v. *Maryland*.[29] White had not been represented by counsel at his preliminary examination, shortly after arrest on a murder charge, and at that proceeding he had pleaded guilty. By the time of arraignment, counsel had been assigned and so White entered new pleas of not guilty and not guilty by reason of insanity. He was convicted and sentenced to death. The United States Supreme Court reversed the conviction because White had not been represented by counsel at the preliminary examination. The decision was based on the "critical stage" theory of *Hamilton* v. *Alabama.*

These two cases clearly established that counsel must be provided at the preliminary examination and at the arraignment in capital cases. Neither dealt with the requirement of counsel at these proceedings in non-capital cases.[30]

AFTER CONVICTION: FIRST APPEALS
AND SUBSEQUENT REMEDIES

Proceedings after conviction fit into two categories. First, there are direct appeals or, as they are sometimes called, appeals of right. Every convicted defendant has the privilege of such appeals. In 1957 the U.S. Supreme Court held that counsel must be assigned to indigent federal prisoners who wish to make such appeals, even though the judge may feel that the appeal is frivolous.[31] In *Douglas* v. *California*,[32] handed down on the same day as *Gideon*, the Court applied a similar rule to state prisoners. Justice Douglas wrote the opinion for the eight-judge majority. He said that, "where the merits of *the one and only appeal* an indigent has as of right are decided without benefit of counsel, we think an unconstitutional line has been drawn between rich and poor."[33] Moreover, Justice Douglas declared:

> The present case, where counsel was denied petitioners on appeal, shows that the discrimination is not between "possibly good and obviously bad cases," but between cases where the rich man can require the court to listen to argument of counsel before deciding on the merits, but a poor man cannot.[34]

The Justice made the limitations of this decision clear: "We are dealing only with the *first appeal,* granted as a matter of right. . . ."[35]

The second type of post-conviction proceeding is often called a collateral attack on the conviction—i.e., a writ of habeas corpus. Normally, such proceedings take place after a direct appeal has failed. Unlike direct appeals, there are no time limits, and the granting of a request for the proceeding is discretionary with the court. Prisoners frequently make repeated collateral attacks and repeated requests that counsel be assigned to argue the matter. But for these situations, the 1963 decisions did not provide clear guidelines for counsel-assignment procedure by courts.

Several of the decisions announced on the same day as *Gideon* did strengthen the indigent prisoner's right to a transcript of his trial, without charge.[36] Since transcripts are essential in proceedings after conviction, these decisions improved the chances for successful attacks on convictions by indigent prisoners—through both direct appeals and collateral proceedings.

Supreme Court decisions on the right to counsel for indigent defendants present an example of the law's developing toward greater protection for individual liberty. By the end of 1963, the following points of law regarding the right to counsel were securely established: Courts must offer assigned counsel to all persons charged with capital and serious non-capital crimes in federal and state proceedings. When a prisoner, convicted in such proceedings, requests the assistance of counsel in making a direct or first appeal, a lawyer must be assigned. Counsel is also required at the preliminary examination and at the arraignment in capital cases.

6
The Defenders

The legal rules regarding the right to counsel provide some protection for the indigent defendant. But even if the rules were followed in every respect, the total nationwide effect would still be dismal. Fortunately, many members of the legal profession have long realized that it is not enough to satisfy merely the formal, minimal constitutional counsel standards. These lawyers and judges, who constitute the moving force behind the American legal aid and defender movement, have attempted to set up defender institutions that would provide an effective defense as early and as late in the proceedings as necessary—regardless of the fact that court decisions do not require many of the services defenders render.

Growth of Defender Systems

The institutional history of legal aid in criminal cases bears similarities to the history of other American social institutions. In the homogeneous, rural society of early America the problem of the defense of indigent defendants was handled strictly on an *ad hoc* basis. Frequently, the accused knew the members of the local bar personally, and one of them agreed to take his case. If not, then it was "every tub on its own bottom," and with this frontier spirit the man faced the Law unrepresented and alone— that is, unless the judge felt that it was a good idea to appoint a local lawyer to take the case without a fee.

The changes that have come about since those days are due to several related developments. The population rise, European immigration, and urbanization are prominent among them. After the Civil War, the population of the United States started to rise and, with the aid of European immigrants in the 1880's and 1890's, it had boomed by 1900. Population increases not only add new dimensions to problems, they also create wholly new problems and, in response, evoke new philosophies.

The first legal aid society in American history was created in 1876 by the German Society of New York City. Its purpose was to provide legal advice to German immigrants. Soon after, legal aid societies evolved in the great urban immigrant centers of the Northeast. At first most of them provided service only in civil cases.

On January 9, 1914, the Public Defender of the County of Los Angeles, California, began operation. This event was a "first" in two respects. The office was the first publicly supported defender agency of the modern type, and it was the first legal aid agency devoted almost exclusively to criminal cases.

By late 1963, there was a professional defender agency operating in 184 counties; in addition, defenders operated in the District of Columbia, the independent city of St.

Louis, and throughout the entire island Commonwealth of Puerto Rico.[1] These agencies have had a profound impact on the defense of the indigent in criminal cases. They have given to hundreds of thousands of indigent defendants the protection of rights that otherwise would have been forfeited because of poverty.

Despite this growth of professional legal aid agencies in the criminal field, the traditional assigned counsel system is still the most prevalent method of affording counsel to the indigent in the United States today.[2] For while defender agencies operate in 184 counties, there are over 3,100 counties in the United States. The assigned counsel system is in exclusive operation, therefore, in approximately 3,000 American counties.

The traditional assigned counsel system does not really deserve to be called a "system." In any fashion he deems wise, the judge simply selects an attorney to represent the indigent person before him.

Experiment in New Jersey

The statewide assigned counsel system in New Jersey is an extension of the Essex Plan, which was initiated in Essex County in 1946. The central idea in this plan is the assignment of the cases of indigent criminal defendants to the lawyers of the county in alphabetical rotation. The support of this plan by Chief Justice Arthur T. Vanderbilt of the New Jersey Supreme Court was invaluable in securing its statewide adoption.

Some insight into the rationale behind the adoption of the Essex Plan for the state is provided by a report on the problem of indigent defendants prepared by a committee of county court judges in the 1940's.[3] The committee considered three alternate methods to provide defense counsel for the indigent. These were: (1) The Catch-as-Catch-Can Plan, which involved assignment of attorneys as cases arose—in other words, the traditional assigned counsel system—with no definite organization. The difficulty with this plan, according to the county judges, was that the burden fell on just a few members of the bar, usually the most inexperienced. This plan was considered far from satisfactory. (2) The Public Defender Plan, which "while appealing on first blush," allegedly had "definite disadvantages." [4] These disadvantages were the financial burden on the taxpayers, and the probability that an official, being on the public payroll, would not be a vigorous and independent protagonist for the defense. (3) The Essex Plan, the most desirable alternative for New Jersey. According to the committee of county judges, the main advantages of the Essex Plan were that the independence of the bar would be maintained, the public would be saved the expense of a public defender's office, and the law clerks and law students assigned to aid attorneys would, in the process, gain experience. The major features of the New Jersey system follow.

THE DEFENDERS: SELECTION

The basic concept of the New Jersey system is laid down in the first paragraph of the rule:

> Where a person charged with crime appears in a trial court, without counsel, the court shall advise him of his right to counsel and of the privilege of having counsel assigned, if indigent, and assign counsel to represent him unless he elects to proceed without counsel or is about to obtain counsel.[5]

Perhaps the most unique provision of the system is that which provides for the assignment of counsel from a master list of all the practicing attorneys in each county "except in cases of murder and where in the opinion of the court the gravity of the offense warrants the assignment of special counsel." [6]

All practicing attorneys are eligible for service. For a variety of reasons, however, the names of all the attorneys in each county are not included on the lists. First, there is a problem in obtaining the names of new attorneys promptly. Second, a large number of attorneys are not eligible for service because of informal county policy. For example, government officials, judges, magistrates, prosecutors, and assistant prosecutors are not eligible for assignment in most counties. One of the court rules made "any partner, employer, employee, or office associate" of a judge or a magistrate ineligible to practice in criminal courts.[7] An amendment to the rule, effective on February 1, 1957, made such partners and associates eligible for assignment to indigent criminal defendants while retaining the prohibition on practice in the criminal courts as retained counsel.

The assignment of attorneys considered eligible for service is a flexible process in most counties so that the alphabetical listing serves more as a rough guide rather than a precise prescription in selection of counsel. This is made necessary, in part, by the economic fact that attorneys are not paid for their time in cases where they represent indigents. For this reason, a request by an attorney to be relieved of an assignment that arrives in the midst of an important private case is usually granted by a judge or his clerk. Otherwise, the assigned counsel system in New

Jersey might become an intolerable imposition on attorneys.

Deviation from the alphabetical listing may be made by a judge for a more important reason than the needs of the attorney's private practice. Where the next attorney on the list is inexperienced in the criminal courts or is a novice in the profession, his assignment to a case, especially where serious charges are involved, may result in great injustice to the indigent defendant. Originally, the problem of inexperienced counsel in serious non-capital cases was not expressly recognized by the rule. The rule provided for the assignment of special counsel only in capital cases where counsel are allowed compensation by the state. Following the survey I made in 1955, the New Jersey Supreme Court amended the rules so that special assignments of attorneys could be made without reference to the alphabetical listing, not only in capital cases, but also "where in the opinion of the judge the gravity of the offense warrants the assignment of special counsel." [8] In this manner there is now formal recognition that one of the basic assumptions of the assigned counsel system—the equal basic competence of attorneys in the criminal courts—has serious limitations in practice. The extent of this limitation was underscored by the questionnaire survey of Essex County, New Jersey, attorneys performed in 1956 by the Special Committee to Study Defender Systems. It revealed that only 9.5 per cent of the attorneys claimed "extensive" experience in criminal practice.[9] This is probably an optimistic percentage, not only for New Jersey, but for the entire country.

The lack of criminal experience among attorneys presents a difficult problem to the judges who select counsel for assignment. The amendment to the rule requires that they deviate from the alphabetical listing in those cases requiring "special counsel." But if only one in ten of the attorneys on the master list has extensive criminal experience, the judges are faced with the dilemma of imposing an extra burden on this small group or of ignoring the precept to be selective in assignments. It is apparent that many judges choose the latter alternative. Nine out of the twelve county judges who answered a questionnaire mailed to them by me in 1957 indicated that they made no deviation from the ordinary assignment procedure in noncapital cases carrying a severe sentence.[10] As a result, it often happens that attorneys with little experience in the criminal courts find themselves defending persons facing prosecution that could bring imprisonment for 10, 20, even 30 years or more. For many attorneys, the very thought of such an assignment is disturbing. I can only imagine what it does to a defendant when he realizes that his legal protector is a novice in the criminal courts.

UNEQUAL TIME

The first contact that many prisoners have with a lawyer after arrest is with a so-called jailhouse attorney. These crafty professionals in the criminal courts frequently operate in a temporary partnership with a bondsman. Such partnership arrangements with non-lawyers are prohibited by Canons 33 and 34 of *The Canons of Ethics* of the American Bar Association, adopted by the Supreme Court of New Jersey as controlling in that state. Both the attorney and the bondsman in such partnerships may make periodic visits to the local jails and to the county jails, where they have relatively free access to the prisoners. On occasion, detectives or jail guards suggest the services of a specific bondsman and attorney to a prisoner and, if the prisoner agrees, may contact them by telephone. The extent of remuneration, if any, given by the attorneys or bondsmen for this service is unknown, although some prisoners claim that "the police get a cut." Many of the interviews these attorneys have with the prisoners involve only one subject—the defendant's ability to pay a fee. Frequently, there is no second interview. From the information supplied by the convicts interviewed, this practice is not widespread but may be more prevalent in certain New Jersey counties than in Philadelphia or in the federal court system.[11]

Unless an indigent defendant has managed to make contact with a jailhouse attorney, he may remain incarcerated, even though convicted of no crime, for months before he has his first conference with his defense attorney. The mean average length of time between arrest and first contact with assigned counsel for the indigent New Jersey prisoners was 56.89 days; while the median average—the point at which exactly half the answers fell above, and half below—was 35 days. The mean average for those men who hired a lawyer was 3.94 days; while the median average was under one day.[12]

A lengthy delay between arrest and first contact with an attorney is common wherever an assigned counsel system operates.[13] In Tompkins County, New York, for example, the Special Committee to Study Defender Systems found that incarcerated indigent defendants often did not consult with an attorney until three months after arrest.[14] On the other hand, the Special Committee was of the opinion that centralized and professional defender systems can and frequently do provide representation much sooner after arrest. The Criminal Courts Branch of the

New York Legal Aid Society usually is able to contact an
indigent client within forty-eight to seventy-two hours
after arrest.[15] And the publicly financed defender agency
in Alameda County, California, is in most cases able to
interview an indigent defendant within forty-eight hours
after arrest.[16] Not all professional defender systems can
be this prompt because of limitations of budget and, con-
sequently, of personnel.[17]

In various studies I have made since 1955, I found that
assignment invariably took place at the time of arraignment or later in New Jersey, as in most states. The Supreme
Court of New Jersey amended the court rules in 1956 to
the effect that "whenever practicable, counsel shall be
assigned before arraignment." [18] At first, it seemed that
judges treated this amendment as only a mild admonition.
There is still much evidence to this effect. But there also
are now some indications that a number of county judges
are making a genuine attempt to assign attorneys to indigents before arraignment. But the evidence on this point
is neither strong nor conclusive.[19] If the practice of early
assignment were to become statewide, however, it would
raise the standard of defense provided by the New Jersey
assigned counsel system over that of most other states.

It is frequently said, as it was by one county judge in
answer to a questionnaire, that a prisoner who requests
assigned counsel before the usual time—arraignment—will
have his request granted. However, not one of the men
interviewed in prison stated that he took advantage of
this policy. Many of these men did not know that their request would be granted. In addition, the communication
system between a prisoner in the county jail and the
county judge is most often imperfect. In many counties
it is almost impossible for a defendant to get such a mes-

sage to a judge. This is not as significant as the fact that most defendants find it inconceivable to think that by merely making a request they will receive appointment of counsel before the regular time. In this belief they are supported by those jail guards and county detectives who tell them they will get counsel only when they decide to "co-operate."

These, then, are the facts regarding the vital interval between arrest and first contact with a defense attorney. They show that the New Jersey assigned counsel plan has not been able to remove from the criminal process a defect that has affected the traditional assigned counsel system for centuries—the inequality of time. The sooner an accused person confers with his attorney, the less likely it is that the defendant's rights will be jeopardized or his defense destroyed. Every day that a defendant spends in official custody without the guidance of an attorney is a day fraught with peril. On this ground alone, indigent defendants in a jurisdiction that has an assigned counsel system are at a distinct disadvantage compared with those defendants who can afford to hire counsel or with those who are represented by the better professional defender systems.

INDIGENCY AND COMPENSATION

The determination of eligibility for assigned counsel in New Jersey is usually made so as to favor the defendant. In most cases, all that is necessary to establish indigency is a statement to that effect signed by the defendant, coupled with the fact that he is detained in the county jail without bail. But the fact that he has been released on bail does not bar the assignment of counsel to him. In this respect, the New Jersey system is more liberal than those many assigned counsel and professional defender systems that will not provide a defense to any defendant who is able to produce bail.

In any jurisdiction, the criteria of "indigency" and bail requirements are directly related on other grounds. Most defendants are in that large, marginal economic group of people who have no cash reserve and do have many debts. If they are taken away from their jobs for several weeks or several months, these defendants must be considered indigent within the frame of reference of the assigned counsel system; that is, they do not have sufficient available capital to pay an attorney's fee. Whether or not they are taken away from their jobs depends largely on whether they are able to pay the bail bondsman's fee. This frequently amounts to less than $100. To break this closed circle, then, $100 in funds or a piece of real estate to pledge is required early in the case. If the defendant produces bail, this unlocks the door for him to return to his employment and, in the long months between arrest and arraignment or trial, to earn enough money to pay an attorney's fee in installments. But most men charged with major crimes do not have the key to this door. They do not produce bail, or, in the case of certain heinous crimes, are not allowed bail by the committing magistrate.[20] They lose their jobs and become another statistic in the indigency tabulations. A change in the rules governing bail might lessen greatly the number of "indigent" defendants who require legal aid.[21]

However, the release of certain defendants under more liberal bail requirements would not always take them out of the indigency group, because of insufficient income from their work. The salary of these defendants is barely adequate to produce living expenses for themselves and their families. There is no excess to pay an attorney's fee. In most cases, however, a defendant at liberty on bail is able to retain an attorney who will accept small installment payments.

Another group of defendants stand a cut higher in the financial scale. These are the so-called white-collar defendants. They have just enough capital in the bank to pay a bondsman's fee and a minimal attorney's fee. However, even if they deplete their small store of savings, which they frequently will do in a criminal case, the effectiveness of the defense they receive is often questionable. According to Judge Jerome Frank and Barbara Frank,

> . . . if the accused is a white-collar worker, neither poverty-stricken nor well-to-do, then ordinarily his lawyer will be incompetent. For then neither the court nor anyone else will provide him with a lawyer. He must hire his own, and his inability to pay anything but a small fee means that usually he will be represented by a counsel who lacks ability.
>
> There are a few well-equipped lawyers willing to defend the white-collar accused. But in most large cities their number is small. There the bulk of the "criminal bar" consists of lawyers with scant legal education. They prey on accused men of modest means. By picking up a few dollars from each client, each of these lawyers earns a meager living. Feeling little responsibility to do much for a small fee, he conducts the defense in careless, slapdash fashion. He will neglect to call witnesses whose testimony might well prove the defendant's innocence, or to cross-examine prosecution witnesses who, by careful questioning, might be shown up as unreliable.
>
> The innocent white-collar defendant in a large city is thus, ordinarily, more likely to be convicted than if he were

wholly destitute. This miserable situation the legal profession should rectify.[22]

Many of the men classified in the indigent group by the courts of New Jersey and of other states and practically the entire white collar group are potential clients for a lawyer's reference service. Such agencies are controlled by bar associations and provide for the services of attorneys at lower than standard fees. But most communities do not have a lawyer's reference service.

The New Jersey policy in regard to the acceptance by assigned counsel of compensation from "indigent" defendants is unclear. By implication, the New Jersey court rules indicate that the system is an *unpaid* assigned counsel system. This was the opinion expressed in interviews by many judges, prosecutors, and attorneys throughout the state. The law provides for compensation only in capital cases.[23] But there is no express prohibition against an assigned counsel receiving a fee. In my 1955 study of the assigned counsel system in New Jersey for the Administrative Office of the Courts, I found that in thirteen counties an attorney was generally not allowed to receive compensation.[24] There were eight counties, however, where compensation by the defendant of his counsel was allowed by the judges under certain circumstances. In six of these counties the county judges advised defendants to pay their assigned attorneys at once or at some time in the future when they were able to do so. A policy statement that allows the acceptance of a fee upon the approval of the court was issued in 1956 by a committee of attorneys and judges in Hudson County.[25] In the absence of a lawyer's reference service, therefore, there is growing up within the structure of the assigned counsel system in certain counties a similar procedure. The main points of distinction are that it is more or less informal, and it is somewhat controlled by the county judges rather than by bar associations.

Because of the lack of a formal lawyer's reference service and the lenient attitude toward claims of indigency, among other reasons, it is unavoidable that certain defendants who could afford a minimum attorney's fee take advantage of the assigned counsel system. It is not surprising, therefore, that one of the main complaints of attorneys in New Jersey is that the indigency test is not strict enough. A recommendation for a tighter indigency test was mentioned as a necessary improvement in the assigned counsel system by a number of Essex County attorneys who answered a questionnaire submitted to them by the Special Committee to Study Defender Systems in 1956.[26] Most attorneys are aware that there is no real screening of a defendant's financial status before assignment. A majority of the Essex County attorneys answered that they felt it necessary to question "indigent" defendants regarding their financial status.[27]

The problem of compensation to attorneys assigned to the supposedly indigent defendant has plagued the assigned counsel system since its inception in this country. When the Special Committee to Study Defender Systems published its report in 1959, it reported that 27 states, including New Jersey, did not provide compensation for counsel assigned in non-capital cases.[28] Other states provided for some payment, but it was usually inadequate.[29] At the present time most states provide compensation, but it is still usually insufficient to adequately compensate the lawyer for the time and effort he must invest in a criminal defense. So it seems fair to say that the most common method for providing counsel to the indigent in this country is the *under*paid assigned counsel system.

In order to prevent non-indigents in New Jersey from claiming the privilege of assigned counsel, the court rules require that defendants sign an affidavit of indigency.[30] Most of the indigent New Jersey prisoners I interviewed remembered signing an affidavit or a statement about their financial condition before receiving assigned counsel. However, 36 per cent claimed that they were questioned about their finances but could not remember signing a statement.[31] The affidavit of indigency may be executed by a county detective or a county prosecutor in the prisoner's cell as part of the copping out process; by the warden of the county jail, who may question men as to counsel at regular intervals after they have been committed; or by the clerk of courts shortly after arraignment. These officials are frequently notaries public. "Investigations" of indigency by county detectives do not ordinarily go beyond an interview with the defendant.

Some professional defender agencies have developed sophisticated procedures for determining indigency and for answering the claims of attorneys, similar to those made in Essex County, that the defender system is making incursions into the ranks of fee-paying clients. The Public Defender of Alameda County, California, provides one of the best examples.[32] In cases where there is any doubt of the defendant's indigence, the defender assigns one of his detectives to investigate. Such investigations of indigency usually remove all doubt. But where there is any question that the accused might have sufficient funds to interest a local private attorney, the public defender refers the case to a panel of three lawyers selected from a list maintained by local bar associations. The main purpose of this procedure is to further screen the defendant's financial status. Any of these attorneys may assume the defense, accepting the usually small fee available. Very often all three attorneys certify that the defendant is, for all practical purposes, indigent and should be defended by the public defender. But even where the panel of attorneys recommends the acceptance of a case by the public defender, the defender may, where he remains doubtful of indigency, present the case to the court for a final decision. This may seem like an unnecessarily long and involved procedure, but it is a reliable method for the determination of indigency—and for creating good relations with local bar groups, as well.

The Defender's Function

It is generally assumed that the function of the defense attorney—whether he serves indigents or fee-paying clients —is to be an adversary. Is this time-honored idea still realistic? My answer is affirmative for the reasons given in the following discussion.

At least four theories may be suggested to describe the defender's function. These are the adversary theory, the truth theory, the negotiator theory, and the lawyer-criminologist theory. The adversary, or fight, concept has roots that go back to the political turmoil of early England. The courts were accepted by judges at the time of Coke as an arm of the Crown in political prosecutions. The prosecution was given every advantage in these cases while the defense was tied down at every turn. In other cases also, many of which involved capital punishment, "a criminal trial in those days was not unlike a race between the

King and the prisoner, in which the King had a long start
and the prisoner was heavily weighted." [33] During the six-
teenth and seventeenth centuries in England, prisoners
accused of major crimes were not even allowed legal
counsel.[34]

These restrictions have left marks on American procedure that are clearly visible to this day. According to
Roscoe Pound,

> What chiefly affected American criminal procedure was
> memory of the unfair advantage it [English procedure at
> the time of Coke] gave the crown, as brought out in the
> prosecution of Whigs and Dissenters under the Stuarts.[35]

The rules governing American trials, therefore, were
drafted by men who remembered painfully those English
trials where the prosecution had an unfair advantage and
where the defense was greatly hindered.

The adversary system casts the defense attorney as a
warrior in the cause of a verdict of not guilty. The function of the defender-as-warrior is to shield his client from
the javelin thrusts of the prosecution by presenting all
legal defenses; the warrior then must sally forth with evidence of innocence, thus destroying the prosecution's
guilty allegations at their base. On the other side of the
battlefield stands the enemy, the prosecution warrior, who
casts the bolts of guilt at the defendant. The judge functions during the trial-battle as a legal umpire who prevents infractions of the rules of evidence. But unlike the
judges under the Stuarts, he is a disinterested party to
the outcome of the case. The achievement of this trial-by-
battle situation, with approximately the same legal advantages given to each side, was a notable landmark in the
progress of individual freedom.

It might be argued that the fight theory was related to a broader line of thought that emphasized freedom from governmental restraint. This was the "invisible hand" notion of Adam Smith and classical social-economic theory of the eighteenth century. It assumed that if you allowed human atoms to interact freely under the eyes of an overseer, whose sole function was to keep the struggle free, social justice would result. As the late Judge Jerome Frank wrote:

> [T]he fighting theory of justice is not unrelated to, and not uninfluenced by, extreme laissez-faire in the economic field.
>
> "Classical" laissez-faire economic theory assumed that, when each individual, as an "economic man," strives rationally, in the competitive economic struggle or "fight" to promote his own self-interest, we attain public welfare through the wisest use of resources and the most socially desirable distribution of economic goods. The "fight" theory of justice is a sort of legal laissez-faire. It assumes a "litigious" man.[36]

As the laissez-faire theory served the cause of individual freedom, so has the fight theory. But as limitations have been found in laissez faire as a method of achieving justice in society, so have limitations been found, it is claimed, in the adversary method for achieving justice in the courts. Perhaps the strongest argument against the fight system was made by Judge Frank in his *Courts on Trial,* published in 1949. Frank expressed strong opposition to the methods used by certain attorneys and, moreover, attacked the entire adversary system that "virtually compels their use, a system which treats a law suit as a battle of wits and wiles." [37] This attack went squarely to the purported strong point of the fight system, the notion that the two adversaries will in their conflict produce all of the evidence that could influence the court in reaching an informed decision. Actually, Judge Frank claimed,

> the lawyer aims at victory, at winning in the fight, not at aiding the court to discover the facts. He does not want the trial court to reach a sound educated guess, if it is likely to be contrary to his client's interests. Our present trial method is thus the equivalent of throwing pepper in the eyes of a surgeon while he is performing an operation.[38]

For the fight theory Frank suggested the substitution of the "truth theory." [39] Under this theory, attorneys would be forced by new rules and judicial pressure to play a more positive trial role. Both defense attorneys and prosecuting attorneys would have greater responsibility placed on them to clarify, not cloud, the facts. The realization of this theory in actual trial practice would be no small achievement.

But, it is important to remember, the outcome of a rather small percentage of serious criminal cases—at most, two in ten—actually is determined by a trial in the courtroom.[40] In most cases, therefore, defense counsel do not function as fighters in the traditional sense, for there is no real contest in progress as to guilt or innocence. The only point at issue is the disposition of the defendant. A favorable disposition would be a light sentence or probation, not acquittal. Professor Donald J. Newman wrote in 1956 that "bargain-justice appears as a natural, expedient outgrowth of deficiencies in the administration of our 'trial by combat' theory of justice." [41] Under these circumstances, the attorney, it may be claimed, operates not as a warrior but as a negotiator.

In most cases, trial by combat simply does not occur in the traditional sense, as present rules assume. And, as I have already argued, the present adversary rules exert almost no control over one of the most important phases of the entire process: the process of negotiation between prosecution and defense.

Does this mean that the adversary system has been subverted? Definitely not. Even in negotiated decisions an adversary posture may be, and frequently is, still maintained. The attorney may "fight" for the best deal possible. And the possibility that the defendant may choose trial-by-combat rather than accept the prosecution's offer is a strong factor in the process of negotiation. Trial in court under the fight theory rules remains the ultimate test of a market-place position taken in the prosecutor's office.

Like the truth theory, the lawyer-criminologist theory has only a slight relation to present reality and, if implemented, would probably result in even more fundamental changes than the truth theory. This concept of the defense function may be inferred from the treatment theory of the criminal law, which makes rehabilitation of offenders the guiding precept for the criminal courts.[42] At the present time, the treatment theory of the criminal law has had a significant effect on the court institution only after conviction. Application of the concepts of penology, psychiatry, and sociology to the procedure leading up to conviction would force prosecutors and defense attorneys to perform their function with an awareness of their responsibility for the furtherance of a rational scheme of individual rehabilitation. They could no longer act as old Anglo-Saxon warriors in a battle for whose final outcome they have no responsibility.[43] And the negotiated achievement of a certain disposition of the defendant, such as by probation instead of by institutional treatment, would not be purely a matter of horse-trading ability.[44] This disposition would be based on the concept of individualization of treatment.

It would be difficult to imagine a concept that would have a more profound effect on the function of defense counsel in the criminal courts than the lawyer-criminologist theory. Our bills of rights and our rules of criminal procedure were motivated by an intense concern to erect a barrier between the individual and his government. Here the government would be invited not only to break down this barrier to an unknown extent, but would be called upon to set the direction of the individual's entire future life! In the words of criminologist Nathaniel Cantor,

> The immediate problem . . . is to determine the implications of a treatment theory of the criminal law on the rules of criminal procedure. Will a code of criminal procedure premised upon individualization of treatment interfere with the traditional safeguards of individual liberty? [45]

Put in other words, would it be possible for a defense counsel to serve the treatment ethic and, at the same time, protect the constitutional rights of the defendant—and provide an effective defense?

This is a difficult question to answer. But of a few things we can be certain. Both the truth theory and the lawyer-criminologist theory have within them the seeds of greater restrictions on the rights of the defendant. In a world that is becoming increasingly organized, increasingly conformist, and increasingly machinelike, it is only with great reluctance that we should incorporate into any governmental institution a practice that tends further to break down individual rights. This is not to ignore the criticisms that have been made of the adversary system. These criticisms are significant and point the way to future reform. It might well be possible, at some time in the future, to blend the best part of the venerable adversary tradition with modern social science and the realities of bargain criminal justice. But no one has yet suggested such a comprehensive and well-balanced scheme. Until this is done, the function of the defense counsel should continue to be that of an adversary: at times, a bargaining adversary; at other times, a fighting adversary in the traditional manner. But still an adversary.

7

The Facts and the Plea

Investigation

Investigation before trial is a "must." The attorney who begins the trial of a case without finding out the facts beforehand might as well practice law with his head in a sack.[1]

The former public defender who wrote those words knew what he was talking about. He does not practice law with his head in a sack. But too many attorneys do.

TWO FORGERY CASES

Clifford Shephard was a partner in a prosperous Philadelphia fund-raising organization.[2] He commuted daily from North Plainfield, New Jersey, where he lived in a boarding house owned by Mrs. Betty Lester. At five o'clock in the afternoon of April 18, 1935, Shephard had taken the train to Plainfield and was on his way back to the boarding house. As he waited for a light to change on the street corner, Mrs. Lester met him on her way home from marketing. Shortly thereafter a man ran up to Shephard and said, "That's him! I'd know him anywhere!" And then the man looked at Mrs. Lester and shouted, "That's the same woman, too. She was with him then." Shephard and Mrs. Lester were then arrested by two detectives, who offered no explanation of the arrest.

In the county prosecutor's office they were told that they were being charged with forgery of checks they had allegedly passed to local merchants. Ten merchants identified Shephard and Mrs. Lester as the forgers. They were indicted for forgery and spent seven months in jail awaiting trial. It was not until November of 1935 that their case was called. As Judge Jerome and Betty Frank wrote:

> Since the defendants had been impoverished by the months in jail, they could not pay a lawyer to defend them. They were represented by a court-appointed counsel, a recent law school graduate. Despite his inexperience, no doubt this lawyer thought of calling a handwriting expert to testify, but, lacking funds, the defendants could not pay an expert's fee.[3]

Defense testimony consisted only of a number of character witnesses and a mechanic who stated that Shephard had been in his garage while one of the crimes was taking place. Upon their conviction by a jury, the defendants received sentences of nine months in jail.

At the expiration of their sentences the prisoners were released, re-arrested outside the prison for another series of forgeries, and retried. Another group of merchants put in evidence another series of forged checks. "The defendants, not able to obtain a handwriting analysis, offered the same pitiful defense."[4] The verdict was inevitable—

guilty. Shephard received a sentence of eighteen months. Mrs. Lester was sentenced to a nine-month term.

On his release from prison the second time, Shephard found that his standing in the community was ruined. He earned his living by doing odd jobs, mowing lawns, and washing dishes. But even this livelihood stopped when he was arrested for forgery a third time. He was again identified by a group of merchants. But in this case his prison sentences produced their sole benefit—they provided him with an airtight alibi, for he had been in prison when this last series of forgeries had been committed. The grand jury refused to return an indictment on this evidence. The third experience was repeated in 1938, when he was charged but never tried for another group of forgeries.

At this point Shephard decided that he would have to prove his innocence at all costs. He borrowed money and hired the Burns Detective Agency to investigate his case. Their detectives came upon Edward Sullivan, who resembled Shephard. More important, Sullivan's handwriting matched exactly the handwriting on the checks allegedly forged by Shephard. Shephard appealed to the New Jersey State Board of Pardons for a full pardon based on this evidence. Nevertheless, the board refused his application without giving any reason. During the next two years, while waiting for another chance to present his application to the Board of Pardons, Shephard prevailed upon Sullivan, the real forger, who was in prison on another charge, to sign a full confession of the crimes. Furthermore, Sullivan's wife signed a written statement in which she admitted that she was the woman who had passed the checks forged by her husband.

It was not until June 14, 1950, that Shephard, with the help of a newspaperman incensed by Shephard's treatment by the authorities, succeeded in obtaining an unconditional pardon from Governor Driscoll.

Approximately twenty years after the arrests in the Shephard case, and a continent away, another man was arrested on forgery charges—similar to those in the New Jersey case—by policemen in Alameda County, California. Like Shephard and Mrs. Lester, he was innocent. But unlike that unfortunate pair, this man was later released by the district attorney. What made the difference? This may easily be discerned in the following brief description of the California case by George Nye, then Public Defender of Alameda County:

> The first case in which we undertook a field investigation outside California arose a few years ago when we represented a man who had been mistakenly identified as a forger operating previously in Alameda County. Mr. Wixson [the public defender's chief investigator] went to the State of Washington and there found hotel and employment records which showed that this defendant had been in the Seattle area instead of in Alameda County at the time involved. The district attorney dismissed the charge in reliance on this new evidence.[5]

So this case was disposed of by the pre-trial investigation, not by an investigation after the defendant had been convicted and had spent years in prison. But had the district attorney insisted on prosecuting, an expert investigator as well as a handwriting expert would have testified for the defense—both of them would have been establishing the facts supporting the claim of innocence, and both would have been paid by the public defender's office.

FACTS FOR THE DEFENSE

When any defense counsel enters a case, he will usually find that there are four important sources of factual information: (1) the defendant, (2) the prosecutor, (3) witnesses, and (4) physical evidence. The defense counsel will ordinarily start his fact-gathering with an interview of the accused, who often is held at that time in a house of detention such as a county jail. Following this interview, the attorney will ordinarily confer with that lawyer in the office of the county prosecutor who has been assigned to the case. An interesting game then ensues. The defense counsel seeks to wheedle out of the prosecutor's assistant every ounce of information he can. For his part, the assistant prosecutor wants to give the attorney every scrap of information that points toward guilt with the hope that the counsel will advise the defendant to plead guilty and save the time and trouble of a trial. This is not to say that prosecutors usually seek to convict the innocent, but many do try to convince the "guilty" to cop out even where the evidence might not stand up at a trial.

During the course of showing how strong his case is, the prosecutor often provides the defense counsel with much valuable information. This is possible because the prosecutor usually has most of the vital facts in his file by the time the defense attorney enters the case. The prosecution file will contain the results of the local police investigation and also, in certain cases, reports of investigations by the prosecutor's own detectives. The file may also contain reports on physical evidence such as ballistic and medical analyses. And in many, if not a majority, of cases the county prosecutor will have a confession from the defendant. All of this confronts the defense counsel when he enters the case.

When the defense attorney walks out of the prosecutor's office, he has a good deal of information about the case, since he has now interviewed both the defendant and the prosecutor's assistant. He has reached, at least to a limited extent, the first two sources of information. Let us assume that the defendant claims that he was at the scene of the robbery, but that he was an innocent bystander picked up by the police because of his juvenile record, and that two drinking companions known only as "Flop Ears" and "Peanuts" will support his story. And let us further assume that the prosecutor has just finished reading to the defense attorney portions of a full confession, which his client allegedly gave voluntarily to the local police, and portions of two witnesses' statements implicating the accused. This is a common type of situation. It would be logical for the defense attorney then to go beyond the first two sources of information, the defendant and the prosecutor, to commence a search for the witnesses "Flop Ears" and "Peanuts"—and to find physical evidence, perhaps at the scene of the crime. But many attorneys do not go beyond the first two sources, and, therefore, their fact-gathering efforts do not deserve to be called an investigation. Why do so many attorneys fail to perform an effective investigation?

Let us first take, for example, the situation confronting an assigned counsel in New Jersey. Except in capital cases, where the New Jersey courts may grant expenses, the assigned counsel is provided neither compensation for his advice nor for the time and expense he may spend on an investigation of the facts. This is the situation found in many states. In others, the remuneration provided by the court is not adequate to cover an investigation. Moreover, no constitutional provision, law, or court decision regarding the right to counsel requires an out-of-court investigation of the facts. Our evolving legal system simply hasn't evolved that far. Thus, the average attorney assigned to defend the indigent finds himself with neither funds nor an explicit legal duty to make an effective factual investigation.

(The case of *State* v. *Horton*, 34 N.J. 518, 170 A.2d 1 [1961] suggests that attorneys should be paid for some investigative costs, but it is not clear how extensively this is being done. Moreover, the essential defect—lack of compensation for *time* spent by lawyers—was in no way affected by the *Horton* case.)

Yet many assigned attorneys may wish to perform such an investigation in order to live up to the *spirit* of their attorney's oath—and because they may be touched by the plight of the poor wretch cooped up in a foul cell at the county jail. Such an idealistic attorney may come back to his office, after having consumed the lion's share of the day at the county jail and in the prosecutor's office, determined to spend the time necessary—perhaps two to four days—to find the elusive "Peanuts" and "Flop Ears," last names unknown. Our attorney then looks at his desk and sees the following matters: letters from two clients asking why he hasn't filed court proceedings against an insurance company in cases that promise fees of several thousand dollars; four notes indicating that important clients have called with urgent questions about pressing business deals; a jumbled pile of long, yellow legal note paper covered with writing about legal research he has been doing almost simultaneously on three separate tax cases; a notice from the building manager that the monthly rent on his office will go up to $400 a month starting with the first of the year; weekly salary checks, totaling $165 for the two secretaries, requiring his signature; a bill for $210 from his oldest son's orthodontist; and an $800 annual dues notice from his country club.

Despite these practical brakes on idealism, there are those attorneys who put in as much time as is necessary to gather all of the facts. Those who work in firms may have a younger office associate detailed from important remunerative business to conduct an investigation. Some may even hire a private detective. I met one such attorney in the halls of the Essex County, New Jersey, courthouse a few years ago. He told me that he had paid a private investigator $200 to gather the facts in this assigned case, and that he considered that fee a small personal contribution to the public welfare.

But all too many attorneys assigned to defend the indigent find the pressures of meeting office expenses that may easily reach $100 per day, plus the pressures of family expenses, plus the desire of wanting to get ahead in a materialistic society too much to resist. Their "investigation" does not go beyond the defendant's county jail cell nor the county prosecutor's office. As the Special Committee to Study Defender Systems pointed out following its nationwide survey, considering the pressures under which most assigned counsel work, "it would be almost miraculous if detailed investigations of fact were made in each case where such an investigation was necessary." [6]

Many assigned attorneys simply tell the defendant, if he is at liberty on bail, to investigate the case himself and to find the witnesses. When I asked a prisoner in the New Jersey State Prison if his assigned counsel had investigated the facts, he replied:

> I did all the running around myself. I ran myself silly looking for witnesses. I spent so much time investigating that I lost several good jobs which I had. I spent 120 days looking for people—witnesses—and evidence.

When I said incredulously, "That's an awfully long time to spend on an investigation," he answered, "If you only knew how much I wanted to stay out of jail."

I have spoken to a number of county prosecutors who were willing to admit that the lack of independent defense facilities created an imbalance in the scales of justice and tended to silently endanger constitutional rights. For example, five of the sixteen New Jersey county prosecutors I interviewed in my 1955 study for the Administrative Office of the Courts of New Jersey cited the lack of investigatory facilities as having an adverse effect on the defendant's case. Use by the defense of the prosecutor's investigation file did not, they maintained, satisfy the need for independent investigation.[7] Also, the lack of investigatory assistance was one of the major criticisms of the New Jersey assigned counsel plan made by the attorneys of Essex County in answer to the questionnaire mailed to them by the Special Committee to Study Defender Systems in 1956.[8]

The situation confronting most attorneys retained to defend criminal defendants is not markedly different from that facing assigned attorneys. Most of those accused of crime who are not totally indigent are near-indigent. They pay a minimal fee and are provided with a minimal investigation—and a minimal defense. Of course, if the attorney is one of those few paid an adequate fee, there is every possibility that he will perform a thorough investigation. But such fees are rare. It is the poor man who sets the tone in the criminal courts.

Finally, let us examine the situation facing the attorney who works in a professional defender office. It should not be assumed that defender offices invariably perform effective investigations. Most defender offices in this country are so strapped for funds that they cannot afford to hire investigators. While exact figures are not available, it is probable that no more than eighteen defender agencies have even one full-time, paid investigator. Since the attorneys in all defender offices are paid a salary to defend the indigent, however, there is more elbow room for idealism. Some attorneys in defender offices that have no investigators will themselves perform fairly adequate investigations in many cases.

An attorney who works in a properly financed and well-staffed defender office can call upon investigative assistance that would make the average assigned attorney—and his client—extremely envious. One of the best examples is found in Los Angeles County, California, which boasts the largest professional defender system in the country.[9]

The Los Angeles County Public Defender Office puts nine investigators with a total of over one hundred years of criminal investigation experience on the defense side of the scales of justice. Each investigator has a specialty. One of the men handles homicide and sex crime investigations. Another is an expert in the field of forgery and handwriting; this investigator is called upon in all cases where the authenticity of a document is questioned. Other investigators handle general investigations in the field. These men have years of experience in such general assignments—in examinations of the scene of a crime and in criminal photography.[10]

The purpose of these investigations is not to contrive a defense at all costs but to get the truth. Even where facts are adverse to the defendant, they are reported to the defender attorney handling the case. According to former Chief Investigator Edward Bliss, this has a two-fold advantage. First, where the defendant still insists on going to trial, the counsel knows what to expect from the prosecution. "Secondly, if all the facts follow the same line and it is obvious that the defendant is lying and that you are fighting a hopeless cause, armed with this information the defendant can be contacted, apprised of the situation, and made aware of the futility of a fight." [11] The result is pressure from the defense attorney on the defendant to avail himself of bargain justice, but it is pressure based on a full understanding of the facts and with the intention of advancing the defendant's best interests—not the prosecutor's.

According to Public Defender Ellery Cuff, zealous investigation by Los Angeles defense detectives has uncovered facts proving the defendant's innocence even in the extraordinary circumstance where he had formally confessed the crime to police and reiterated his confession to defender attorneys. Investigation proved in one case that a young man was lying to shield his mother, who he thought had committed a murder. Investigation also proved that he was mistaken about his mother's guilt.[12]

But independent defense investigation facilities like those in Los Angeles are the rare exception in this country. Were Clifford Shephard and Mrs. Betty Lester to be tried in any New Jersey county today, it is extremely likely that the quality of defense investigation would not be markedly different than it was in 1935. Indeed, were they to be tried in any of those many American counties that do not provide adequate investigative facilities for impecunious defendants, the odds that they might be convicted are embarrassingly high.

Discovery: Ally to Investigation

"Discovery" is the formal method by which a defense attorney may force a prosecutor to divulge facts in his possession. It is an important aid to the defense, especially to the assigned attorney, so hard-pressed for time to gather facts. The theory underlying discovery is that the defendant should be aware of the salient features of the prosecution's case so that he may properly prepare his defense. However, the idea of giving information before trial about prosecution evidence and witnesses to "criminals" has produced many grave doubts in the minds of judges and lawyers. As a result, the power of discovery has many limitations.

When I began this study of the criminal process in 1955, I found that, like many states, New Jersey had a restrictive discovery doctrine. The New Jersey court rules did, and still do, have a provision covering discovery and inspection by the defendant; it states that the courts

> . . . may, if the interests of justice so require, order the prosecutor to permit the defendant to inspect and copy or photograph written statements or confessions made by the defendant and designated books, tangible objects, papers or documents obtained from others except written statements or confessions.[13]

Although there is room within the provisions of this rule for a liberal discovery procedure, in the early 1950's New Jersey courts repeatedly said that any request by the defendant for discovery and inspection was addressed to the "sound discretion" of the court.[14] In practice, this judicial verbiage meant that even the defendant's own confession was ordinarily not available to his counsel! [15] Thus, the courts of New Jersey held that "the interests of justice" did not require that the defendant be apprised of the facts in the prosecution's case. Discovery existed only in the court rules.

The reason for that restrictive discovery procedure was found in a "fundamental" difference allegedly existing between civil and criminal cases; this was explained by Chief Justice Arthur T. Vanderbilt in 1953:

> . . . the criminal defendant who is informed of the names of all the State's witnesses may take steps to bribe or frighten them into giving perjured testimony or into absenting themselves so that they are unavailable to testify. Moreover, many witnesses, if they know that the defendant will have knowledge of their names prior to trial, will be reluctant to come forward with information during the investigation of the crime. . . . All these dangers are more inherent in the criminal proceedings where the defendant has much more at stake, often his own life, than in civil proceedings. The presence of perjury in criminal proceedings today is extensive despite the efforts of the courts to eradicate it and constitutes a very serious threat to the administration of criminal justice and thus to the welfare of the country as a whole.[16]

This is a widely held philosophy among American judges. Professor Robert Knowlton of the Rutgers University Law School in New Jersey pointed out in 1956 that perjury has not been a problem limited to those states that allow full discovery in criminal proceedings.[17] And in one of the leading works on criminal procedure Professor Lester B. Orfield claimed that the perjury argument "has been long ago discredited." Orfield went on to state:

> With the assistance of cross-examination, the knowledge previously obtained by the defendant will not seriously reduce the probative force of the evidence, if the theory of the prosecution is correct. It will give the defendant an opportunity to demonstrate that the theory of the government is incorrect. In fact the defendant might argue that to deny the right to inspect would be out of harmony with the policy of the state to give every defendant a fair and impartial trial, and an opportunity to meet every charge preferred against him.[18]

Many students of the law have found it exceedingly odd that while discovery is slow in coming to the criminal courts, it has been widely used for years in the civil courts. An attorney trying a civil case may use all sorts of devices —discovery, depositions, interrogatories, and inspection— to apprise himself of his opponent's case so that he can prepare an adequate answer. As a result, it could be said back in 1928 that "in the trial of a civil action one plays the game with the cards face up." [19] Reflecting on this dichotomy, Judge Jerome Frank wisely prodded his judicial brethren:

> [O]ne would think that, since life or liberty is at stake, we would be more generous in helping the accused in a criminal case to defend himself than the defendant in a non-criminal case who stands to lose only money.[20]

In his dramatic book, *One Man's Freedom,* Washington attorney Edward Bennett Williams portrayed this inverse situation more graphically than any account I have read. In 1947, Williams related, he was assigned by the District of Columbia court to defend an indigent accused, Paul Collins, on a charge of embezzling $700 from a dairy. Williams' investigation convinced him that his client was innocent, for "while he might have been a bad bookkeeper, he was not a thief." [21] In preparing the somewhat complicated defense, Williams was confronted with the sharp contrast between civil and criminal cases:

> If the dairy had filed a civil suit against Collins for $700 alleging that he owed them this as a result of a shortage in his accounts, he would have had available to him all of the procedural safeguards that any civil litigant can employ. He could have ascertained the names of all the witnesses against him and taken their depositions before trial to find out what their testimony at trial would be. In other words, in the defense of $700 he could have availed himself of what we lawyers call pre-trial discovery procedures.
>
> But this was a criminal case. His liberty was at stake. He faced a possible sentence of five years in the penitentiary, the loss of his civil rights and the destruction of his reputation. Under the criminal rules, the procedural safeguards available to the parties in a civil case were not available to him. We were flying blind as we prepared for trial.[22]

Despite these difficulties, Williams, a skillful trial attorney, won the case.

Fortunately, the arguments against the lack of adequate discovery procedures are beginning to have their impact. For example, in 1958 the Supreme Court of New Jersey held that pre-trial applications by a defense attorney, for inspection of statements given by his client to police or prosecution officials, will be granted unless the prosecutor shows good cause for their denial.[23] But there is still a long way to go in New Jersey and in other states before discovery in criminal cases approximates discovery in civil matters, where property rights rather than personal liberty hang in the balance.

"How Do You Plead?"

Arraignment in a second-level or trial court (the county court in New Jersey) is, on the surface, a rather simple proceeding at which the defendant enters his plea.[24] But through a combination of constitutional interpretation and court practice the arraignment has taken on a significance that goes beyond a pleading session.

Up to this point the right to counsel is in darkness, or, at the very least, in the shade.[25] The Supreme Court of the United States has indicated that under the Fourteenth Amendment, it is not until the arraignment that a state judge has a duty to bring up the subject of counsel. This is not to say that the conviction will be reversed if the judge does not inform the defendant of his right to counsel. The Supreme Court hasn't been as definite as that. It does mean that the judge runs the *risk* of having the conviction overturned if the judge does not make it clear to the defendant that he has a right to hire counsel or to have counsel assigned—and, in certain cases, if counsel is not actually assigned. In many, if not most, right to counsel cases that are brought to appellate courts, it is the transcript of the words spoken at the arraignment upon which the decision rests.

This constitutional doctrine is supported by practice. It is at the arraignment that the trial-level judge usually appoints an attorney to defend the indigent accused appearing before him. Few municipal court judges assign counsel. No matter how many months elapse between arrest and arraignment, the assignment of an attorney is not made until arraignment in the great majority of criminal prosecutions throughout the United States today. Although the United States Constitution does not explicitly require an arraignment, it is assuming increasingly greater significance. It is here that the battle between prosecution and defense is formally joined. Here the accused is formally taken within the jurisdiction of the court that has, unlike the municipal court, full jurisdiction over crimes of a serious nature. Here the defendant is informed of his rights, especially of the right to assigned counsel. And it is here that the defendant announces formally and for the record whether he intends to plead not guilty and to fight the case by going to trial—or whether he will publicly admit his guilt to a crime, an admission that could result in his imprisonment for many years, perhaps for life.

Therefore, the defendant's plea is one of the most vital formal steps the defense must take.[26] It involves a decision that should take into account every significant factual and legal detail of the case.

The plea involves more than the question of the legal guilt or innocence of the accused. In many cases, especially where first offenders are involved, justice in a broad sense would be better served by an acquittal. But where the defense attorney feels no such compulsion to serve a higher ethic, his duty is clear. Even though his client admittedly committed the act, the Canons of Ethics require that if there is a legal defense to the charge, it be presented by the attorney.[27] Thus, in many doubtful situations attorneys should advise a plea of not guilty and risk a trial.

GUILTY PLEA: A QUICK WAY OUT?

There is some evidence that the guilty plea is used as a quick way out by certain assigned counsel harassed by the pressure of private business and embarrassed by the procedure of an unfamiliar court.[28] Where the plea is suggested without adequately considering all of the legal defenses that might possibly be presented, this is a dereliction of duty, even when the defendant is obviously guilty. One prisoner claimed that his assigned counsel walked into his cell and said, "There's only one thing I can do for you on this charge. The prosecutor told me to tell you to plead guilty. I can't do too much for you. The state appointed me." Many other prisoners maintained that their assigned attorneys had suggested guilty pleas to them during their first or second interview.[29]

In and of itself, such advice during a first or second interview is not improper. It is quite possible that after one or two interviews of twenty minutes each, unsupported by an independent investigation, an attorney is able to advise his client properly on the plea in a given case. However, at least one of the cases I studied in detail as they were being tried suggests that this is not always possible. This case involved the arrest of several young men for robbery in Essex County, New Jersey. One claimed that he was at the scene of the crime but had not taken part in it. This man had a criminal record, although he was by no means a habitual criminal. Soon after being arrested and incarcerated in a local jail, this defendant decided to plead guilty for two reasons. First, he was at the scene of the crime. He doubted very much if he could convince anyone that he had not participated. Secondly, he had a criminal record. This, in itself, is sufficient to convince a large number of prisoners every year to cop out rather than fight the charge. A prisoner with a record knows, as does any competent defense attorney, that few juries ever acquit a man with a criminal record. Such men are easy targets for the prosecution's offer of a "deal" in return for a guilty plea. The assigned counsel entered this case several weeks after arrest. He interviewed the defendant twice and then agreed, as a preliminary matter, to follow the defendant's original decision to plead guilty.

Yet this decision was constantly reviewed by the attorney and his associates up to the date of arraignment to plea in the county court. By the time of arraignment several more interviews were held with the prisoner, and an investigation was carried out by the attorney's younger office associate. On the basis of these subsequent interviews and the investigation, the attorney decided that a trial was a good risk, thus reversing the original decision taken after the second interview. As a result of this careful consideration, I saw the defendant walk out of the courtroom—a free man. He was ordered acquitted by the judge after the prosecution rested and before a single defense witness was heard.

READING THE JUDICIAL MIND

The defense attorney who wishes to advise his client properly on the plea must be able to predict with some degree of accuracy what the sentence will be upon a guilty plea. On the other hand, the attorney must have some notion of the sentence that would be imposed following conviction by trial. The stumbling block is that sentencing is exclusively a judicial function. Of course, it is well known that prosecutors and defense counsel have conferred with judges regarding the sentence to be imposed on a particular defendant and have received advance information. These promises-in-chambers are never binding, however. At the present time in New Jersey, such informal conferences are somewhat eclipsed by the pre-sentence report made by the probation department on almost every defendant convicted in the county courts.[30] The pre-sentence report contains an extensive history of the defendant's personal background and criminal record. Since the investigation by the probation department does not commence until after the final plea, or after conviction at a trial, it would appear on the surface that no advance notice on the sentence is possible. But this is not entirely the case.

The county prosecutor continues to be a major source of advance information for defense attorneys. This is especially true for assigned counsel without extensive experience in the criminal courts. The prosecutor's advance calculation of the sentence is frequently quite accurate. Having seen each judge impose sentence in numerous previous cases, prosecutors become fully cognizant of many of the judge's more pronounced sentencing habits. Moreover, as discussed previously,[31] the prosecutor has virtually unlimited discretion to drop charges or to reduce criminal accusations to a lesser degree. The county prosecutor is in a pivotal position at this stage of the case. He can advise the assigned attorney on the consequences of a guilty plea, on the "terrible" consequences of a conviction after a trial; and in return for a guilty plea he can offer to drop charges with the possibility of a lower sentence, the precise extent of which he may estimate for the assigned counsel. It is usually after such a conference with the prosecutor that assigned counsel advise their clients on the plea. But it must be emphasized again that no promises made by the prosecution are binding.

BETWEEN GUILTY AND NOT GUILTY

The *non vult* plea presents special problems. In the criminal process, this plea is equivalent to the plea of guilty. But for some reason, it is a catchword among the prison population. Many prisoners feel that by pleading *non vult* rather than guilty they will obtain a lighter sentence. One of the first things men learn upon being arrested and placed in the local jail is the term *non vult*. There is absolutely no substance to the notion that the *non vult* plea will affect the sentence in any way different than a guilty plea. Yet the myth persists. The myth finds strong support in the fact that so many attorneys advise their clients to plead *non vult*. This plea was entered more frequently than any other plea by the New Jersey prisoners interviewed.[32]

Many defendants are convinced by their attorneys that a *non vult* plea will have a different effect on the sentence than a simple plea of guilty. One of the prison chaplains offered some proof of this during an interview in Trenton. Of the many complaints he had heard in private consultations with approximately 1,400 men over a period of several years, the one most frequently heard was that the prisoner pleaded *non vult* at the suggestion of his attorney without fully understanding the consequences of this action. Even where the attorney has the best of intentions, the plea is confusing. Regardless of explanations made to them by their attorneys or by the judge in open court, prisoners ask, in effect, "How can *non vult* mean 'guilty' when it doesn't say 'guilty'?" I asked one prisoner, who had pleaded *non vult*, what the term meant; he replied in characteristic fashion: "I don't really know. My attorney said it's twix and between guilty and not guilty."

According to the prisoners, a practice commonly utilized by defense attorneys is to advise a *non vult* plea as a precondition to a specific, low sentence: "If you plead *non vult*, I can get you off with six years." (This statement may be based on sound professional calculations, or it may be motivated by baser considerations.) But on sentencing day the judge announces that the minimum term will be ten years. The defendant's trust in attorneys is destroyed. His original notion—held by many prisoners—that the courts are for the rich or the big-time racketeer is confirmed and strengthened. And an extra wall of bitterness is placed between the inner man and the rehabilitative efforts of the prison authorities. It is worthwhile to note that the plea of *nolo contendere*, the equivalent of *non vult*, is discouraged in federal courts by judges and by prosecutors. This is graphically illustrated by the responses of the federal prisoners—not a single one indicated that he had pleaded *nolo contendere*. Almost half of the New Jersey group entered a plea of *non vult*.[33]

HOMICIDE CASES: THE HIGHEST STAKES

It is in homicide cases that the need for expert and conscientious legal advice before pleading, based on a thorough factual investigation, is illustrated most dramatically. A man's life hangs in balance even though the ultimate sanction is actually imposed in only a small percentage of homicide prosecutions. The death penalty is used rarely, not only because of the distaste and revulsion

it evokes among jurors, but also because the facts rarely
point to a cold-blooded murder. There are few such crimes.
In my opinion, most murderers are not "criminals"; they
strike but once in a moment of irrational fury. (I found
murderers to be the most likeable human beings, as a
group, of any of the hundreds of prisoners I have interviewed; robbers, the worst. Only one convict I interviewed
even implied that he had committed a murder in a cold,
rational fashion. In fact, this gangland slaying had been
carried out so rationally that he had never been caught
and was then serving a sentence on another charge! Unlike
many of the murderers I interviewed, he had, of course,
not contacted the nearest police station and promptly reported his crime.)

Where the accused admittedly caused the death of the
victim, there is ample room for a conscientious attorney
to take one of two courses. The defense attorney may offer
to enter a non-contesting plea while making a concentrated
effort to present facts to the prosecutor that would tend to
convince him to lower the charges to second-degree murder or even manslaughter. After that plea has been entered, the attorney may also offer evidence in mitigation
of the sentence to the probation officer making the pre-
sentence report or directly to the judge.

The second alternative is to go to trial. This decision
may be made originally or may hinge on the willingness
of the prosecution to reduce the charge. At the trial the
defense strategy may be aimed at convincing the jury that
the act was in self-defense, that the defendant was temporarily insane, or that the guilt of the accused is only
"technical"—"Morally, my client is blameless." Because of
the harsh penalties involved after a verdict of guilty, even
of a lesser degree of homicide, the latter appeal injected

into a case may have a weighty effect on the jury's deliberations. This is not unethical on the part of the attorney. It will be a dark day indeed when moral considerations are purged from our judicial system.

The attorney who takes the second alternative and goes to trial is often taking the more hazardous path. Death sentences are not common where the defendant pleads guilty to first degree murder. In New Jersey the law forbids them under such circumstances.[34] A conviction of the same charge by a jury is more apt to result in the extreme penalty.

Whereas the pressure of earning a livelihood may act as a brake on the zeal for justice of an attorney assigned in non-capital cases, it is much less difficult in capital cases for counsel to take the time necessary to prepare a truly effective defense and to go to trial if necessary. For example, New Jersey law provides for "reasonable compensation" to counsel assigned in capital cases.[35] Judges usually base their interpretation of this phrase and calculate the payment to the assigned counsel on the amount of time and energy the attorney invested in the case. For only advising an indigent on the plea, a fee of $500 is common. For a protracted trial, attorneys assigned in capital cases may receive $4,500 or more under the "reasonable compensation" formula.

Because of the high stakes involved, the defense attorney's decision on the plea in a homicide acquires an awesome significance. A plea of guilty may very well save the defendant from the death chair, but it may doom him to life imprisonment. A not guilty plea and a trial may result in either one of two extremes—the death penalty or freedom.

Most counsel show the proper degree of concern for

their clients in capital cases. Other attorneys, both assigned and retained, reveal what amounts to a callous
haste to plead their clients guilty. One of the most striking examples of the importance to the defendant of every
act of commission or omission by his attorney is provided
by a homicide case that came to my attention. The defendant was a colored man with little formal education. Because he was indigent, counsel was assigned to him by the
court. The crime charged was that he had beaten a man
to death with a baseball bat. Both the defendant and the
victim were allegedly competing for the affection and company of the same woman.

At the first arraignment in the county court, the defendant's counsel entered a plea of not guilty. Several months
later the defendant came into court, retracted his plea of
not guilty and, following the advice of his counsel, entered
a plea of *non vult*. At this arraignment the defendant's
assigned counsel described the events leading up to the
murder and the murder itself. According to the records,
this was the only time the counsel made such a lengthy
statement to the court. This argument, as reported in a
transcript of the proceedings by a certified shorthand reporter, did not contain one favorable fact about the defendant.

The attorney commenced his statement by assuring the
court that he had made a thorough investigation of all the
facts. He then described the crime. According to the defense counsel, the victim drove his car past the defendant,
who was standing on the sidewalk, and made some insulting remarks to him. The defendant and another man obtained two baseball bats and went down the street looking for the victim. On their way, they went into a store
where the defendant told the proprietor that he was going

to kill somebody. The two men found the victim in a parking lot. The defendant walked up to the victim, according to the attorney's story, and struck several blows with the bat, which caused the victim's death.

Going into the background of the crime, the counsel stated that the victim was the common law husband, broadly speaking, of a woman whose home the defendant was also frequenting. The victim and the defendant had argued over this situation. Then the assigned attorney stated:

> They had illicit relations, that is the defendant and this woman—*the woman is a white woman*—so it can readily be seen just what prompted the defendant to do what he actually did. This man was in his way, the victim, in continuing with his illicit relationship with this woman. [Emphases added]

If it seems that these words are out of place coming from the defense counsel in open court, the statement immediately following sounds all the more like a prosecutor's plea to a jury. The defense counsel continued, "There is not the slightest doubt from all the evidence in this case that this was murder premeditated and wilfully carried out. Am I stating the facts, Mr. Defendant, right?" The defendant replied, "Yes, you are stating the facts."

Shortly thereafter the defense counsel again asked, "I would like to ask the defendant whether what I stated are the facts." The defendant replied, "Yes." Apparently the answer was made in a low voice. For the attorney immediately asked again, "Are they the facts?" The defendant replied, "Yes, that's right."

Throughout the proceedings the defendant answered very briefly except for one short question, and he at no time challenged what his attorney had to say. This is typical of many defendants, who are awed and silent when they are brought into a courtroom. The plea of *non vult* was thoroughly explained by the court and the counsel to the defendant. It appears clearly on the record that the defendant was told that a plea of *non vult* is the equivalent of a guilty plea.

The only statement made by the defense counsel later at the time of sentencing was, "I believe your honor is in full possession of all the facts and circumstances and also the report of the probation office. There is hardly anything further I need to say for your honor to be able to impose the proper sentence in this case." The "proper sentence" was life imprisonment.

In a letter from prison to the county judge who had sentenced him, the defendant claimed that the plea of *non vult* was entered at the insistence of the defense counsel. According to the defendant, the attorney had told him in a consultation that if he, the attorney, were on a jury in a case such as this, the defendant would be sent to the electric chair. In fear of his life the defendant changed his plea from not guilty to *non vult*. The defendant further claimed that he was told by his assigned counsel that if he saved the state the expense of a trial, he would receive a light sentence. When the defendant finally agreed to plead *non vult*, he was under the impression, given by his counsel, that he was thereby pleading to some lesser degree of homicide such as manslaughter. As for the victim, according to the defendant, he was not unarmed but had a weapon superior to the defendant's baseball bat, an iron-tipped club. With this iron-tipped club the victim had severely injured the defendant in the course of their fight, which necessitated stitches in the scalp of the defendant.

The defendant maintained that there was a record of this injury and of the attention given him at the county clinic. At some time previous to this assault, the defendant had been beaten by the victim and by a police officer for some unexplained reason. The victim carried a gun in his car with which he had previously threatened to kill the defendant. There was what amounted to a private feud between the defendant and the victim. This is the defendant's story.

However, none of these facts, even if they are completely true, presents a legal basis for reversal of the conviction—once the conviction has been established on the record. For maximum effect in cases of this nature, the peculiar shadings in the factual situation must be fully considered and utilized *before* the plea is entered.

A FEW FATEFUL WORDS

It is only at the end of a long process—starting with arrest, and going through a lengthy interrogation; perhaps a beating by the police; a preliminary examination; incarceration for as long as six months, perhaps, in a small cell with insufficient food, no recreation, and an occasional beating; the pressure of the prosecution for a guilty plea through the periodic visits of the county detectives; and conferences with a defense attorney explaining the intricacies of the criminal courts—that the defendant is brought into the county court to plead at the arraignment. He is brought before the bench and formally informed that there is a charge accusing him of a specific crime. The clerk of court may read the indictment, accusation, or—in the federal courts and in some states—the information. Either the judge or the clerk will then ask the defendant, "How do you plead?" It should be apparent by now that the defendant's answer—a few words, but fateful ones—is not based purely on a rational appreciation of his guilt or innocence of the acts charged, for the plea is dictated by all sorts of pressures that have been building up since the moment of arrest. Much of what has happened before, and even the consequences of the plea, are not fully understood by many defendants.

Nevertheless, the defendant must state a plea, and after he does so, it is entered into the record. If he pleads guilty or *non vult,* the judge or the prosecutor will explain that he can expect no consideration in return for entering the plea; that the plea of *non vult* is equivalent to guilty; and that there remains nothing further for the court to do except to pass sentence. Not only is the plea recorded but also the statements made by the judge, the prosecutor, the defendant, and his counsel. If the defendant later objects that he pleaded *non vult* or guilty because the prosecutor or his counsel told him that he would receive a light sentence, the record stands as virtually unimpeachable testimony to his understanding. The truth is, however, that the transcript is a bleak description of a human situation filled with anguish, fear, and uncertainty. The typical defendant is scared and completely awed by the judge sitting up on a high bench, clothed in black robes, and possessing tremendous power to affect his future. He frequently only half listens to what the prosecutor, the judge, and his defense counsel say to him. The entire situation renders him speechless, even embarrassed. He pleads a certain way because he was induced to do so—weeks or months previously. If the judge, the prosecutor, or the defense counsel makes a statement in open court that is contrary to what he has been led to believe, especially as to promises by the prosecution or his defense counsel, or as to the effect of a *non vult* plea, he would no more challenge that statement in open court than he would challenge a clergyman's sermon from the pulpit.

8
Trial and Sentence

Trial

In October, 1958, a penniless circus roustabout, Robert A. Jamison, was arrested in Santa Barbara, California, on a charge of murder. Although he protested his innocence to a deputy district attorney, prosecution was recommended. An Alameda County grand jury indicted him. Since Jamison was indigent, he was defended by the Alameda County Public Defender office. Because of the seriousness of the case and because of a desire to get back into a courtroom again after an absence of many months occupied by administrative duties, the Chief Public Defender, George Nye, took personal charge of the case.

A review of the facts showed Jamison's plight to be almost hopeless and portrayed him as a kind of ghoul. Jamison had married a divorced woman in 1956 when both were nineteen years of age. His wife had two children from a previous marriage. Within two years there were two more children. When Jamison was arrested in October of 1958, three of these children had died under rather strange circumstances—the two from his wife's earlier marriage and one from the current marriage. While his wife had made no complaint originally, she finally went to the police of Bellingham, Washington, where the family was then living, and made a complaint alleging that Jamison was responsible for the deaths of her three children. Mrs. Jamison repeated her story before the Alameda County grand jury that subsequently handed down the indictment. She was rated as the main prosecution witness —and a formidable one.

The first death had taken place on January 7, 1957, in South Toms River, New Jersey. Raymond Lee, aged 18 months, had died while Jamison was taking care of him. Jamison had explained that the baby had choked on a cookie he had given him. The child had been hurt and bruised a week earlier in falling down a flight of stairs—according to Jamison's explanation. Mrs. Jamison later claimed before the Alameda County grand jury that her husband had previously slapped this child repeatedly and had maltreated him in other ways. The New Jersey coroner, however, had ruled that Raymond Lee died of bronchial pneumonia.

Slightly more than nine months after this death, Ronald Edward Jamison, 16 months of age, had died on September 25, 1957, in Alameda County, California. From a defense counsel's viewpoint, the similarity in facts was chilling: Jamison had been alone with the child and claimed that the boy had accidently fallen down some steps. The local coroner this time had ruled death due to a ruptured liver and broken ribs. But in late 1958 Mrs. Jamison testi-

fied before the Alameda County grand jury that when she
returned from an errand:

> Ronnie was lying in his crib. He was deathly white. His
> eyes wouldn't focus. Bob was sitting in the chair.
> Q. What did your husband say?
> A. He proceeded to tell me Ronnie had been crying . . .
> and Bob got mad and lost his temper and hit him.
> Q. Did he say where he hit Ronnie?
> A. I remember definitely he said he hit him in the face and
> in the chest and head, around the head.

Almost a year later, on September 1, 1958, Jody Marie
Jamison had died at the age of six weeks in a Pocatello,
Idaho, motel where her parents were staying briefly. The
coroner's report was that death came from asphyxiation,
apparently brought on when the baby choked on her
formula. But again Mrs. Jamison's testimony strongly suggested that her husband had something to do with the
death. She told the grand jury that from her bed she observed Jamison leaning over the child's crib before he
went to work; that she fell asleep again; and that she
awoke to find her baby girl dead in the crib.

To all of these allegations Robert Jamison had maintained his complete innocence, both to the grand jury and
to Public Defender George Nye. But Nye might have
been forgiven had he disbelieved his client, for the facts
seemed to damn the man—and like most defenders, Nye
had heard many fervent protestations of innocence from
guilty persons.

Fortunately for Robert Jamison, Public Defender Nye
was a competent and zealous attorney who had on his staff
trained investigators, a crew of able lawyers who put in
hundreds of hours of unpaid overtime on this case, and a
county board of supervisors who believed enough in justice

for the poor to advance the extra funds necessary for the factual investigation, even though it involved proving that the district attorney of the county, also supported by an appropriation from the board of supervisors, was wrong.[1]

It was this factual investigation that probably made the difference in the case—that and Nye's determination to be a defender of the rights of the accused, whatever the odds. The major task of investigation was carried out by the public defender's chief investigator, Clifford Wixson, Jr., a former investigator for the district attorney. To understand the subtle facts and motives involved, it was necessary to trace the lives of Jamison and his wife almost from birth. In the pursuit of these elusive facts, Wixson went to New Jersey, Florida, Idaho, Iowa, and Washington. On these travels he interviewed almost one hundred witnesses. Nye located one witness by long distance telephone on a submarine at Guantanamo Bay, Cuba, where a Naval legal officer took a deposition that was sent to the public defender. Help in the investigation was sought and obtained from the Criminal Courts Branch of the New York City Legal Aid Society; the Public Defender of Omaha; a public defender in Rhode Island; a chief assistant district attorney in Bellingham, Washington; an assistant attorney general of Rhode Island, who assisted in obtaining subpoenas and depositions from witnesses, as did private attorneys in New Jersey, Idaho, and Washington; Navy personnel, who obtained hospital records, located and arranged interviews with sailors, and took the deposition in Cuba; the Red Cross, which located a potential witness in Korea; and a group of doctors who acted as consultants, some of whom testified later at the trial for only a nominal fee. In addition, a group of University of California law students did legal research and other tasks. One may wonder if such wholesale cooperation and assistance would have been rendered if Nye had not displayed a conviction that the man was innocent and if he had not had the prestige that the title "Public Defender" carries with it.

After this extensive investigation, which occasioned fourteen postponements in the trial date over a period of eight months, Nye was ready for trial. But the final decision on trial and trial tactics was left to the man who had most to lose—the defendant. He made his decision after Nye explained that if they went to trial and let the prosecution bring in facts only about the Alameda County death, the verdict would probably be second degree murder or manslaughter, nothing worse. But if the defense allowed the prosecution to go into the other deaths, Nye calculated, there were eighteen chances in twenty of getting a first degree murder verdict with a life sentence, one chance of a death sentence, and one chance of an acquittal. So only if the trial was thrown wide open to include the other deaths was there a chance of an acquittal—for only then could the real facts and the wife's motives in accusing her husband be revealed to the jury. But only then was there a chance of the death penalty. The defendant was thus fully apprised of the shoals in the channel ahead. His reaction: "I'm innocent. Let's go whole hog." And this is what the public defender did.

The trial began in July, 1959. Most defense attorneys want jurors who are underdogs, who have emotional dispositions and can sympathize with the plight of a small man caught in the toils of the criminal law. Public Defender Nye worked in the opposite direction—he attempted to select jurors who could think in analytical terms. On the jury finally empaneled were three engineers and two businessmen.

Another unusual tactic was Nye's opening statement, made before the prosecution offered any evidence. Nye dealt with all three deaths and told the jury that they were due primarily to the mother's neglect of the children and that she had finally accused her husband because she was afraid that the deaths would be blamed on her. Most surprising of all, he admitted that the death of Ronald Edward Jamison in Alameda County was due ultimately to the action of the defendant, but then offered to prove that this happened accidentally when Jamison clumsily applied artificial respiration in a frantic attempt to save the child's life.

Public Defender Nye succeeded in proving all of these points at the trial. His cross-examination of a doctor testifying for the prosecution brought out that it was possible for a 160-pound man such as Jamison to have caused Ronald's fatal injuries—six broken ribs and a torn liver—by applying his full weight in attempting artificial respiration. This expert opinion was strongly supported by a defense witness who was a respected thoracic surgeon and an expert on artificial respiration.

The cross-examination of Mrs. Jamison revealed that when Jamison stated that he was going to the police in Bellingham, Washington, she pleaded, "Don't go to the cops—you'll get me in trouble"; and that she was indifferent to the fate of her one remaining child because of her intention to marry her boyfriend.

The defense witnesses, including the defendant, claimed that Jamison was a good husband who loved the children and never hurt them; that Mrs. Jamison was an indifferent mother who cared little for her children and slept till noon every day; that she gave five different versions to acquaintances of how Ronald died. Her own brother testified that she had a bad reputation for truth and honesty. Defense investigation also made it possible for Nye to bring out at the trial that Mrs. Jamison had enclosed a small picture of the defendant in the casket of the first child; that she had written letters in 1958 stating that Jamison loved the children as if they were his own; and that she had once accused her first husband of the same kind of mistreatment of which she now accused Jamison—and that threatened him with California's gas chamber.

After nearly eight hours, the jury returned a verdict of not guilty.

In his last annual report before leaving his public defender's post for private practice Nye, a skilled trial tactician, explained why he was able to prove the subtle points set forth in his opening statement at the trial. For the public defender cited the Jamison case as "Another example of the absolute necessity for pre-trial investigation, if the truth is later to be established in the courtroom." [2]

But the Jamison case clearly supports two more points. First, the protection and strengthening of constitutional rights take place at two levels—in the decisions of appellate courts, especially the United States Supreme Court, and in the largely unknown day-to-day efforts of many dedicated attorneys and investigators.[3] The appellate courts are important for establishing broad philosophical points and for overturning the relatively few outrageous convictions. The work of defenders and investigators is in many respects more important for it operates as a shield directly between the rights of the citizen and the sword's point of the invader; it prevents invasions that could not be proved nor remedied by an appellate court decision months later—after the damage had been done. In one sense, the worst way to vindicate a person's right is through an appellate proceeding following a conviction. While this may be a good method of making constitutional gains for the future, a reversal of a conviction on appeal does not actually erase it from the record—although the exorcism takes place in legal theory. If the defendant is not tried again, the conviction stays on the indelible record kept by society. And if he is tried again, as often happens, the voided conviction may induce a second set of jurors to return a guilty verdict—although legal theory demands that jurors not consider the invalid conviction in their deliberations.

Second, the Jamison case shows that the assurance of constitutional rights is no assurance of an adequate defense. The definitions of constitutional rights, as declared by appellate courts, establish only minimal standards. Such standards may be labeled "reversal standards," for the most powerful weapon that an upper court has in the maintenance of constitutional rights is the reversal of a specific conviction obtained by methods that fall below the absolute minimum. But courts are loath to overturn convictions. Therefore, much can occur in a criminal case that is unfair, unwise, and that prevents an adequate defense from being presented—but these practices may be constitutional. Public Defender Nye was not compelled by the constitutional interpretations of the right to counsel, as set out by any American court,[4] to perform an investigation, even a skimpy one. Nor did any constitutional provision prevent him from demanding that Jamison plead guilty without investigation or trial.

It should not be inferred, however, that attorneys assigned in capital cases by the courts of states other than California are usually negligent. Some of them apparently do take a cavalier attitude toward the rights of the accused. But whether the charge is capital or non-capital, many assigned attorneys are zealous advocates because of a sense of responsibility; and in capital cases this sense of responsibility is even more acute. Nevertheless, the high odds against Jamison would have been that much higher had he been tried in a state that had an assigned counsel system or an organized defender system without trained investigators available. And there are many cases of both a capital and non-capital nature where the line between circumstances and truth, between criminal intent and non-criminal negligence, is just as thin as it was in the case of Robert A. Jamison.

The basic right involved in a trial is the right to a fair hearing—described by Professor David Fellman as the "Siamese twin of the due process guarantee of notice." [5] Supporting this right, and at the same time a part of it, are the rights to confront accusers and to a speedy and public trial free from a biased judge or mob domination. [6] These are extremely important rights in our scheme of democratic freedom. But few attorneys want to contest the case by going to trial if it can be avoided. Popular fiction gives a picture of a superior and confident defense advocate, able to grasp the jury like a violin and deftly draw a tune of "not guilty" from it. The truth of the matter is that experienced attorneys approach a trial in many cases as they would a roulette table: no one knows where the wheel of chance will stop—and the stakes are years of a life, not replaceable lucre.

Such reluctance is much more understandable for the assigned counsel serving without compensation in New Jersey and so many other states. Counting all preparations, research, investigation, and delays in the courtroom before the case is called, a trial may easily add seven days to the length of the attorney's gratuitous service, forcing the attorney to ignore the interests of clients upon whom his livelihood depends. This combination of legal considerations and personal business pressures is a powerful force operating in the assigned counsel system against decisions to go to trial, even in those cases where such a course might be highly advisable. The defense attorney paid but a minimum fee is in almost the same predicament.

TACTICS OF AVOIDANCE

A large part of an attorney's activity upon entering a case may involve tactics to avoid a trial because of the high risks involved for his client. These tactics are part of the negotiation process and usually take place both before and after a not guilty plea has been entered. I have observed such tactics continuing until a few minutes before a trial.

If there is evidence of the defendant's innocence, his attorney may present this evidence to the prosecutor (as occurred in the Alameda County, California, "forgery" case described in the last chapter) and thereby attempt to induce the prosecutor to dismiss the charges. Of course, the defense attorney could hold the evidence in secret until the time of trial and then produce it dramatically before a jury. But the former course is obviously preferable. In this manner, the client will be saved further anguish and, in the case of the clients of most assigned counsel, the defendant will be released from an unjust and perhaps wretched confinement in the county jail. Every effort should be made to avoid the shame and disgrace often attached to a public trial.

There is another very persuasive reason for bringing

strong evidence of the defendant's innocence to the prosecutor before trial. Even a fair-minded prosecutor may remain sufficiently convinced of the veracity of his witnesses to demand a trial. Later at the trial, however, if cross-examination of the prosecution witnesses reveals weaknesses in their testimony, the pre-trial activity of the defense counsel may bear fruit. With the seed of doubt already planted in his mind, the prosecutor may make a motion during the trial to dismiss the charges.

A frequently utilized method of avoiding trial is for the defense attorney to confront the defendant with the evidence indicating the hazards of going to trial. Defendants are often told that there is strong evidence indicating guilt; that the prosecutor appears ready with a convincing case for the jury; and that the prosecutor might accept a plea to a lesser charge. Attorneys will often tell their clients, moreover, that judges tend to give a lighter sentence following a plea of guilty than that imposed after conviction by a trial jury of the same charge.

PREPARATION FOR TRIAL

If these tactics of avoidance are unsuccessful, the steps that must be taken by the defense to prepare for trial may be placed into three broad categories. First, the attorney must research the law governing the crime. He must prepare the points of law that he intends to emphasize while examining witnesses. The defense attorney must, furthermore, prepare the instructions he will request the judge to insert in his charge to the jury at the end of the testimony.

Second, the attorney must decide exactly how he is to present his case in the courtroom. He may determine that it will be necessary to call an expert witness—a doctor, an accountant, or a handwriting specialist. Professionals in any field of knowledge may be vital props to an otherwise shaky defense structure.

A high percentage of the people who are brought before the bar of justice in criminal courts suffer from some mental disorder. This brings up the question of whether or not the defendant was sane and responsible for his criminal act. Where the prosecution desires to be informed of the defendant's sanity, it has at its command the huge mental health establishment of the state. Moreover, an examination by a state psychiatrist often involves questions concerning the guilt or innocence of the accused. Results of such an examination frequently turn up later at the trial and point the finger not only at the sanity but at the guilt of the defendant. Without an expert to take the stand for the defense, the word of a psychiatrist in the employ of the state may go substantially unchallenged. This often happens when the accused is indigent, for then there is no provision for the fees of expert witnesses in non-capital cases in many states.

The question of whether to put the defendant on the stand as a witness in his own behalf must also be decided. Like many other decisions of trial strategy, this may not be finally determined until the trial is well under way. A defendant with an unstable personality or a hostile attitude may make a very bad impression on a jury, even if he is innocent. Moreover, attorneys are especially reluctant to place on the witness stand a defendant who has a prior criminal record. It is basic to our concepts of justice and fairness, of course, that a previous conviction of crime should not be considered as evidence of the guilt of the defendant at the trial of another charge. At the same time, if a defendant takes the witness stand, the prosecution usually manages to bring out the fact of the previous conviction. Here there is operative a legal fiction to the effect that although the jury should not consider the defendant guilty of this crime because of prior criminal acts, the defendant, being "a criminal," is more apt to lie *as a witness*. On this basis, it is allowable to inform the jury of the defendant's criminal record.[7] It is generally accepted, however, that the purpose of impeaching the defendant's credibility as a witness by introducing his previous record is to convince the jury of his guilt in the current prosecution.

A full understanding of the facts of court life in this regard was expressed by Judge Frank in a dissenting opinion,

> In the states of this country, . . . and in the federal courts as the decisions now stand, if the accused elects to become a witness, the prosecutor, on cross-examination, may bring out the fact that the defendant had been previously convicted. Virtually all experienced lawyers and judges acknowledge that, almost invariably, the jury will treat such evidence as evidence of the defendant's guilt of the crime for which he is on trial, despite the judge's instruction that they must consider it as bearing on the defendant's credibility only. On that account, usually the lawyer for an accused with a criminal record will advise him not to testify. Yet his failure to do so is likely to convince the jury of his guilt. Either way he is likely to be convicted.[8]

In New Jersey, the problem is aggravated by the rule, not followed in many states, permitting the prosecutor and trial court to comment upon the defendant's failure to take the stand in his own defense. His failure to testify, it is said, can permit the inference, but not the presumption, that he could not truthfully deny the charges against him.[9] It is doubtful if many jurors are affected in their deliberations by the fine line between an "inference" and a "presumption."

Third, the attorney may decide to investigate the list of prospective jurors. This is not often done with thoroughness by defense attorneys because it may require checking into the background of one hundred people within the few days between the day the list of jurors is served on the defendant and the first day of trial.[10] The expense for checking the jury list is out of the question, therefore, for most defendants—who are either indigent or in a marginal income bracket. The county prosecutor, on the other hand, may assign this task to his detectives or legal assistants.

Because many prospective jurors will not reveal their biases and prejudices upon the *voir dire* examination in open court, investigation of their backgrounds may be a vital part of the defense case. A trial may be won or lost while the jury is being empaneled. In many serious cases, the prosecutor has before him a detective's report on each juror to guide his questions and challenges, while the defense operates in the dark.

The New Jersey court rules provide that the defense shall have unlimited challenges of jurors for cause (personal interest in the outcome of the case, bias, and so on) and twenty peremptory challenges in trials involving serious charges.[11] A peremptory challenge allows the defense attorney to strike a juror from the panel without explanation. In such serious cases the state has six challenges for every ten allowed the defense.[12] Since it is frequently difficult to obtain the consent of the judge to excuse a juror for cause, both the defense and the state husband their peremptory challenges. In the use of peremptory challenges, therefore, a rather complete dossier on each prospective juror allows the counsel to use his challenges with the greatest effect. Furthermore, facts hidden in the background of a prospective juror that would induce the judge to excuse him for cause may be brought out by a cross-examination guided by an extensive investigation.

THE ASSIGNED ATTORNEY ON TRIAL

With the empaneling of the jury, the stage is set for one of the most ancient of human dramas. Once an assigned counsel enters the courtroom for a criminal trial, how effective is he in the performance of his adversary role? This question has always been most difficult to answer. In its *Plan for Survey* of the administration of criminal justice in the United States, the American Bar Foundation observed that: "The evaluation of the trial practice of defense counsel can be little more than an expression of personal opinion. There are no objective standards by which this part of a lawyer's work may be measured." [13] To an extent, I agree with this statement. For when the defense wins the case, what lawyer can identify with certainty those tactics that were most persuasive with the jury? And when the defendant is found guilty, a Monday morning legal quarterback may argue that a certain line of questions would have saved the day, but it would be difficult to find two lawyers agreeing on this issue. And when the matter is considered, not from the viewpoint of victory or defeat, but in light of the manner in which the defense attorney raised all legal defenses, an objective judgment is also extremely difficult. Moreover, it could be argued that the role of trial advocate is indeed a *role*, not unlike the part played by an actor in a staged drama; that it will always be an open question as to whether Orson Welles' Macbeth was better than that portrayed by others; and that the final judgment is a subjective one found in the minds and hearts of each member of the audience.

But there is another side to this matter. In the first place, while the evaluation of assigned counsel at the trial reduces itself to a matter of opinion, the opinion of some people should have at least a modicum of additional weight over that of others. Judges observe trial after trial and attorney after attorney. Several New Jersey judges have told me that on occasion the performance of assigned attorneys has been absolutely pitiful. In these cases, the judges said, in order to assure a minimal standard of defense they have had to virtually descend from the bench, cast aside their judicial robes, and become co-advocates for the defendant.

In the second place, the observation that evaluation of defense trial practice is largely a matter of opinion is true only to the extent that this conclusion is confined to events in the courtroom itself. But pre-trial events have an immense effect on events in the courtroom. The disadvantages in the pre-trial stage that are suffered by attorneys in the assigned counsel system follow them into the courtroom. It might be presumed that the trial presents an opportunity for an attorney with a fighting attitude and some trial ability to stand on a par with the prosecutor despite the advantages the prosecutor has had up to this point. To a certain extent this is true, but in many cases even the most zealous assigned counsel cannot overcome at the trial the disadvantages that he suffered in preparing for trial. Ellery Cuff, the Public Defender of Los Angeles County, made this emphatic statement regarding the relationship between adequate investigation and competent defense at the trial:

> I have noted with disgust, from time to time, remarks made by appellate justices in which they asserted that a certain defendant who had assigned counsel was given the finest defense. From my experience, I do not see how a judge can tell whether a man had good defense, because what goes on in court possibly represents only 50 per cent of the actual work done in the preparation of a trial. The investigation, the running down of sources of information, sometimes demands that you go beyond the range of the knowledge of the defendant in gathering this information. Unless this was done a cross-examination, however vigorous, would never bring out information that might be revealed upon proper investigation.[14]

Under a certain set of circumstances, however, the assigned counsel system in New Jersey and in other states does provide a high standard of defense at the trial. This occurs when an investigation is not necessary to establish all of the key facts because they may be elicited from the defendant or from the witnesses who appear at the trial; and, furthermore, where the counsel assigned has had extensive trial experience, either civil or criminal.[15] Since civil trial experience is sometimes transferable to the criminal courts, an able counsel may put up an excellent defense under these circumstances despite the handicaps of the assigned counsel system.

But these elements are not always present in the same case. Vital facts may be needed to prove an alibi. The attorney may have had little trial experience. Many civil attorneys rarely enter the courtroom, even to try cases in their own field. When such a "chamber attorney" attempts to try a criminal case, his performance is frequently awkward and insufficient. The effectiveness of assigned counsel as adversaries at the trial must be rated, at best, as uneven. In certain cases, they are quite effective; in many others, assigned counsel seriously jeopardize the rights of the defendant. The blame rests upon lack of an adequate provision for investigation as well as the fact that too many attorneys lack criminal trial experience.

Sentence

The only important issue in many cases is not guilt or innocence but the length of sentence. A defendant may receive one of a large variety of sentences, ranging from the suspended sentence, which involves immediate release, to a term of years, or, in rare cases, death. The decision is made by the sentencing judge within the limits imposed by law. In making this decision the judge considers not only the nature of the crime but also the background of the criminal. This reveals a partial acceptance of the new theories of individualization of punishment.

PRE-SENTENCE REPORT

So that the judge will have some information about the defendant, New Jersey, like many other states, provides for a pre-sentence investigation of all defendants convicted in second-level courts. This investigation is made by the county probation department. The final report covers the defendant's personal and social background, his criminal record, if any, and his mental and physical condition. Within one week to a month after a defendant has been convicted or has pleaded guilty, the judge has this report in his possession. Although it is in no way binding on the judge, the pre-sentence report may contain recommendations as to the sentence. Whether specific recommendations are made or not, the report is a highly significant factor in the final determination of the sentence.

When judges imposed sentences immediately following a conviction or a plea of guilty, the last-minute impassioned plea of the counsel for leniency may have had some effect. But in almost every county court case in New Jersey and in many other states today, the judge decides upon the sentence by studying the pre-sentence report in the quiet of his chambers long before the day when sentence is formally imposed. It would appear, therefore, that the role of counsel in the sentencing process is severely limited by the pre-sentence report.

DEFENSE COUNSEL AND PROSECUTOR

This does not rule the defense counsel out of the sentencing process entirely. He can participate in this process in two ways. First, in making arrangements with the prosecutor for a guilty plea, the defense counsel may have a significant effect on the sentence. This emphasizes again that the various steps in the criminal process bear a close relationship to one another. As shown previously, the pre-trial bargaining over a plea of guilty usually involves attempts by the defense to enter the plea in return for a lessening of the charges. If there is only one charge involved, the defense counsel may ask the prosecution to drop the charge to a lesser count carrying a shorter sentence. In this manner the sentence the defendant finally receives may be largely decided by the prosecutor, rather than by the judge who formally imposes the sentence.

Closely allied with the prosecutor's power to lessen

charges is the unique position he holds in the court structure. The relationship between judges and prosecutors appears from the outside to be a very distant one. In many respects, such as in ruling on the evidence to be admitted at a trial, this impression is quite correct. But in many other respects, the prosecutor and his staff are the staff for the court. For example, the prosecutor has a good deal of discretion as to the dates when certain prisoners will be arraigned and sentenced. In counties where several judges are sitting, selection of these dates amounts to a selection of the judge. This may have a great effect on sentences. Judges develop sentencing habits and are more severe on certain types of crimes than others. The implications of the informal power of the prosecutors in this regard are obvious. It is not known to what extent the use of this power enters into the bargaining process. Moreover, it is not known to what extent this power is used. But it is known that some prosecutors consciously select judges because of their sentencing habits. Graphic evidence was provided one day when I was sitting in the anteroom to the county prosecutor's office in an urban New Jersey county. The detectives were just returning from a sentencing session involving many prisoners convicted on narcotics charges. One detective fairly exploded, regarding the judge:

Did you see what that —— did? He just patted them on the wrist. From now on, let's not give him these kinds of cases!

In many instances a prosecutor may openly suggest to a judge a specific sentence for an offender. Such a suggestion is frequently, of course, made at the request of the judge. A prosecutor may, therefore, suggest a definite sentence to the judge, and, although the court is not bound thereby, this advice may determine the sentence in a doubtful case. Many bargains between prosecution and defense are struck with the understanding that in return for a guilty plea the prosecution will suggest to the judge a sentence lower than the maximum. Such an offer becomes almost irresistible where the prosecutor promises both to reduce the charges so that they fit into a category where a suspended sentence and probation are possible and also to suggest such a sentence to the judge. Few defendants who face the possibility of even a few months in jail can resist an offer that, if accepted, will place them "on the street" again. In this connection, Professor Donald J. Newman concluded in his study of "bargain justice" in a Midwestern county,

> Selection for placement on probation is determined by the skill of the offender or his lawyer in bargaining, rather than on factors of the case which would have more relevance to successful rehabilitation by field rather than institutional placement.[16]

DEFENSE COUNSEL AND PROBATION OFFICER

Second, defense counsel may affect the sentence after a guilty plea or after conviction by concentrating his efforts upon the probation officer assigned to perform the presentence investigation and upon the judge who will impose sentence. In general, this is a much less effective method for influencing the sentence than bargaining with the prosecution before a plea is entered. But it may well have some effect, and in those cases where the prosecution will not negotiate, it may be the only method for the counsel to affect the sentence.

Since the probation officer's report is such an important factor in the determination of the sentence by the judge, the competent defense attorney will make certain that the investigator is aware of every scrap of information favorable to the defendant. Certain information is not sought by the overworked probation officers in most counties, but if it is made available to the officer, it may be included in the report.[17] Character references from clergymen and other respected members of the community may be sought by a diligent counsel. A host of information may be supplied to the probation officer bearing, not on the question of legal guilt or innocence, but on the degree of culpability of the defendant, his lack of viciousness, and his possibilities for rapid rehabilitation. Witnesses to the incident, unknown to the police or the probation officer, may be produced for the purpose of showing that the defendant played a minor part in the commission of the crime. Such arguments have less effect, of course, where the defendant is not a first offender but a "repeater"—the judge has already heard his plea that this was but a single wayward step.

A dramatic example of how a diligent assigned counsel may affect the sentence by supplying information to the pre-sentence investigator was supplied by the attorney in a recent case. In a written communication to me, the attorney explained that several years ago he was assigned by the court in an urban New Jersey county to defend a man accused of murdering a friend over a money problem. In this assigned attorney's own words:

Defendant admitted shooting the deceased, but claimed that only an unhappy coincidence placed him in possession of a gun, at the precise moment he chanced to meet the latter. Plagued by financial problems, defendant said that the day preceding the killing, he had arranged to sell an acquaintance a gun which defendant had possessed since his days in the army. Defendant could not remember the name of the acquaintance, nor his exact street address; he was able only to describe the latter's residence and approximate its location. The next morning, defendant said he put the revolver in his pocket and went across town to deliver it to the unidentified would-be purchaser. Unfortunately, no one was home; defendant then retraced his steps to the neighborhood "hang-out," and there by coincidence ran into the deceased. An argument developed over a long-standing debt of the deceased to defendant; one word led to another—in the heat of the moment, defendant pulled out his gun and shot the deceased.

The explanation with respect to defendant's possession of the gun was, on its face, unbelievable. Yet, the undersigned through devious investigation which led from one address to another ultimately found the alleged purchaser, who did not even know defendant by name, but who, on interrogation, instantly recalled that around the time in question, he had told a person, whose physical description and first name matched the defendant's, that he would purchase the latter's revolver for $10, delivery to be made the following day. The next day, this witness stated, "Bob" never showed up, and the witness often wondered what had happened to him. Indeed, he did not even know of the killing until the undersigned told him. Ultimately defendant pleaded to murder in the second degree, but his story about the coincidental possession of the gun (ruling out a deliberate, planned murder), now was corroborated by an affidavit from the witness. This information submitted to the Probation Department and ultimately to the court was of considerable significance in bringing about a relatively light sentence.

DEFENSE COUNSEL AND JUDGE

Attorneys may concentrate their efforts after conviction and before sentence on *either* the probation officer or the judge. After sentence has been imposed, however, attempts by counsel to influence sentence usually focus on the judge because the work of the pre-sentence investigator is finished. According to the rules in New Jersey, the judge may alter the sentence within sixty days following its original pronouncement.[18] Many counsel cease their activities on behalf of their client as soon as the sentencing session ends, but others, I was told by several county judges, continue their efforts to get a lower sentence up to the end of the sixty-day period following sentence.[19]

In its most significant aspects, the function of the defense counsel in the sentencing process, as in other stages of the proceeding, is performed outside the courtroom itself. The presence of counsel in most American courts on the day that sentence is imposed is perhaps less necessary, in an adversary sense, than at any other stage of the proceedings. The question of guilt or innocence has been decided. The judge has read the pre-sentence report of the probation department investigator and has prepared the sentence. Little is done at the sentencing session save the pronouncement of sentence by the judge. It is only in the rarest of circumstances that the defense attorney has any effect on the sentence by his presence and plea in the courtroom on sentence day, but such cases do occur.

One of these rare cases occurred in Essex County in early 1956. A former convict, Albert Trowbridge, was brought up for sentencing on two counts of armed robbery. Because of his record, it appeared that he was about to receive a very severe sentence. However, Trowbridge's court-appointed lawyer had done more than prepare a general plea for leniency. Going into the background of the defendant and his prior record, the lawyer found that Trowbridge had spent four years and eight months in New York's Dannemora Prison for two crimes, robbery and parole violation, that had never occurred. At the sentencing session the assigned counsel urged that the judge take this into consideration. There was no legal necessity for the judge to do so, but after hearing the plea of the counsel, the judge deferred sentence. In doing this he said, "If society owes him something, I want to take that into consideration."

Several weeks later the defendant was brought up for sentencing again. In the interval the judge had checked the story of the assigned counsel, *which did not appear in the pre-sentence report of the probation department,* and imposed a sentence of nine to thirteen years. The judge explained that for two such armed robberies the sentence for a man with a record would ordinarily have totaled fourteen to twenty years. By taking into account the previous sentence served wrongfully in another state, the judge thus reduced the sentence. This reduction is directly attributable to the work of the court-appointed counsel. This last-minute plea was not purely an oratorical adventure in the old tradition but was based upon evidence that was new to the judge.[20]

A further reason for the presence of defense counsel at the sentencing is the administrative and clerical errors made at this time. Such mistakes are subsequently straightened out only with a great deal of difficulty. At the sentencing defense counsel can make certain what the sentence is, whether it is a legal sentence, and whether, in the case of two or more sentences, they are consecutive or concurrent. It may seem surprising that errors are made by the judge or clerk in regard to such an important thing as the length of sentence. Yet prison administrators have stated in interviews with me that these mistakes are not at all uncommon. Few defendants are sufficiently alert on this fateful day in their lives to question erroneous statements by the judge or the clerk of courts.

Finally, many defense attorneys appear at the sentence session purely out of sympathy for the defendant. This is completely understandable and quite commendable. If ever a person needs to feel that someone has a good word to say for him, and if ever a person needs to feel one other individual at his side, it is on the day when he is to receive a prison sentence.

ASSIGNED COUNSEL: EFFECTIVENESS

The effectiveness of unpaid attorneys appointed under the assigned counsel system in the sentencing process is, as with trial, adversely affected by the lack of investigatory facilities. Where certain facts would establish extenuating circumstances if they were known, the assigned counsel may be in no position to discover these facts and thereby obtain a lower sentence. Since the pre-sentence report is not usually made available to the defense, the assigned counsel must be his own private detective. However, much of the information ordinarily used to influence sentence— statements of character witnesses, psychiatric reports, and medical reports—may be obtained by telephone calls or letters. If he is willing to make this effort, the assigned counsel may be just as effective in this regard as a well-paid retained counsel or a public defender attorney. Moreover, some assigned attorneys have displayed heartening zeal in quests for mitigating evidence. But for every assigned counsel who takes time from his practice to aid a "criminal," there are several whose role in the sentencing process is almost entirely passive.

9

The Convicted

When the prison doors close behind a convicted man, they usually cut him off from all of his constitutional rights. This is not dictated by legal theory, but by the practical facts of the situation. Provisions for supplying convicts with legal advice in the United States compose the weakest part of the entire legal aid and defender structure. This has been allowed to happen because of popular notions that a man convicted of a crime has no legal rights and because this attitude has affected many judges and attorneys, who should know better. We are rapidly coming to the point where we realize that men in prison deserve competent medical treatment, psychiatric guidance, spiritual assistance, and sanitary living conditions. But it has not yet been driven home to the American public and, most important, to the American Bar, that a man in prison is entitled to avail himself of all those legal rights not directly abrogated by his conviction.

Because their earning power is virtually non-existent, people in prison comprise one of the most impecunious groups in society. The need of prisoners for legal guidance is greater than that of any other group of people—not only because of their wholesale state of indigency, but also because the fact of imprisonment produces many perplexing legal problems.

Since 1957 I have had discussions with at least five hundred convicts, either singly or in groups. I was surprised how many of them wanted desperately to confer with a lawyer and how many had not been able to arrange such an interview. Like Paul Jenkins, large numbers of them indicated that I was the first lawyer that they had spoken to since they were imprisoned. As a result of these many discussions with prisoners, I believe that there are five types of situations involving criminal law [1] regarding which many prisoners need competent legal assistance.

Legal Problems of Prisoners

The first type is the most serious and the least widespread —where the prisoner is innocent of the crime for which he is confined. Almost all men in prison are guilty of some crime. However, occasionally our courts do make mistakes. Despite the protestations of prosecutors and judges in New Jersey and elsewhere that only the guilty get convicted, Professor Edwin M. Borchard in 1932,[2] and, more recently, Judge Jerome Frank and Barbara Frank [3] filled two volumes with sixty-five examples and thirty-six examples, respectively, of cases in which the innocent were convicted. There *are* men in prison who are innocent. The need of these men for legal counsel is most urgent and compelling.[4]

Second, there are other men who may have been guilty

of some crime but were convicted and sentenced by an illegal procedure. That they were guilty in fact does not mean that prisoners can be held if they have not been properly convicted in a court of law. Our legal tradition does not stress conviction at any cost.

A third type of situation is that in which a broad sense of justice would seem to require reduction of the sentence by executive action. The men who fit into this category generally admit that they committed the crime but allege highly extenuating circumstances. Many of these cases involve crimes carrying relatively light prison sentences, but even two years in prison is severe for some offenses. An example is the case of a man I interviewed who received a two-to-three-year sentence for atrocious assault and battery upon a woman with whom he was living and whom he was supporting. According to the prisoner, he pushed the woman during an argument and she fell against a door, breaking her jaw. Although the couple had not gone through the formality of a marriage ceremony, this was a domestic quarrel. The prisoner claimed that shortly after the incident the woman attempted to withdraw her complaint, but he had already entered a plea of *non vult*. Apparently, the prosecutor could not see how justice would be done if the charges were dropped. The man was sent to prison, and the woman and her two children went on relief, eagerly awaiting the return of the family breadwinner.

An additional example may be cited. A thirty-two-year-old Negro with no criminal record was stopped by the police on the road shortly after he entered a northern New Jersey county. His car was searched, and a pistol was found. The man had technically committed the crime of carrying a concealed weapon, but there was no indication that he intended to use it for a criminal purpose. Even had he intended to apply for a gun permit in New Jersey, the man could hardly have had a permit at the time he was stopped and searched, for he had just arrived in the state. Although this crime is in the statute books and it can readily be admitted that the possession of deadly weapons should be discouraged, a plea for clemency in this case would seem to be in order.

The fourth type of situation is the most common—where the prisoner has groundless grievances about the legality of his conviction or sentence. The extent of misunderstanding concerning the criminal courts among prisoners, especially as to the more theoretical aspects of the criminal law, is extensive. These prisoners are generally aware that they have no legal basis for complaint, but almost every one of them carries a pet grievance concerning his trial, conviction, or sentence. Over the long years these grievances are nursed into a cancerous knot of hatred toward society. Living in an atmosphere of distrust, these men are unable to obtain unbiased legal advice on matters that might put their minds at rest and that would allow them to cease building up a reservoir of bitterness. Advice from the institutional authorities, whom the inmates regard as "the opposition," is not sufficient.

For example, I spoke to one man in the New Jersey State Prison who was under the impression that American law did not apply to illegal immigrants. This man had shot and killed a man whom he had suspected of having illicit relations with his wife. He did not believe that any punishment was due him because the victim was in this country illegally. The law, of course, makes no such distinction between victims rightfully in this country and those illegally within the jurisdiction of the United States.

A more frequent complaint among prisoners is that the judges took their prior criminal records into account in the determination of their sentences. This is a very widespread and perfectly legal practice. Although one may or may not agree with the notion that a fourth offender should be sent away for life,[5] it is understandable that a judge may be more lenient with a first offender than with a recidivist. Yet many prisoners look upon the law as a credit agency. Their argument amounts to this: All that is required to pay for each conviction is a certain amount of time put into the state collecting agency. This payment entitles a man to another withdrawal, free and clear of prior incumbrances. Prisoners who have this impression are, therefore, shocked when their co-defendant, a first offender, receives a lesser sentence for the very crime in which both have participated.

Each of these types of situations involves a need for legal advice concerning matters beyond the walls of the prison. The fifth and final type is one rarely mentioned in discussions of the right to counsel—where a prisoner desires to exercise his "rights" regarding administrative rulings and punishment by prison and parole officials.[6] Much like the period before arraignment, it is not clear to what extent the Constitution applies procedural safeguards after conviction. Whatever the legal formalities of the matter, it seems reasonably clear that prisoners are, in fact, very much at the mercy of prison and parole officials. This can have an effect on the amount of "good time" taken from their sentence for good behavior; on when they are released on parole; on punishment such as solitary confinement; and on their work assignments. No one should assume from this that the prisons visited in this study were run by characters out of *Oliver Twist*. Many prison personnel, at all levels, are real humanitarians. The point is that when a prison or parole official uses the administrative powers that he possesses, the prisoner is almost powerless to oppose him.

These, then, are the types of situations in which prisoners need the advice of an expert legal counselor. A prisoner who can arrange to pay a fee will usually manage to get a message to an attorney and obtain his assistance. The great difficulty arises, of course, from the fact that most convicts are penniless. In order to get legal advice, these men usually must request a judge for an assigned attorney. As will be seen in this examination of post-conviction court procedure in New Jersey, their requests create many serious problems for American courts.

Counsel for Convicts

Appeals by assigned counsel are rare, and the indigent defendant himself is usually not sufficiently aware of his rights to appeal within the designated time—in New Jersey, three months from the final judgment.[7] Therefore, most post-conviction proceedings by prisoners are by way of the writ of habeas corpus, which is not restricted by any time limit. The procedure in New Jersey, as in most states, involves two steps. First, the defendant must submit an application for a writ to a judge in the county where he was convicted. The judge may deny this application, whereupon all further proceedings under it are terminated, or he may order a writ of habeas corpus to be issued. This writ directs that the prisoner be produced in court at a certain date for a hearing. At this hearing the judge makes a final determination on the legality of the confinement. The standard of proof of an illegal procedure required at the hearing is much higher than that required for a successful original application for a writ. At the hearing on the writ the defendant must generally show that either through intent or omission such a manifest injustice occurred in his case that he was prevented from receiving a "fair trial." [8]

Provisions for appeals *in forma pauperis* are made by the New Jersey court rules.[9] That is, the rules provide for a waiver of filing fees and costs in the appellate court and allow the indigent prisoner to submit typewritten papers. In this manner, the cost of court fees and printing does not stand as a bar to a post-conviction application. However, even the cost of typing the court reporter's transcript of the record and trial proceedings is prohibitive for many prisoners. In the past this effectively prevented post-conviction action in many non-capital cases unless, as happened on rare occasions, the trial judge allowed—without an express statutory provision in support of his action—the printing of a transcript at public expense.

In capital cases the rules provide that when a person has been sentenced to death he may, if indigent, be supplied by the trial judge with a copy of the transcript of all proceedings. Furthermore, the rules provide that a person convicted of a capital offense—who was not sentenced to death—may be supplied with a transcript upon a showing to the trial judge that such is necessary for his defense.[10] A new statute now extends this policy to non-capital cases. Judges are empowered to grant the cost of transcripts when they are satisfied with the "sufficiency" of the appeal.[11] This statute was passed after the United States Supreme Court, in *Griffin* v. *Illinois*,[12] decided that the state must supply indigent appellants with a transcript or an equally effective remedy.

Although it does not completely fulfill the need, the New Jersey provision for post-conviction assignment is one of the most enlightened in the entire country.[13] The rules provide that the judge to whom a request for counsel is addressed by a prisoner "may" assign new counsel for appellate proceedings. Since the duties of original assigned counsel terminate with sentencing,[14] the judge determines, in large measure, whether there will be any post-sentence proceedings in the case.

If the application for the writ alleges facts that are un-contradicted by the record and that, if proven, would pro-vide a valid basis for overruling the conviction, counsel is assigned by the judge. On the other hand, if the judge takes the position that the defendant has absolutely no basis for a complaint, the judge is empowered both to deny the writ and to deny the application for assignment of counsel on the grounds of indigency. This preliminary finding means that the judge has arrived at a conclusion based on the crude papers submitted by the prisoner as to the merits of the application. These papers are frequently incoherent and sometimes cite inapplicable principles of law that may hurt rather than help the case. Furthermore, the facts of the complaint and its legal basis—even though they be valid—are not always made clear by the pris-oner in this original application. Many applications for counsel and, therefore, all post-conviction proceedings, are cut off, at least temporarily, by a decision based only on these very crude papers. In order to receive any legal assistance whatsoever, therefore, an indigent prisoner must himself compose a letter or an application for a writ that will convince a judge that he might have a valid legal complaint with his conviction or sentence.

This procedure clearly does not provide for legal assist-

ance in three of the five types of situations requiring legal
advice—for judges simply do not assign counsel and send
them down to one of the state's prisons to confer with
men who have a case requiring executive clemency, who
have groundless grievances, or who are fighting a ruling
of the prison administrators. As for the remaining two
types of situations, only in one of them—where there was
a legal defect in the proceedings—is there a clear basis for
the assignment of counsel. For even when a man claims
innocence, this does not preclude a conviction according
to the rules of law.

Moreover, where a man has a valid legal complaint,
there is no guaranty that he will be assigned an attorney,
for, as indicated above, state judges generally do not assign
lawyers to prepare the original applications for writs.
Many men want such guidance while drafting these applications and can usually pay a fee of only a few cartons
of cigarettes—which explains why prison "lawyers" are
rarely out of tobacco. But if assignments of professional
attorneys were made to all the convicts who actually
needed legal advice in drafting original applications for
writs, this would be a terrible burden on this country's
lawyers. Nevertheless, the need for such advice exists. It
is not being met. I do not know precisely how many applications are rejected by judges without assignment of counsel because prisoners are not knowledgeable enough to
draft a convincing original letter or application. But interviews with prisoners convince me that this is an extensive
problem.[15]

When a judge in New Jersey is satisfied, as a preliminary
matter, that a prisoner might have a valid basis for complaint, he may select an attorney for post-conviction assignment in one of two different ways. First, assignment

after sentence is usually made by choosing the next attorney on the county master list. When an assignment is made in this manner, it is seen to be similar in procedure to the assignments made before trial.

A second method of assignment involves special selection of an attorney. Such assignments are similar to those pre-trial assignments made by certain judges in cases involving a severe sentence or a capital offense. In the latter instance, of course, compensation is allowed. No compensation is allowed for attorneys assigned in non-capital cases, whether the services are rendered before or after conviction.

The function that an attorney assigned after conviction is expected to perform has undergone some changes in recent years. The New Jersey court rules once provided that before a court could assign counsel for the purpose of going forward with a habeas corpus application, there had to be a showing of "reasonable doubt" as to the validity of the conviction. In order to have "preliminary reviews made to determine the existence of reasonable doubt," it was further suggested that an attorney be assigned from one of the Habeas Corpus Advisory Committees of the Junior Section of the State Bar Association. The role of the attorney selected was, therefore, to examine the evidence and to present his conclusions on the question of "reasonable doubt" to the judge. At the outset of his duties, at least, this attorney was not expected to begin preparation of the application for the writ.

This procedure presented serious problems. First, it forced an attorney who supposedly was an advocate for the prisoner to report adverse information about his case to the judge. A rule amendment has apparently done much to clear up any confusion on this point. The section concerning the necessity for a showing of reasonable doubt has been stricken. Secondly, the rule provision gave the appearance that there was something binding about the report of the attorney to the judge. As to this problem, it has since been made clear in a 1954 decision, that, as a matter of law, the report of an attorney assigned to an indigent prisoner is merely advisory; it is no substitute for the court's own independent opinion.[16]

Despite these rulings, the practice in many county courts regarding the preliminary finding made by a judge remains unchanged. Before a judge will order assignment of counsel, he must be satisfied that there is reasonable doubt that the conviction and imprisonment were completely legal. Once assignment is made, furthermore, the attorney may still find himself on the horns of a dilemma where his investigation results in a conclusion unfavorable to the prisoner:

> If . . . [the attorney] cannot conscientiously go forward, he appears to have no course but to present his conclusions to the court and ask to be excused. The court must then make its own independent examination, and while this may give a satisfactory result in many cases, there always remains the possibility, in the event of an adverse decision, that other more astute or ingenious counsel might succeed in persuading the court of the merit of the applicant's position.[17]

In light of the discretionary control that judges exercise over the assignment of counsel after conviction, it is disturbing to find a sense of annoyance expressed by judges regarding habeas corpus petitions and applications for counsel. The attitude with which all too many American judges approach their task in this area was summed up in the following excerpt from a 1954 New Jersey case:

[E]xperience has disclosed that it is time to deplore the conspicuous abuse of the liberality with which whimsical and spurious appeals . . . are transmitted *in forma pauperis* to this Division.

The responsibility for this generous and burdensome practice has been ours. In our desire to aid any indigent prisoner in our penal institutions whose incarceration might be discovered to be unlawful, our courts have in recent years encouraged a current flow of petitions for writs of *habeas corpus* which are sham and baseless and in which the fictitious factual allegations are falsely verified. Prisoners have become a distinctive class of litigants to whom special and exceptional privileges are accorded. The payment of filing fees is excused. The court rules are uniformly relaxed in such cases. Counsel is sometimes appointed to represent a prisoner without compensation. Experience has now revealed that the benevolent opportunities so afforded most of these prisoners with the best of intentions are being notoriously abused by too many who are manifestly unworthy of such leniencies.[18]

The judge does not recognize, however, that it is high time that our society ceased to look upon the opportunities presented to men to challenge their confinement in generally inadequate institutions as "generous" or "benevolent," and considered them a matter of absolute necessity and justice. Furthermore, the only manner in which most prisoners can receive an answer from an attorney about a legal problem is to file an application for a writ of habeas corpus and on that basis ask for the assignment of counsel. Many of these complaints would never result in court proceedings if the prisoners had easier access to counsel. This is not to overlook the possibility that many more prisoners might make applications for writs, some of which might be successful, if counsel were freely available, and that others might continue to abuse the privilege. The judicial attitude expressed in the last quotation should be further criticized on the basis that it lacks that elemental quality supposedly attributed to judges in a civilized nation—the quality of mercy.

But this is not to suggest that the post-conviction problem is easily solved. As illustrated by this analysis of the situation in New Jersey, the problem is an extremely complex one. Every time that the Supreme Court of the United States hands down a favorable decision in a review of a state habeas corpus case, the problem is increased by the sheer weight of the number of applications that follow from other prisoners. An overly liberal attitude by the state courts would make of the existing flood an overwhelming deluge. But a restrictive view, now held by many state appellate courts, smothers meritorious applications for relief.

Prison Conditions

The prisoners in all four institutions I visited were treated humanely. They seemed well fed and clothed. The physical plants at the Reformatory in Bordentown, New Jersey, and at the Federal Penitentiary in Lewisburg, Pennsylvania, were modern and clean. Those of the New Jersey State Prison in Trenton and the Holmesburg Prison in Philadelphia were much older, but they also were clean and generally well maintained. Higher ranking personnel in all of these institutions appeared to be enlightened individuals. The worst that can be said about the guards is that some of them showed little sympathy for the rehabilitative role of the prison. In general, the guards appeared to be fair-minded men who wore their authority lightly and treated the inmates like fellow human beings. Although all of the prisoners were not queried specifically on this point, there was not a single claim of brutality levied against prison personnel. This was a healthy contrast with the many charges of ill-treatment against local policemen and county jail guards. It is heartening to observe that reports from other sections of the country indicate that these four institutions are not unique.

But it must also be observed that some American penal institutions are little better than slave camps. The 1961 *Justice* report of the U.S. Commission on Civil Rights gave brief but chilling glimpses into three institutions. In Florida's Raiford Prison, sadistic guards subjected Negro and white prisoners to inhuman punishment for minor rules infractions, sometimes for no apparent reason. There was no criminal prosecution of the guards by local authorities. The sum total of local action against the guards was the discharge of two head guards at the order of the governor. When the federal government prosecuted fourteen guards under a civil rights act in 1960, the judge directed a verdict for the defendant-guards because it was not shown that in beating the victims they had intended also to violate their constitutional rights. The Commission on Civil Rights reported:

> At the trial, James Donald Brown, a 21-year-old Negro inmate of Raiford Prison, made allegations typical of those made by other prisoners. He said that he had been caught with a pencil (a minor violation) and informed by a prison lieutenant, one of the defendants, that he was going to be shackled to the bars of a cell as punishment. His testimony continued:

A. I started to resist from being handcuffed to the bar and he hit me with a blackjack.

Q. Did they complete chaining you at any time?

A. Yes, they chained me.

Q. In what position were you chained?

A. I was sitting down with my legs up on the bar and my hands up on the bar sitting down on the floor nude.

Q. How long did you remain in that position?

A. About 41 hours. . . .

A. After I had been chained . . . [the officers] shot water on me, and poured salt on me.

Q. What did he do with the hose?

A. Shot water all down on my privates, all in my face and all over my body.

Q. How was the nozzle adjusted?

A. It was pretty powerful.

Then, Brown continued, after 2 or 3 hours, one of the guards gave him another hose "treatment" under the direction of the prison lieutenant. Later he was chained to the bars again for several hours.[19]

The Commission report also revealed that a few years ago prisoners in Alabama's Atmore Prison stopped work to draw attention to bad conditions; this culminated in a riot. Those who participated in the riot and those who had signed a petition for a redress of grievances were allegedly forced to run between rows of guards who beat them with bats and clubs. Prisoners managed to get word to the Department of Justice, and as a result an FBI investigation was made. After the agents left the prison, reports got to Washington indicating that prisoners were subjected to serious beatings because of the federal probe. A state investigation did not result in any prosecution. The Department of Justice closed its case on May 2, 1960, and did not institute a prosecution.[20]

Another case reported by the Commission on Civil Rights involved the State Training School for Girls in New Mexico. The housefather of that institution was charged with imposing harsh punishments on the inmates and with forcing them to engage in sexual intercourse with him. The state initiated a prosecution but eventually closed the case because of lack of evidence. Since the Department of Justice had deferred to state action while the case pended in state courts for over eighteen months, it, too, was forced to close the case—on December 16, 1959—for lack of evidence.[21]

Had such savagery been reported in the prisons of an Iron Curtain country—especially to American citizens—there would have been indignant outcries from the press, the pulpit, and the public. But little public indignation greeted these revelations in the Commission's report, perhaps because the victims were convicts.

"I Cannot Sleep Well"

A guide to dealing with post-conviction court and counsel problems is this simple and time-worn postulate: When there is doubt in a conflict between authority and liberty, decide on the side of liberty. No person should be confined behind the walls of a prison, sometimes under brutal conditions, and be denied the advice of counsel and even liberty itself when there is the slightest doubt that he ought to be enjoying these hallmarks of civilization. If adjustments must be made in the court

institutions—in the number of judges, in defense practices after conviction, and so on—then these changes
should be made. The spirit that should motivate this
reform was well expressed by Judge Jerome Frank in
1956:

> The way out of this apparent dilemma is to consult the
> interest of justice: Surely, even if but one out of a hundred
> attempted appeals by indigents has merit, justice compels
> the conclusion that that appeal shall be heard. It is no
> answer that so many appeals will result as to "crowd the
> docket." If so, more judges should be appointed. True,
> the cost of running the government will somewhat in-
> crease. But I, for one, cannot sleep well if I think that,
> due to any judicial decisions in which I join, innocent des-
> titute men may be behind bars solely because it will cost
> the government something to have their appeals consid-
> ered.[22]

10

The Institutions of Freedom

If rights are to have real meaning for the great mass of people, we must not only inscribe them in constitutions and statutes—we must support these freedoms by powerful institutions as well.

When protections of personal freedom are set down in constitutions, in statutes, and in court decisions, the ideals of rights are established, but not the realities. The institutions of freedom provide the most important bridge between the ideals of the law and the stark realities of the police station, the county jail, and the criminal court. Although many official practices threaten the rights of those accused of crime, I will restrict my discussion to reforms of three broad problems in the administration of criminal justice because, in my opinion, these problems demand immediate relief: the ineffectiveness of present defender systems, especially the assigned counsel system; the threat to freedom posed by much police activity; and the lack of a powerful overseer of American freedoms.

Professional Defender Systems

DEFECTS OF ASSIGNED COUNSEL SYSTEM

The assigned counsel system is an amateur method using "volunteers" to solve a major social and judicial problem that requires a professional solution by career specialists. All of its other weaknesses either flow from this fundamental and inherent defect or are much less significant.

The criminal courts deal largely with the so-called social welfare group in the community. In most aspects of social welfare work, specialized agencies have been established to assist the indigent and near-indigent when they have domestic difficulty or lose a job. Yet when a person in this class gets into difficulty with the criminal law—greater difficulty than anything he has ever known— we allow underpaid or unpaid attorneys, with mainly civil court experience, to fill this most desperate need of all. A poor person in difficulty with the law needs the help of specialists in an agency that is a blend of social welfare organization and law office. Only a professional defender office can completely fulfill this need.

This criticism should not be considered as directed at the integrity or the devotion to duty of American lawyers. On the contrary, thousands of American attorneys have expended considerable effort and have shown commendable zeal in the defense of indigent defendants. Many of these attorneys "consider themselves in a 'fiduciary' role when the courts put the rights of a man in their trust." [1] A zealous "amateur," moreover, may be more effective in certain cases than a bored professional.

Nevertheless, when the fact that most attorneys are amateurs in the criminal courts is combined with the fact that, under the usual assigned counsel plan, they are underpaid amateurs, expectations of a competent defense for the indigent must be found in the zeal of individual attorneys for justice and their conception of their duty as officers of the court. Although both of these elements are motivating factors in the performance of large numbers of assigned attorneys, it must be admitted that attorneys are human; zeal can be tempered by practical necessities such as earning a livelihood; and the duty of an attorney as an officer of the court may be subordinated to these pressing considerations.[2]

It may be argued that whatever shortcomings the system has in regard to the qualifications of assigned counsel, they are compensated for by the fact that, first, individual young attorneys gain experience; and, second, this educational process will, through a bar awakened to its responsibilities, have a beneficial effect on criminal court reform.[3] Neither of these propositions has borne fruit in practice. First, most attorneys are not assigned frequently enough to be "educated" purely by the assigned case they receive once every two to three years. If there were in each county a small panel of attorneys who handled the cases of the poor on a regular basis, there would perhaps be some validity for this claim. But this is not the usual procedure under the assigned counsel system in this country.

There is, furthermore, a more conclusive answer to the argument that emphasizes the educational virtues of the assigned counsel system—even if it were to be admitted that they were present. A sink-or-swim philosophy for young attorneys in the criminal courts—whereby if there is any "sinking" to be done, unfortunately, it is done by the defendant—is fundamentally at odds with the concept of effective defense in an adversary system. When the defendant happens to be indigent, the criminal courts cannot be considered an extension of the law school moot court system. This notion subverts our professed belief in the need for a competent defense for all persons accused of crime regardless of their financial means or social station. Counsel assigned to the indigent may gain experience in the process, but it would be an inverse set of values, indeed, that emphasized this incidental benefit at the expense of the primary function of the defendant's counsel —that of providing a vigorous and professional defense. No man should be placed in the position of the defendant in an English court who was asked after his conviction if he had anything to say before sentence. His reply applies, unfortunately, to many assigned counsel:

Nothing, My Lord, except to plead the youth and inexperience of my counsel.[4]

As for the second argument, after over ten years of the New Jersey system, which has spread assignments among several thousand attorneys, there seems to be no resurgence of interest within the ranks of the state bar in criminal court reform. Most attorneys still consider themselves civil practitioners. Appropriately, they display considerable interest in such matters as the regulation of fees in negligence cases, but find it difficult to feel a sense of injustice concerning the lack of a fully adequate discovery procedure in criminal cases. Reforms in the criminal courts usually originate with the prosecution—in the offices of the police, the county prosecutors, and the attorney general wherein are found the men who are paid to prosecute offenders. Were a professional defender system with paid, full-time attorneys operating in every state there would be, perhaps, a compensatory pressure for reform coming from the benches of a somewhat more organized and coherent opposition. But now, in most states, there is no powerful voice speaking for the defendant—and, thereby, for American liberties.[5]

DEFECTS OF
ORGANIZED DEFENDER SYSTEMS

As a general proposition, an organized defender system employing paid attorneys is an improvement over the assigned counsel system. But many of the organized defender systems, which operate in 184 American counties, are not now providing adequate service. Many of them consist of one lawyer who has a private practice and serves as a defender on a part-time basis for a small annual retainer. For example, out of the 33 defender offices in Illinois, 28 are staffed with part-time lawyers. And in California, which is second to Illinois in the number of defender offices, only the defenders in those counties having a population of over 600,000 are on a full-time basis and prohibited from having a private practice. Moreover, the great majority of defenders handle cases only in second-level courts. These defenders do not enter a felony case at the preliminary examination stage, nor are they able to provide vital post-conviction service.[6] And not more than 18 defender organizations in this country have full-time investigators on the payroll. Indeed, there are probably not more than 50 full-time, paid defender detectives in the entire country—a figure that should be contrasted with the more than 200,000 American police officers.

Neither the American states nor the federal government provide either the assurance of constitutional rights or an effective defense for the great majority of indigent accused persons appearing in their courts. It is high time that they did.

STRENGTHENING THE
DEFENDER INSTITUTION

A professional defender agency should now be operating in every American court. I would not consider a defender agency "professional" unless it had the following attributes: It should provide experienced, competent, loyal, and zealous counsel for every impecunious person who faces the possibility that he will suffer loss of his liberty or some other serious criminal sanction. It should provide investigative services and all other facilities, such as expert witnesses, necessary for a complete defense. It should have a broad scope of operations, starting very soon after arrest and continuing through post-conviction proceedings.[7] The organizational details of the agency are insignificant—if it has these attributes.

There are now three types of organized defender agencies operating in the United States: the public defender plan, the private defender plan, and the mixed public-private defender plan.[8] The main point of distinction between them is the source of finances. The public defender is supported by governmental funds, usually from a county, and operates as a public agency. Private defenders are often supported by community chest organizations and other charitable sources. Finances for the third plan come from both public and private sources. All three are similar to the extent that they are a centralized institution that employs paid attorneys who regularly defend the indigent accused. And any one of these three types could provide effective defender service.

Each community must select that type of defender suitable to its own particular conditions. Because there was much resentment to the idea of a public defender in New Jersey, several years ago I published a detailed proposal for a mixed public-private defender system.[9] While it was tailored for that state, it could be utilized in many others. The basic features of the plan are as follows: The agency would be organized as a single statewide entity and would be registered as a charitable corporation. Defender attorneys would be empowered to enter any criminal or quasi-criminal case, including those in the federal courts, that is heard within the state border. The staff members of the defender system would include attorneys, investigators, and legal stenographers, all of whom would be paid adequate salaries. Originally, the system would concentrate on providing representation at all stages of those criminal cases heard in the county courts and for comparable cases in the federal district courts. Expansion to the municipal courts and the juvenile and domestic relations courts would be accomplished as soon as financing was available, so that defendants in all cases involving a possible deprivation of liberty in a criminal or quasi-criminal proceeding would be represented by competent counsel. Financing and direction of the agency would come from both public and private sources.

It is likely, however, that most defenders will be supported in the future, as they are now, entirely by public funds. This is both financially practical and idealistically sound. Governments are able to provide a greater and steadier stream of funds than private, charitable sources.

Democratic governments should be unabashedly and enthusiastically on the side of freedom—not only on the Fourth of July, but also when funds are being appropriated. Therefore, I have placed the full text of the Model Defender Act drafted by the National Conference of Commissioners on Uniform State Laws in Appendix B. It provides a simple but sound statute establishing a public defender system. If it or some system like it was adopted by every state legislature and by Congress, constitutional rights and an effective defense in criminal cases would be placed on a strong institutional footing.

In a few American counties this institutional foundation for constitutional ideals is now in existence. In Los Angeles County, California, for example, constitutional rights are supported daily by men and public money. The budget during the 1960–61 fiscal year for the Los Angeles County Public Defender Office was $713,294; [10] and there were 71 persons on the staff: 51 defender attorneys (including the chief public defender), 9 investigators, and 11 administrative personnel.[11] All of these people were engaged full time in an organized effort to assure an effective defense and the protection of constitutional rights to the indigent accused. During the 1959–60 fiscal year, they handled 23,626 criminal cases.[12] Full service was provided from preliminary hearings in municipal courts through proceedings after conviction. Where necessary, investigations were performed. The contrast between this massive practical support for constitutional freedom and that found in most American counties, needs little explanatory comment at this point—but it should evoke action.

Professional Police Systems

DEFECTS OF POLICE SYSTEMS

Too many police forces in the United States are led by men who do not believe that they have to follow any law they consider an obstacle to efficient law enforcement. Most police forces have inadequate budgets, no recruit selection standards worthy of the name, and ineffective training programs. It is less than surprising that this unhealthy combination produces millions of rights violations every year. When combined, the measures that alleviate these problems—discussed in the sections that follow—help make professional police systems; they also help provide greater protection for constitutional rights through prevention of violations, rather than often less effective, after-the-fact remedies.

LEADERSHIP

Earlier in this century, a police official said, in a public address, that he had on one occasion left the station while his men were interrogating a suspect. When the official returned, he found that his men had succeeded in obtaining the information they sought. The official then told his audience:

> Now, I *don't know* what Captain O'Haver *did* to secure the information he desired. . . . But . . . I said to Captain O'Haver the next morning, *whatever you did* was right. . . .[13]

Many police leaders today follow the philosophy implicit in this statement but do not say so publicly. At times, some police leaders act as if they are above the law; at times, painfully similar to the French king, they act as if they *are* the law. Even though they wear blue uniforms instead of satin breeches, these police commanders are autocratic throwbacks in this century of democracy's trial. They are often kept in office because many powerful community leaders themselves have no real commitment to the democratic dream and fully agree with the "tough" police policy mainly because it operates only on the other side of the tracks. And many respectable people operate on the assumption that the "rough" elements of society have to be treated roughly or they will get out of hand.

Justification for keeping such police chiefs in office is also often found in the fact that some of them show a high degree of efficiency in running their departments. But it must be remembered that when police leaders encourage illegal conduct by their subordinates, they are engaging in a criminal conspiracy. Even an efficient criminal should not be in charge of a public institution, especially one dedicated to the enforcement of the law. Police leaders who act as if the Constitution did not exist must either be forced to obey it or they must be removed from office.

"Perhaps the single most potent weapon against unlawful police activity is a police commander who will not tolerate it," declared the U.S. Commission on Civil Rights in 1961.[14] Fortunately, there are a number of police commanders in this country who show intolerance toward illegal conduct by their men. One of these is Superintendent Orlando W. Wilson of Chicago.

By 1959 the Chicago Police Department was the target of much justified criticism regarding rights violations and corruption. In 1959 Chicago was disgraced even more when it was revealed that several full-time policemen worked part-time in operating a flourishing burglary ring. Despite the oft-mouthed shibboleth attributed to Alderman Paddy Bawler—"Chicago ain't ready for reform yet" —the city brought in Orlando W. Wilson to reform its police department. Wilson is a rare person in that he combines the intellectualism of the scholar (last job: Chairman of the Department of Criminology at the University of Southern California) with the experience of running three police departments and the craggy-faced toughness of a drill sergeant. Since Wilson took over in early 1960, police efficiency in combating crime has gone up, police corruption and invasions of constitutional rights drastically down.

Why? First, Superintendent Wilson set up a new procedure for handling complaints against policemen. The new machinery was most important, but the second element in this "before and after" story was even more vital. As the Commission on Civil Rights declared, ". . . the major reason for the successful operation of Chicago's system lies not in the fine points of organization, but rather in the determination of a strong, capable leader that it *would* work. . . ." [15]

Police commanders like Orlando Wilson are pushing police work to the status of a profession. By insisting on vigorous enforcement of the law within the law, they also are providing practical support for constitutional ideals where the tests are most severe—on slum streets, in police interrogation rooms, and in jail cells.

THE ULTIMATE FACTOR

The Commission on Civil Rights stated that "The ultimate factor in any study of police misconduct must be . . . the individual policeman." [16] It is dismaying, therefore, to discover that some police departments will hire anyone who will take the hazards, long hours, and low pay—provided that he weighs enough on the hoof.[17]

At the opposite pole we find that many enlightened police leaders are promoting research into more scientific police recruitment tests that will isolate the personal factors that make a man a good prospect—and that will help to discover the unsuitable recruit. The New York City Police Department is engaged in an extensive study of this sort. It is financed primarily by two private foundations. The research is being carried out by a group of scientists from the American Institute for Research, who are dealing with such factors as prejudice and the ability to stand situations of stress. Such studies have helped the armed forces select men who could best stand the rigors of demanding duty assignments. The New York study has now brought twentieth century social psychology to bear, in a massive program, on the twin problems of police efficiency and the observance of constitutional rights.[18]

Related to the need for good recruitment programs is the problem of low pay. FBI Director J. Edgar Hoover put the problem in proper perspective when he recently said:

> One large Southern community pays its patrolmen a starting salary of $279 a month, and the minimum work week is 48 hours. In this same city, 18-year-old stenographers can find government positions offering $337 a month salary for a 40-hour week!
>
> In a medium-sized Western city, the situation is even more ludicrous. Here the starting salary of patrolmen is $175 per month. The Chief of Police of this "enlightened" community earns $400 a month. . . .
>
> When conditions such as these persist, it is no wonder

that many police departments have trouble recruiting qualified personnel and retaining competent officers.[19]

TRAINING PROGRAMS

Training programs are of two types: those that teach modern methods of crime detection and control, and those that deal with human relations. Both can have a significant impact on the extent to which policemen observe the rules of the law and the precepts of fairness. A policeman trained to trap a suspect by matching his fingerprints with those on a pistol will have much less motivation to force a confession by putting toothpicks under his fingernails. A policeman trained to respect people and their rights is more apt to be fair and law-abiding.

Here, again, we find a situation where most police departments are ineffective, while others are reaching to the borders of science for methods to improve their programs. The New York City study includes, in addition to recruitment tests, research into more effective human relations training programs. The Philadelphia Police Department is also engaged in a research and development program aimed at producing a training system based on new insights of social science.[20] Former New York Police Commissioner Stephen P. Kennedy offered great hope for the future when he said:

> We cannot continue to be satisfied with a trade school approach to police training. The police officer must be instructed in human relations, civil rights, constitutional guarantees. In short, he has to be prepared to assume his role as a social scientist in the community.[21]

Every step that we take down Mr. Kennedy's road brings our society that much closer to the point where constitutional ideals will have institutional props at the grass-roots level, where they count the most. Progress down that road will receive a dramatic push if a 1961 recommendation of the U.S. Commission on Civil Rights is followed; the Commission proposed that Congress enact a grant-in-aid program to assist state and local police forces establish and maintain effective recruit selection standards and training programs.[22]

INDIRECT CONTROLS ON POLICE ILLEGALITIES

Professionalization of the police offers the best hope for the prevention of millions of constitutional rights violations every year, but there are other, indirect methods that could have some impact.

Independent Advisory Boards: "When five policemen hear a complaint against another policeman, the policeman is always right." This critical sentence was uttered by Philadelphia City Councilman Henry W. Sawyer III in 1957 about alleged deficiencies in the handling of complaints by the official police board of inquiry.[23] Most large police departments have a procedure whereby complaints against policemen are heard by a panel consisting of fellow officers. Too often, the decisions of these boards have come out on the side of the policeman—leading many responsible citizens to doubt the integrity of the official complaint machinery. Moreover, those policemen who use illegal methods are led to believe that they will be protected by the "system."

In the face of mounting outrage over alleged police excesses, Mayor Richardson Dilworth of Philadelphia established the first police review board in this country on October 1, 1958.[24] Now called the Philadelphia Police Advisory Board, it is composed entirely of distinguished private citizens. Aggrieved persons may now bring their complaints to the Board, which holds hearings, listens to witnesses on both sides, and issues decisions and recommendations. Though these recommendations are not binding on the police commissioner, he has imposed the suggested punishment—usually suspensions without pay for a period of days or weeks—in almost every instance. Therefore, the relatively few policemen in Philadelphia who are inclined toward lawlessness and brutality now face the prospect of being called to account before an impartial group of private citizens.

In those communities where both the citizenry and erring policemen doubt the integrity of the departmental complaint machinery, a police review board may both restore public confidence in the police department and discourage rights violations by officers. Review boards similar to the Philadelphia model are now appearing in other cities.

Stricter Legal Controls: Many students of civil liberties concern themselves primarily with proposals for new legal rules that will promulgate stricter controls on police activity. There is some basis for this concern since the Supreme Court of the United States has laid down only two clearly definable constitutional commands dealing with state or local police activity that have teeth in them. That is, it has made clear that it will overturn convictions only where it can be shown that the defendant was convicted (1) on the basis of a coerced confession or (2) on the basis of property seized in violation of the Fourth Amendment. In addition, the Court will allow suits against police officers who have been brutal, although this will not secure the release of the victim-defendant.

There is, moreover, much concern over the double standard in constitutional jurisprudence. And if we were to adhere closely to the traditional Supreme Court-oriented approach to problems of civil liberties, we would argue for stricter legal rules to control the third degree and other police transgressions. For example, the argument might declare that the solution lies in the application of the *Mallory* Rule [25] to state trials—that is, to rule all confessions taken by the police during a period of illegal detention inadmissible in evidence at a subsequent trial. Following this rule, now applicable only to federal cases, the simple fact that the confession was obtained during a period of extra-long detention would be sufficient to eliminate that statement from the case. State prisoners would no longer have to prove "inherently coercive" [26] conditions of interrogation or a brutal third degree [27] in order to have convictions reversed by the Supreme Court.

For two reasons I would agree that such changes in Supreme Court policy should take place. First, the double standard that now exists in American jurisprudence, which allows different rules under the same Constitution for federal and state criminal procedure, presents a ridiculous picture whatever legal logic may be conjured up to support it. Second, more stringent legal rules are certain to have a salutory effect on the attitude of many officials and the general public regarding the powers of the police. Such rules may also have some effect on the actions of some police officers.

However, a change in the constitutional philosophy of the Supreme Court means only that one set of ideals has been displaced by another. More stringent constitutional standards of criminal justice may be necessary conditions —but they are certainly not sufficient conditions for genuine reform. Fundamental changes will also have to take place in police institutions before these ideals are implemented in practice.

For this same reason, I am both pleased and cautious about the *Mapp* decision, which effected a change in the double standards regarding the use in evidence of property seized in violation of the Fourth Amendment.[28] Pleased because the double standard seemed legally unsound; cautious because I retain sanguine doubts as to how long we must wait until we see concrete results at the precinct level.

As a remedy for the third degree, some might argue for the adoption of the Scottish Rule: only a magistrate may interrogate the prisoner and only in open court.[29] Professor Orfield described the Rule as "the simplest, clearest, and most effective rule against police interrogation." [30] However, as Professor Orfield implied, this rule is totally unsuitable for the realities of criminal prosecution in this country. It would almost cripple the police, who are now struggling under a case load of millions of investigations every year.

Suits Against Policemen: Another form of indirect control is found in the prosecution of criminal and civil suits against officers who resort to illegal practices. It is theoretically possible for an injured person to sue a police officer for false arrest or assault and battery in a civil suit for money damages under state laws. It is theoretically possible for the aggrieved party to sue for damages in a civil suit under the federal Civil Rights Acts when a police officer interferes with the enjoyment of a right protected by the federal Constitution.[31] It is theoretically possible for the police officer to be prosecuted in a criminal court for assault and battery under the state law or for a variety of other state crimes. The same is true regarding a prosecution under the federal Civil Rights Acts, which make it a crime for a policeman or other official to interfere with the enjoyment of a right protected by the United States Constitution.[32]

From this line-up of legal weapons, the arsenal of remedies to which an aggrieved person may resort appears quite adequate. In practice, there are many limitations, and such suits are not at all common. The most outstanding limitation is the fact that even when these suits are brought, they are difficult to win. This is primarily due to the fact that the complainants in these cases are usually members of the lower classes of society, frequently of a minority group; in addition, many of them have criminal records. When they stand up in court and accuse a law enforcement official of wrongdoing, juries rarely decide for them. Of course, even if they were to win in the civil suits, most officers do not have enough money to satisfy a judgment of any sizeable amount,[33] and municipalities are not liable under the doctrine of sovereign immunity.[34]

Further difficulties appear in criminal prosecutions of officers under the federal Civil Rights Acts as interpreted by the Supreme Court in the *Screws* case.[35] In this landmark decision of 1945, which was the first Supreme Court interpretation of this Reconstruction statute, the high tribunal decided that in order to convict an officer it was necessary to show that the man had a "specific intent" to deprive the injured party of a federally protected right. In other words, it is conceivable that an officer might admit that he killed a person purely out of spite and still not be guilty of a violation of the federal criminal statute. It would be necessary for the prosecution to show, in addition to the fact that the person was killed, that the officer had the specific intent, for example, to interfere with the person's right to trial by jury.[36] So it is obvious that, along with more vigorous use of existing legal weapons imposing penalties on police officers, there should be reform of these laws.[37]

The Supervisor of Rights

One day during the summer of 1954, a young private walked into the office of a Fort Dix regimental Information and Education Section, where I was assigned.

The trainee said, "Sergeant Trebach, I'm in trouble and I don't know what to do. I'm afraid I'm going to kill somebody. Can you help me?"

After I asked what he meant, he explained, "I have very bad eyesight, but they are training me to be an infantryman. A few days ago, I was on a combat training range where the trainees fire their rifles in alternate lanes. As I was firing, other men were rushing forward in the lanes beside me. Just like in combat. I was supposedly providing covering fire. But when I went to shoot, I couldn't tell the target in my lane from the backs of the men in the lanes next to mine. I was about to shoot at a target, when it got up and ran."

"Have you told your company commander?" I inquired.

He replied that he hadn't been able to obtain an interview with the captain in charge of his unit but had complained to the ranking sergeant. The sergeant had been quite unsympathetic—an attitude somewhat to be expected, since many men can think of at least one good excuse for getting out of the infantry and usually communicate it to the company sergeant during their training period. Further questioning confirmed my belief that this trainee had exhausted all local remedies.

I picked up the telephone and called the lieutenant in charge of the Information and Education Section, who was then at regimental headquarters. "Sir, there's a trainee in the office who's on his way to the IG. Perhaps someone from regiment should speak to him before he goes," I said.

The lieutenant replied, "Hold him there. I'll be right down."

"What's the IG?" the young soldier asked as I put the telephone down.

I explained that he was the Inspector General. (There is an Inspector General who operates under the Chief of Staff of the Army. Units of the IG are found at almost every army post. They oversee all operations and can inquire into any activity, even if there has been no complaint. Supposedly, any soldier who so requests must be allowed to make a secret complaint to a representative of the IG. The very mention of the name is often enough to make errant commanders hew to the line of fairness—even though the IG has no prosecutive powers. But members of the IG do have the authority to report directly to the highest levels of command.)

Within minutes the lieutenant burst through the door and gave the trainee all the respect due a visiting congressman. The trainee did not go to the IG. The regiment solved this problem itself, after checking into the private's story.

A few weeks later, the soldier walked into my office smiling. He said, "Thanks a lot, Sergeant Trebach. I'm a cook now." There are many soldiers who will argue that this man with blurred vision could wreak more havoc on a kitchen range than on a firing range. Nevertheless, this story makes my point.

I have often speculated on the benefits of an agency of civilian government that could evoke such conditioned responses—and in the cause of individual rights. Of course, the objectives of the army Inspector General are quite different from the protection of the rights of civilians. Yet, there are important similarities between privates in the army and those who suffer abuse in private life.

Indeed, one of the major reasons why reform is so torturously slow in the process of criminal justice is the nature of the clientele. Those most affected by injustice or inefficiency in the criminal process are almost always socially powerless if not insignificant. They stand at the bottom of the social heap. They are the privates of society. They are not movers and manipulators. If they are maltreated, they are often tough enough to get up from the floor but not sophisticated or powerful enough to bring a complaint to the proper authorities and to fight it through successfully.

For this and other reasons, it sometimes seems as if wrongs, rather than rights, in the criminal process are institutionalized.

There are agencies at all levels of government in this country that are doing a creditable job in the field of individual rights. Two units in the national government are almost exclusively concerned with rights: the Civil Rights Division of the Department of Justice and the Commission on Civil Rights. Of these two, only the Civil Rights Division has clear authority to provide some form of relief in response to complaints of unconstitutional action against agents of justice. Its most potent weapon is a criminal prosecution against officers who have violated constitutional rights, by, for example, the use of brutality to coerce a confession. But, as I have already stated, the Civil Rights Acts, which provide the legal basis for such suits, are not effective remedies. In a recent two and one-half year period, there were only six federal convictions of officers on grounds of brutality [38]—a mere fraction of the probable total of such acts during those years. Prosecutions by state agencies for violations of state laws have been equally unsuccessful.[39]

If professional police and defender systems were established throughout the United States, they would go a long way toward institutionalizing freedom by preventing injustice from happening in the administration of criminal justice. But even these reforms would leave unfulfilled the need for a backstop to catch the ones that get away—the instances of injustice that are bound to happen under any system, and that are now happening by the millions under our present system of criminal justice.

A governmental institution that could fill this need would have the following qualities: Its major function would be to observe all governmental agencies within its jurisdiction as to their compliance with law, with basic fairness, and with the demands of efficiency. It would have unquestioned authority to demand full information concerning the activities of officials. It would be plugged directly into the highest levels of power. It would be so constituted and operated as to command universal respect—yes, even fear. In time, it might become a powerful force for the fair treatment of little people by big people.

All of this may impress my readers as the pipe dream of a professional liberal. But is it all a product of imagination? Not at all. A brief look at a Scandinavian institution shows a solid basis in fact, and suggests detailed methods for improving American practices.

In 1713 in Sweden the office of Chancellor of Justice, a representative of the king, was established to supervise the administration of justice and the observance of laws.[40] Finland established a generally similar office. With the adoption of its revised constitution of 1953, Denmark created a supervisor whose title is Ombudsman, or Parliamentary Commissioner for Civil and Military Government. In the *Wisconsin Law Review* of March, 1961, Danish Ombudsman Stephan Hurwitz described the operation of his office in detail.[41]

Hurwitz wrote, "The Parliamentary Commissioner's foremost duty is to provide control of the entire government administration [except judges and municipal administration]. His jurisdiction comprises ministers, civil servants, and all other persons acting in government service."[42] The Commissioner "has been given far-reaching powers."[43]

First, upon receipt of a complaint "or on his own initiative" he may "examine any civil or military activity performed in the service of the state."[44]

Second, "he may inspect any government office, and all who work in government service are obliged to furnish him with information and produce documents or records which he may require in the discharge of his duties."[45] Some exceptions are allowed regarding this power, such as information containing state secrets.

Third, if he finds that a minister or former minister of the cabinet has violated the law, the Ombudsman may make a suitable recommendation to Parliament for corrective action; but if such evidence concerns another, lesser-ranking official, "he may order the prosecuting authorities to institute a preliminary investigation and bring charges against the persons concerned before the ordinary courts." [46] And if he believes that a civil servant should be disciplined, the Ombudsman "may order the administrative authority concerned to institute a disciplinary investigation." [47] These three categories of power alone would have a beneficial effect on present American practices.

A fourth category of authority allows the Parliamentary Commissioner to "state his views on the matter to the person whom the complaint concerns." [48] This provides for informal negotiation, sometimes the best method for the correction of practices that threaten freedom. According to Ombudsman Hurwitz, this power "has proved to be of the greatest practical importance." [49] In the United States, U.S. Attorneys sometimes perform a mediative function with local justice officials, but the results have not been impressive.

Fifth, "the Commissioner may recommend that free legal aid be granted to a complainant who wishes to bring an action against a state authority." [50]

Significantly, the Commissioner "has no authority to change an administrative decision. His duty is to act as a supervisor of government administration and not as a special court of appeal. The administration is not obliged to follow his recommendations, but from the very beginning it has shown great deference to them, both in specific cases and general questions regarding administrative practice and procedure." [51]

It is of especial importance to the administration of justice that "any person who is deprived of his or her personal liberty has the right to address written communications in sealed envelopes to the Commissioner. This right has been used quite frequently." [52] Moreover, visits are made periodically to prisons and institutions where the inmates may have private interviews, if they wish. [53]

Conversely, it is extremely rare for an American official of, for example, the Department of Justice to make an uninvited trip to a state prison.

One of the largest categories of cases taken up for investigation by the Ombudsman involve "The Police and the Prosecuting Authorities." [54] Ombudsman Hurwitz explained: "In the Administration of Justice Act—primarily for the protection of . . . persons charged—there are a number of rules for the conduct of the police during the investigations of crimes. For example, there is the rule that the party charged, before being interrogated, shall be informed that he is not compelled to make a statement, and there are rules concerning procedure during seizure and search. The Commissioner has on several occasions criticized police who failed to comply with such rules, with the result that the prosecution authorities enjoined the police to observe the rules of seizure and search." [55]

"Summing up after five years' work," Mr. Hurwitz declared, "it may be said that the office of the Parliamentary Commissioner in Denmark has proved to be an institution acknowledged by all sections of the Danish community as a natural and beneficial unit in our democratic form of government." [56]

This, then, is the Ombudsman in Denmark. No such institution exists in this country. Could such agencies be created here?

There are at least four important differences between Denmark and this country. Denmark has a unitary system of government, while we have a federal system. At the national level, Denmark has a parliamentary system, while the United States has a presidential-congressional system. The population of Denmark has a relatively homogeneous character—especially regarding attitudes as to rights—compared with the United States. Finally, there is an immense difference in size, both in terms of geography and population, between the two countries. All of these differences could be used to dismiss any further consideration of the Ombudsman in the United States.

But differences between countries do not mean that one cannot learn from the other. There is no substantive reason why agencies with many of the functions of the Ombudsman could not be created in this country. A supervisor of rights could be created by act of Congress or by a Presidential order for the purpose of supervising federal officials. Such an official would examine not only the activities of federal officials vis-à-vis the citizen, but also the enforcement of federal laws against state officials who have violated citizens' rights. He could also directly supervise state agencies as to their observance of federally guaranteed rights. The Scandinavian models provide detailed guides for both this federal agency and also for similar agencies in every state—which would exist primarily to supervise the enforcement of rights guaranteed by state constitutions and laws.

Epilogue:
The Injured and the Indignant

Solon's ancient prescription to secure justice in Athens was "Those who are not injured [must] feel as indignant as those who are."

But one of the stumbling blocks for social improvement throughout history has been that those best in a position to redress invasions of rights rarely have their own rights invaded. They are rarely injured, even more rarely indignant. Of course, when rights violations are obvious and flagrant, they are more apt to make indignant those people not directly affected.

A major impediment to reforms in the administration of criminal justice today is that the defects are almost invisible to influential members of our society. Even lawyers, as a group, do not appreciate the terrible social portent contained in many present practices—for few lawyers practice in the criminal courts. Fewer still have ever been arrested, subjected to the third degree, and prosecuted for a crime.

The great mass of liberals in America, whatever their

profession, simply seem incapable of working up a sweat, even in intellectual terms, over indignities and denials of rights in the process of criminal justice. My less phlegmatic attitude, I am sure, results from the fact that my work on criminal justice has involved, not only theoretical research, but also hundreds of face-to-face contacts with those who have felt the sting of state power. I do not think about criminal justice only in terms of Supreme Court decisions or constitutional concepts or in terms of opinions generally held by those who are living comfortably ignorant lives, but rather in terms of people I have known—some "good," some "bad," but all deserving of civilized concern: The widow in a backwoods Georgia county whose husband had been lynched by local policemen. The lifer in the New Jersey State Prison who, when I asked why he was in prison, barely was able to mumble that he had drowned his infant son in a pail of water while drunk—a man who cannot be punished enough in his own eyes. The retired policeman in Detroit who, amazingly enough, had himself twice been subjected to police brutality. The sixteen-year-old boy in the New Jersey Bordentown Reformatory who had somehow gone wrong and had committed a series of crimes, which he freely admitted to me; his major worry on the day I spoke to him was how to fend off the many homosexual advances of fellow inmates.

Millions of American citizens live in a constitutional underworld that is almost everywhere found beneath the quasi-constitutional world in which most of us live. It is an underworld because it is hidden from the sight of most Americans. The underworld dweller may, at any given time, be arrested on suspicion and spend a night in jail. Once arrested and accused of a specific crime, the man of low social standing may be held in a detention cell by the police for days before they get ready to move in his case. The dweller in this risky world knows that the odds are a bit too high for comfort that he may suffer police violence, either at the time of arrest or later while being interrogated. If prosecuted, the underworld dweller may know that a "state" lawyer will appear for him and perhaps provide a perfunctory defense. And once placed in prison, the underprivileged citizen will find it extremely difficult even to talk to a lawyer.

Despite these distressing facts—and they are facts beyond dispute—whenever it is proposed that we increase the protection of the rights of those accused of crime, the cry is instantly raised that criminals will go free, and that the jobs of policemen and prosecutors are difficult enough under present conditions. I agree that we should fight crime, but this fight by society must be carried on within the boundaries of the Constitution and fair play. As the Supreme Court of the United States pointed out some two decades ago: "History teaches us that there have been but few infringements of personal liberty by the state which have not been justified . . . in the name of righteousness and the public good." The argument against greater protection for the rights of the accused reduces itself to an argument for violation of the law in order to enforce it. It is a crime to violate the rights of any person. Yet, well-trained officials can usually catch and convict criminals without, in the process, becoming criminals themselves.

A most shocking fact is that if all violations by policemen and other officials of the agencies of justice are counted, many, perhaps the majority, of those "injured" are innocent. But whether the victims are innocent of any crime or guilty of the most heinous acts, in the final accounting we protect not only persons but a *system* of rights that makes our society better than it would be without it. And, when more fully observed, this system will help make our society a "good" one.

It would benefit American society immensely, therefore, if those who live in the world of the country club and the six-bedroom ranch house were indignantly aware of the stakes in the game now silently played in the constitutional underworld. The support of influential though uninjured people is vital to enlightened reforms in the administration of American criminal justice and thereby in our society as a whole.

Note on Convict Interviews

Interviews with convicts provide a view of the criminal process that is unique. I did not start out with a plan to interview prisoners about their cases, but intended to observe court proceedings and to contact judges, lawyers, policemen, and other agents of criminal justice. As the work slowly progressed, it seemed natural that I should ask some questions of the main actors in the criminal process—the defendants. Since it was not possible to interview defendants while their cases were in progress, I interviewed former defendants who were prisoners.

Initially I was doubtful that the prisoners would tell me anything significant, and I was quite prepared to hear a succession of biased and untrue stories. I asked myself, "How can a man in prison be objective about the people and the process that put him there?" It turned out that, to an extent, my doubts were justified. Many of the men did tell me biased stories, for it *is* impossible for a man to be completely objective about the process that put him behind bars. The saving feature for my research was that almost every prisoner had one grievance that stuck out in his mind above all the others, that acted as a lightning rod for his complaints. In the overwhelming majority of cases, the lightning rod was the length of sentence. Few prisoners will sit back in their chairs and judiciously pronounce that, in light of all the circumstances, the sentence they received was harsh but proper.

On most questions, however, I found no patterns of group bias that would distort the mass picture presented by the prisoner responses. Many prisoners displayed an objective attitude on numerous questions regarding rights, perhaps because their expectations as to the protection of their rights were not high—or because they were ignorant of their rights, like the man who thought the police had a right to use violence in order to extract information from a suspect. Others were able to distinguish between a proper use of violence and violence that was unnecessary. When I asked one prisoner, during an interview in 1957, how he had been treated by the police, he replied, "O.K. Except that they shot me here." He pointed at a spot just below his heart but then went on to explain, without rancor, that he had stolen a policeman's gun and had tried to escape from a police station, and that in the ensuing fight he had been shot.

The individual stories of each convict were not as important as the patterns of official action revealed by the answers of large numbers of prisoners. (Only those individual stories were related in the text that were representative of a pattern.) On many questions there were remarkable similarities between the responses of men from a particular county, and those responses of men arrested by a particular police force. Therefore, the effect of individual convicts' giving untruthful answers to individual questions was greatly reduced.

Interview Techniques

All of the interviews with convicts took place within the walls of a prison. In the 1957 interviews the prisoners were questioned individually, and their names were recorded. Because I wished to obtain more data, the 1959 interviews were handled in groups of from fifteen to fifty. During these group interviews, I stood at the front of the room and explained the form, question by question. The men filled in the answers themselves and were told not to sign their names unless they wished to do so.

I was gratified by the rapport and air of frankness that generally prevailed in my discussions with the convicts. During my opening words to them I took great pains to establish that atmosphere. I said that I had no official position (which was, of course, true at that time), that all answers would be voluntary on their part, and that after I was finished with the introductory talk, anyone who wished could leave the room. (Approximately 10 per cent of the total number brought to the interview room did so.) Moreover, I told them that I had no illusions about the characters of many of those sitting there: "Some of you may be among the worst S.O.B.'s that ever walked the face of the earth, but I'm not interested in that. I want to find out what happened in your cases and to see if your rights were violated in any way. This probably isn't going to do you a bit of good, but it might help some guy who comes along the same path later." I used the same approach when questions were asked. For example, during a mass interview in 1959, a prisoner complained that he had been unfairly sentenced to a term of ten to twelve years for armed robbery. After listening to the facts, which indicated that his partner had fired his weapon during the course of the robbery, I said, "While I do not like to see anyone receive a sentence of that length, you might have killed some poor fellow who was sitting in that bar minding his own business drinking a beer. You're lucky that you're not pushing up daisies." He was upset somewhat by my reply, but the other prisoners in the room immediately expressed sentiments similar to mine and in much stronger language.

The questionnaires of some men were eliminated when I concluded from the answers that they had not understood my questions. This lack of comprehension arose from a variety of reasons: because of emotional disturbances, exceptionally low intelligence, or inability to understand the English language. The final total of usable questionnaires was 359, divided among the institutions as follows:

New Jersey State Prison, Trenton, New Jersey	146
New Jersey State Reformatory, Bordentown, New Jersey	99
Holmesburg Prison, Philadelphia, Pennsylvania	39
United States Penitentiary, Lewisburg, Pennsylvania	75
TOTAL	359

Two matters should be clarified at this point. First, most of the men were selected by prison officials although I selected some from a convict register. Ideally, of course, they should have been selected by a completely scientific random process. Had it been felt that there was enough to be gained, that procedure would have been followed. But since this was not a study of the prison but of events that occurred before the men came to prison, there seemed little reason for prison officials to attempt to stack the deck. My general impression of the prison officials encountered was that they were high-minded men of good faith. It is my belief that they followed my request to select men "at random" from the prison population. Even if the men brought to the interview room were those who would present a favorable picture of the police and the courts, this only suggests that the edge of criticism in this study should have been even sharper.

Second, the fact that some men were allowed to leave the room without being interviewed suggests that a piece of the criminal universe was not explored. The reason for this procedure was the hope that the number of truthful responses would thereby be increased. Every man who remained to answer the questionnaire was a volunteer. The guards could have made the reluctant prisoners stay, but they couldn't or wouldn't have forced them to answer the questions truthfully. Moreover, an air of compulsion would have destroyed the rapport that I tried to build with each man and with each group of men.

May it be said that the 245 prisoners interviewed in New Jersey were typical of other prisoners in the state? All of the other evidence available—and it is to be emphasized again that the prisoners represented only *one* source of information for this study—suggests that these men in many respects were typical. Moreover, the comparisons between these statistics and official statistics on age, race, and offense in Items 1, 2, and 3, while revealing some differences, do not show any disparities that would markedly alter the picture of the criminal process presented by these men.

Methods of Calculation

For most questions the prisoners were asked to check their preference of answers that were printed on the questionnaire. But in a few cases only the questions were provided, and the men were asked to write out their answers. These answers were later placed in categories. For example, in Item 12, B, the prisoners were asked to explain why they had confessed. Their answers were then analyzed and placed in categories such as "Thought I had to answer, and/or ignorant of rights," "No explanation," "Violence," and so on.

The statistics in the tables have been rounded off into whole numbers, with the exception of Item 23, wherein fractions might have some value. I did this to drive home the point that the purpose of these statistics is to provide some new quantifiable data regarding broad trends in the criminal process. The statistical part of this study was not conducted like the opinion polls that attempt to predict elections. As the presidential "cliff-hanger" of 1960 proves, the calculations to the right of the decimal point are of more than passing interest in such statistical ventures. That is not the case in this study.

For the sake of consistency, all of the percentages were made to add up to 100. This produced slight inconsistencies, which arose from the fact that all figures were rounded off into whole numbers. For example, if the responses to a question were 20, 20, and 20, the percentages were calculated as 33, 33, and 34 (rather than 33).

Appendix A

Appendix A

Statistical Tabulations of Prisoners' Responses

I. GENERAL INFORMATION

Item 1. AGES OF PRISONERS

	Sample Interviewed	Official Statistics *
A. New Jersey State Prison		
Mean	32	41
Median	27	41
Number of prisoners included in calculations	(137)	(100)
B. New Jersey State Reformatory, Bordentown		
Mean	22	28
Median	20	28
Number of prisoners included in calculations	(97)	(100)

* In questions 1, 2, and 3, the official New Jersey statistics come from a random sample compiled for this study by the Department of Institutions and Agencies, State of New Jersey; the official Philadelphia statistics come from the Department of Public Welfare, *Philadelphia Prisons, Annual Report, 1959;* and the official federal statistics come from the Bureau of Prisons, *Federal Prisons, 1959* (El Reno, Oklahoma: Bureau of Prisons, 1960).

Item 1 (continued)

	Sample Interviewed	Official Statistics *
C. Philadelphia Prisoners		
Mean	34	(Not
Median	49	available)
Number of prisoners included in calculations	(100)	
D. Federal Prisoners		
Mean	31	31
Median	26	26
Number of prisoners included in calculations	(75)	(33,669)

Item 2. RACE

	State Prisoners (New Jersey and Philadelphia)		Federal Prisoners	
	Official Statistics	Sample Interviewed	Official Statistics	Sample Interviewed
	PERCENTAGES			
White	54	52	70	49
Nonwhite	46	47	30	44
Did not answer	0	1	0	7
TOTAL	100	100	100	100
Number of prisoners	(200)	(284)	(17,281)	(75)

Item 3.   OFFENSES *

A.   New Jersey Prisoners

	Official Statistics	Sample Interviewed
	PERCENTAGES	
Homicide	7	5
Robbery	22	17
Rape and sex crimes	7	7
Atrocious assault and battery	7	5
Burglary	26	26
Larceny	10	10
Narcotics	5	8
Others	16	22
Did not answer	0	0
TOTAL	100	100
Number of prisoners	(200)	(245)

B.   Federal Prisoners

	Official Statistics	Sample Interviewed
	PERCENTAGES	
Larceny	28	28
Drugs	8	12
Forgery	10	16
Immigration	9	1
Juvenile delinquency	5	0
Liquor laws	14	7
Others	26	29
Did not answer	0	7
TOTAL	100	100
Number of prisoners	(17,281)	(75)

* Information not available for Philadelphia prisoners.

Item 4. EDUCATION: HIGHEST GRADE COMPLETED

All Prisoners

PERCENTAGES

No school	0
Grades 1–6	12
7–9	38
10–12	39
College 1–2	4
3–4	2
Graduate work	0
Did not answer	5
TOTAL	100

Number of prisoners (359)

Item 5. NORMAL OCCUPATION

All Prisoners

PERCENTAGES

Professional	Less than 1
Skilled	11
Semiskilled	54
Unskilled	19
Agriculture	1
Other	2
No normal occupation	3
Did not answer	10
TOTAL	100

Number of prisoners (359)

Item 6. FINAL PLEA TO CHARGE

	New Jersey Prisoners	Phila- delphia Prisoners	Federal Prisoners	Total
		PERCENTAGES		
Guilty	36	38	74	44
Non vult or *nolo contendere*	46	3	0	32
Not guilty	18	59	21	23
Did not answer	Less than 1	0	5	1
TOTAL	100	100	100	100
Number of prisoners	(245)	(39)	(75)	(359)

Item 7. TRIAL

	New Jersey Prisoners	Phila- delphia Prisoners	Federal Prisoners	Total
		PERCENTAGES		
Yes	19	67	32	27
No	79	33	63	70
Did not answer	2	0	5	3
TOTAL	100	100	100	100
Number of prisoners	(245)	(39)	(75)	(359)

Item 8. GUILT OR INNOCENCE

"What do you now have to say about your guilt or innocence?"

	New Jersey State Prison	New Jersey State Reformatory	Philadelphia Prison	Federal Prison	Total
			PERCENTAGES		
"Claim complete innocence of crime for which convicted this time"	23	14	31	16	20
"Admit I committed the acts charged, but there were special circumstances in my case which should be considered, such as the fact that I was drunk, that the other guy insulted me, that I got angry for a few seconds, that I had no real criminal intent, and so on"	45	38	46	37	42
"Admit I committed the acts charged; no sad story, no song and dance that I had no criminal intent. I knew damned well what I was doing"	30	43	23	40	34
Did not answer	2	5	0	7	4
TOTAL	100	100	100	100	100
Number of prisoners	(146)	(99)	(39)	(75)	(359)

II. THE POLICE

Item 9. INCOMMUNICADO DETENTION

	New Jersey Prisoners	Philadelphia Prisoners	Federal Prisoners	Total
		PERCENTAGES		
Requested to make outside contact				
But not allowed to contact anyone	30	18	21	27
Told by police in effect, "No outside contacts until after statement or confession is signed"	20	10	3	16
Were allowed to contact relative or attorney	27	62	49	35
Did not request to make outside contact and was not advised that he could	16	8	16	15
Did not answer	7	2	11	7
TOTAL	100	100	100	100
Number of prisoners	(245)	(39)	(75)	(359)

Item 10. KNOWLEDGE OF RIGHTS

"If you had been asked the following question at the time of your arrest in this case, how would you have answered:
'When you are arrested and questioned by the police, what does the law require that you tell them?'"

	All Prisoners
	PERCENTAGES
Nothing	32
Personal information only, nothing about alleged offense	23
Every question they ask, including signed statement	24
Every question they ask, but no signed statement	1
Don't know	17
Did not answer	3
TOTAL	100
Number of prisoners	(359)

Item 11. RESPONSES TO POLICE INTERROGATION

"What did you, in fact, tell the police when they questioned you in this case?"

	All Prisoners
	PERCENTAGES
Nothing	16
Personal information only, nothing about alleged offense	17
Every question they asked, including signed statement	44

Item 11 *(continued)*

	All Prisoners
	PERCENTAGES
Every question they asked, but did not sign statement	15
Some questions—not all—and signed statement	2
Did not answer	6
TOTAL	100
Number of prisoners	(359)

Item 12. CONFESSIONS AND REASONS FOR MAKING THEM

A. "If, in the last question, you stated that you answered every question and signed a statement, does this mean that you signed a written confession for the police to the offenses charged?"

	New Jersey Prisoners	Phila-delphia Prisoners	Federal Prisoners	Total
	PERCENTAGES			
Yes	53	15	51	48
No °	22	31	19	22
Did not answer °	25	54	30	30
TOTAL	100	100	100	100
Number of prisoners	(245)	(39)	(75)	(359)

° Many of the 185 prisoners who answered "no" or did not answer this question responded on Item 11 that they had told the police "nothing" or "nothing about alleged offense."

B. *Reasons for Confession*

	New Jersey Prisoners	Phila-delphia Prisoners	Federal Prisoners	Total
		PERCENTAGES		
No coercion claimed				
Police caught me red-handed or had solid case against me	12	0	39	18
Confederate had already confessed and implicated me	15	0	0	11
Felt badly about crime and did not want to hide it, or wanted to speed up trial	11	83	24	16
Thought I had to answer and/or ignorant of rights	2	17	11	5
Felt no crime committed	3	0	0	2
No explanation for confession	19	0	13	17
Coercion claimed				
Violence by police	22	0	5	18
Threat of violence by police	5	0	0	3
Resistance weak due to intoxication, dope, long questioning, or psychological pressure	11	0	8	10
Did not answer	0	0	0	0
TOTAL	100	100	100	100
Number of prisoners	(130)	(6)	(38)	(174)

Item 13. TREATMENT BY POLICE

A. *Kind of Treatment*

"How were you treated by the police?"

	New Jersey Prisoners	Phila- delphia Prisoners	Federal Prisoners	Total
		PERCENTAGES		
Treated well, no complaint	41	56	70	49
Threat of violence	25	38	11	24
Violence ("actually hit you")	29	3	11	22
Did not answer	5	3	8	5
TOTAL	100	100	100	100
Number of prisoners	(245)	(39)	(75)	(359)

B. *Reason for Such Treatment*

"If the police threatened violence or actually hit you, did they do so to force you to sign a confession?"

	New Jersey Prisoners	Phila- delphia Prisoners	Federal Prisoners	Total
		PERCENTAGES		
Yes	70	56	44	66
No	30	44	56	34
Did not answer	0	0	0	0
TOTAL	100	100	100	100
Number of prisoners	(132)	(16)	(16)	(164)

Item 14. TREATMENT BY SPECIFIC POLICE AGENCIES

A. "How were you treated by the police?"

	Newark	Jersey City	Paterson	New Jersey Cities	New Jersey Cities	New Jersey State Police	New Jersey County Detectives	Philadelphia	Federal Bureau of Investigation Agencies	Military Agencies	Other Federal Civilian Agencies
Population in thousands (1950 Census)	438	299	139	60–130	less than 60	—	—	2,071	—	—	—
					PERCENTAGES						
Treated well, no complaint	22	0	15	39	47	36	47	56	96	33	80
Threat of violence	26	13	31	27	20	36	23	42	0	33	0
Violence ("actually hit you")	52	87	46	31	15	28	15	2	0	17	20
Did not answer	0	0	8	3	18	0	15	0	4	17	0
TOTAL	100	100	100	100	100	100	100	100	100	100	100
Number of prisoners	(27)	(8)	(13)	(33)	(68)	(25)	(13)	(36)	(25)	(12)	(20)

A total of 70 prisoners failed to adequately identify the police agency.

B. *"If the police threatened violence or actually hit you, did they do so to force you to sign a confession?"*

	Newark	Jersey City	Paterson	New Jersey Cities	New Jersey Cities	New Jersey State Police	New Jersey County Detectives	Philadelphia	Federal Bureau of Investigation Agencies	Military Agencies	Other Federal Civilian Agencies
Population in thousands (1950 Census)	438	299	139	60–130	less than 60	—	—	2,071	—	—	—
					PERCENTAGES						
Yes	71	75	90	69	92	81	40	56	0	50	50
No	19	0	10	26	8	13	60	44	0	33	50
Did not answer	10	25	0	5	0	6	0	0	0	17	0
TOTAL	100	100	100	100	100	100	100	100	0	100	100
Number of prisoners	(21)	(8)	(10)	(19)	(24)	(16)	(5)	(16)	(24)	(6)	(4)

Item 15. INSTRUCTIONS AND ADVICE BY POLICE

A. *"Did the police tell you that you did not have to answer any of their questions?"*

	State Prisoners	Federal Prisoners	Total
	PERCENTAGES		
Yes	16	40	21
No	77	52	72
Did not answer	7	8	7
TOTAL	100	100	100
Number of prisoners	(284)	(75)	(359)

B. *"Did the police tell you that you could hire an attorney while in their custody?"*

	State Prisoners	Federal Prisoners	Total
	PERCENTAGES		
Yes	18	32	20
No	77	64	75
Did not answer	5	4	5
TOTAL	100	100	100
Number of prisoners	(284)	(75)	(359)

Item 16. SUGGESTIONS REGARDING ATTORNEY OR BONDSMAN

"Did policemen, court officers, or jail guards suggest that you hire a certain attorney or bondsman in this case?"

	State Prisoners	Federal Prisoners	Total
	PERCENTAGES		
Yes	15	5	13
No	74	83	76
Did not answer	11	12	11
TOTAL	100	100	100
Number of prisoners	(284)	(75)	(359)

III. PRELIMINARY EXAMINATION

Item 17. STATEMENTS AT PRELIMINARY EXAMINATION

"In this case, what did you say at the 'first hearing'?"

	All prisoners
	PERCENTAGES
Pleaded guilty only	23
Pleaded not guilty only	34
Pleaded guilty and related facts of crime	7
Pleaded not guilty and denied guilt in testimony	Less than 1
Not given opportunity to talk by judge or commissioner	10
Did not answer	26
TOTAL	100
Number of prisoners	(359)

Item 18. KNOWLEDGE OF RIGHT
TO RETAIN COUNSEL

"Did you know at the time that you had the right to hire a lawyer to talk for you at that first hearing?"

All prisoners

	PERCENTAGES
Yes	62
No	23
Did not answer	15
TOTAL	100
Number of prisoners	(359)

Item 19. COUNSEL AT PRELIMINARY
EXAMINATION

A. "Did you hire counsel for that hearing?"

All prisoners

	PERCENTAGES
Yes	21
No	54
Did not answer	25
TOTAL	100
Number of prisoners	(359)

Item 19 (*continued*)

B. *"Did the judge or United States Commissioner at that first hearing assign a lawyer to help you?"*

	All prisoners
	PERCENTAGES
Yes	10
No	68
Did not answer	22
TOTAL	100
Number of prisoners	(359)

IV. COUNSEL

Item 20. TYPE OF COUNSEL

	New Jersey Prisoners	Philadelphia Prisoners	Federal Prisoners	Total
		PERCENTAGES		
Retained	34	56	34	36
Assigned	46	8	40	40
Assigned:				
Legal aid organization	0	28	7	5
Waived, no counsel	16	5	12	14
Other answers *	4	3	7	5
	Less than			Less than
Did not answer	1	0	0	1
TOTAL	100	100	100	100
Number of prisoners	(245)	(39)	(75)	(359)

* Other answers broken down as follows:

No counsel, but did not waive counsel	7
No counsel, no further explanation	3
Assigned counsel, but I gave him money	1
Had counsel, no further information given	5

Item 21. SUGGESTIONS BY LAWYER REGARDING PLEA

"If your lawyer suggested that you plead guilty, non vult, or nolo, during what interview did he do so? (First, second, etc.?)"

All Prisoners: According to Type of Counsel				
Interview	Assigned	Assigned (Legal aid organization)	Retained	Total
	PERCENTAGES			
First	34	50	17	27
Second	18	13	25	21
Third	3	0	5	4
Fourth	1	0	5	2
Fifth and above	1	0	2	1
Did not answer	43	37	49	45
TOTAL	100	100	100	100
Number of prisoners	(145)	(16)	(131)	(292)

Item 22. PROSECUTION-DEFENSE NEGOTIATIONS

A. *"Did you or your lawyer talk or bargain with the prosecution (with detectives, county prosecutors, probation officers, etc.) with the idea of making a deal over some part of this case?"*

	All prisoners
	PERCENTAGES
Yes	30
No	40
Did not answer	30
TOTAL	100
Number of prisoners	(359)

Item 22 (continued)

B.   "If yes, during the talk over the deal, did the prosecution suggest that you waive either indictment, trial, or the right to counsel and that you plead guilty in return for some favor?"

	All prisoners
	PERCENTAGES
Yes	90
No	10
Did not answer	0
TOTAL	100
Number of prisoners	(107)

C.   "If answer was yes to question B, what was the favor or consideration offered by the prosecution?"

	All prisoners
	PERCENTAGES
Drop certain charges completely	39
Reduce certain charges to lesser offense	13
Suggest to the judge lower sentence than maximum	33
Suggest to the judge or probation officer that he be put on the street on probation	15
Did not answer	0
TOTAL	100
Number of prisoners	(96)

V. TIME INTERVALS

Item 23. TIME INTERVALS BETWEEN ARREST AND FURTHER ACTION

	New Jersey Prisoners			Philadelphia Prisoners			Federal Prisoners		
	Mean Average	Median Average	Number of Prisoners	Mean Average	Median Average	Number of Prisoners	Mean Average	Median Average	Number of Prisoners
A. "How many days between arrest and the first time that you had a private interview with your lawyer?"									
Retained counsel	3.94	less than 1	72	13.88	7	16	16.88	7.50	16
Assigned counsel	56.89	35	100	81.67	95	3	35.26	15.00	23
Assigned Counsel: Legal aid organization	—	—	—	18.40	20	10	31.50	29.00	4
Combined averages	36.95	15	172	22.45	15	29	27.00	15.00	43

	New Jersey Prisoners			Philadelphia Prisoners			Federal Prisoners		
	Mean Average	Median Average	Number of Prisoners	Mean Average	Median Average	Number of Prisoners	Mean Average	Median Average	Number of Prisoners
B. "How many days between arrest and original plea in the big court (*trial-level court, county court, district court,* etc.)?"	81.71	65	210	55.61	25	38	41.26	25.00	57
C. "How many days between arrest and first court hearing (the preliminary examination)?"	6.58	4	163	1.13	less than 1	30	2.30	less than 1	29*
D. "How many days between arrest and trial, if any, in the big court?"	178.08	150	39	145.91	125	22	60.42	65.00	19

* Figures for 23 C exclude military cases.

VI. JAIL AND PRISON CONDITIONS

Item 24. TREATMENT: COUNTY JAIL
VS. PRISON

"Where were you treated better, in the jail where you waited around to enter your final plea (or for your trial) or in this prison?"

	New Jersey Prisoners	Philadelphia Prisoners	Federal Prisoners	Total
		PERCENTAGES		
Jail	5	0	9	5
This prison	59	77	55	60
Treated the same	5	3	9	6
Did not answer	31	20	27	29
TOTAL	100	100	100	100
Number of prisoners	(245)	(39)	(75)	(359)

Appendix B

MODEL DEFENDER ACT

Drafted by the

NATIONAL CONFERENCE OF COMMISSIONERS ON UNIFORM STATE LAWS

AND BY IT APPROVED AT ITS

ANNUAL CONFERENCE
MEETING IN ITS SIXTY-EIGHTH YEAR
AT MIAMI BEACH, FLORIDA

AUGUST 17–22, 1959

WITH PREFATORY NOTE AND COMMENTS

The Committee which acted for the National Conference of Commissioners on Uniform State Laws in preparing the Model Defender Act was as follows:

JAMES K. NORTHAM, 827 Lemcke Bldg., Indianapolis, Ind., *Chairman*.
F. REED DICKERSON, Indiana University Law School, Bloomington, Ind.

ROBERT J. FARLEY, School of Law, University, Miss.

ARIE POLDERVAART, University of New Mexico Law School, Albuquerque, N.M.

HOMER B. HARRIS, Lincoln, Ill., *Chairman, Section B.*

Copies of all Uniform and Model Acts and other printed matter issued by the Conference may be obtained from

NATIONAL CONFERENCE OF COMMISSIONERS ON
UNIFORM STATE LAWS
1155 East Sixtieth Street
Chicago 37, Illinois

[The Prefatory Note to the Model Defender Act
has been omitted. A.S.T.]

MODEL DEFENDER ACT °

[Be it enacted. . . .]

1   SECTION 1. In any county [the appropriate governing au-
2   thority] may establish the office of public defender. A county
3   may join with one or more other counties to establish one office
4   of public defender to serve those counties.

COMMENT

Provision for securing counsel for indigents charged with criminal offenses has been accomplished in various patterns:

1. By statute setting up the office
   a. as mandatory for every county;

° The National Conference of Commissioners on Uniform State Laws in the promulgation of its Uniform Acts urges, with the endorsement of the American Bar Association, their enactment in each jurisdiction. Where there is a demand for an Act covering the subject matter in a substantial number of the states, but where in the judgment of the National Conference of Commissioners on Uniform State Laws it is not a subject upon which uniformity between the states is necessary or desirable, but where it would be helpful to have legislation which would tend toward uniformity where enacted, Acts on such subjects are promulgated as Model Acts.

    b. as permissive for every county;

    c. as mandatory in counties of a stated population and permissive for others.

2. Appointment by the court in individual cases with compensation

    a. under legislative scale;

    b. fixed by the appointing court.

3. By legal aid and defender organizations in certain municipalities supported by public funds, private philanthropy, or both.

It seems wise, therefore, to create the office by an enabling act with the county as the appropriate unit, so that local requirements and wishes can be carried out.

Throughout the act, the county is made the governmental unit. In some jurisdictions this will necessarily require changes.

1   SECTION 2.

2   (a) The public defender shall be a qualified attorney licensed
3   to practice in this state selected by [the appropriate appointing
4   authority]. He shall represent, without charge, each indigent
5   person who is under arrest or charged with a crime, if:

6   (1) the defendant requests it; or

7   (2) the court, on its own motion or otherwise, so orders and
8   the defendant does not affirmatively reject of record the op-
9   portunity to be so represented.

10   (b) Before arraignment the determination of indigency may
11   be made by the public defender. At or after arraignment the
12   determination shall be made by the court.

COMMENT

It is recognized that the criminal codes of the several states vary widely with respect to what specific acts constitute offenses against the state. Therefore, it should be left to each jurisdiction to determine what crimes are to be covered in this act.

Careful thought should be given to the method of selecting the public defender. A method other than by election will shield the public defender from the hazards and expense of campaigning for office. In some jurisdictions, a judicial selection is made; in others, the public defender is chosen by the legislative division. Sometimes he is under civil service.

If local conditions are such that election of the public defender must be the method of selection in order to get the bill passed, additional safeguards may be set up.

Many lawyers who have studied the various defender systems feel that the method of selecting the official is the key to the success of the plan. The objective, whatever the method, is to make certain that not only a qualified lawyer holds the position but that he will also have the independence to serve his clients with complete professional loyalty.

Former drafts embodied the thinking that it was appropriate to pattern the office after its so-called counterpart, the office of the prosecuting attorney, and subject to the same restrictions respecting salary, private practice, etc. Debate has shown this provision to be inelastic, difficult to create, and provocative of controversy.

1   SECTION 3.

2   (a) The term and compensation of the public defender shall
3   be fixed by [the appropriate governing authority].
4   (b) The public defender may appoint as many assistant at-
5   torneys, clerks, investigators, stenographers, and other employ-
6   ees as [the appropriate governing authority] considers neces-
7   sary to enable him to carry out his responsibilities. Appoint-
8   ments under this section shall be made in the manner prescribed
9   by [the appropriate governing authority]. An assistant attorney
10   must be a qualified attorney licensed to practice in this state.
11   (c) The compensation of persons appointed under subsection
12   (b) shall be fixed by [the appropriate governing authority].

COMMENT

This section should be flexible enough to cover jurisdictions of varying size and population, as some counties may need only a part-time defender while others may require more than one lawyer and additional clerks, etc., on the staff. In the more populous counties, the effectiveness of the office will be greatly reduced unless there is provision for an investigator.

1   SECTION 4. When representing an indigent person, the pub-
2   lic defender shall (1) counsel and defend him, whether he is held
3   in custody without commitment or charged with a criminal
4   offense, at every stage of the proceedings following arrest; and
5   (2) prosecute any appeals or other remedies before or after con-
6   viction that he considers to be in the interest of justice.

COMMENT

This wide authority is given to permit the defender to represent indigent clients at every stage of the proceedings and to appear for those charged with felonies and misdemeanors. One of the chief criticisms of the assigned counsel system is that the defendant's lawyer is selected too late in the proceedings to render the most effective service. Too, there are many situations where indigent defendants with misdemeanor charges need a lawyer as much as those facing more serious offenses. This is particularly true where the defendant is young or is a first offender, and in jurisdictions where misdemeanors carry a heavy penalty.

1   SECTION 5. For cause, the court may, on its own motion or
2 upon the application of the public defender or the indigent
3 person, appoint an attorney other than the public defender to
4 represent him at any stage of the proceedings or on appeal. The
5 attorney shall be awarded reasonable compensation and reim-
6 bursement for expenses necessarily incurred, to be fixed by the
7 court and paid by the county.

COMMENT

It seems desirable to provide a plan for handling those cases where a conflict of interest or other legitimate reason makes it desirable to appoint counsel other than the public defender.

1   SECTION 6. The public defender shall make an annual report
2 to [the appropriate governing authority] covering all cases
3 handled by his office during the preceding year.

COMMENT

This requirement is self-explanatory. The justification of the office as well as a history of its efficiency makes this regulation a requisite.

1   SECTION 7. The [appropriate administrative official] shall
2 provide office space, furniture, equipment, and supplies for the
3 use of the public defender suitable for the conduct of the busi-
4 ness of his office. However, [the appropriate governing author-
5 ity] may provide for an allowance in place of facilities. Each
6 such item is a charge against the county in which the services
7 were rendered. If the public defender serves more than one
8 county, expenses that are properly allocable to the business of
9 more than one of those counties shall be pro-rated among the
10 counties concerned.

COMMENT

If the defender serves more than one county, the last two sentences are
desirable to clarify the division of cost and expense.

1   SECTION 8. If [the appropriate governing authority] deter-
2 mines not to create the office of public defender, then it may, at
3 county expense, either:
4   (1) authorize the court to provide the services prescribed
5 by this Act by appointing a qualified attorney in each case and
6 awarding him reasonable compensation and expenses; or
7   (2) arrange to provide those services through nonprofit legal
8 aid or defender organizations.

1   SECTION 9. This Act may be cited as the Model Defender
2 Act.

CHAPTER 1

The Police: Arrest and Detention

1. National Commission on Law Observance and Enforcement, *Report on Lawlessness in Law Enforcement* (Washington, D.C.: U.S. Government Printing Office, 1931), p. 4.

2. *1961 United States Commission on Civil Rights Report*, Book 5: *Justice* (Washington, D.C.: U.S. Government Printing Office, 1961), hereafter cited as *Commission Justice Report*.

3. State education officials may challenge policemen for this dubious honor, since, for example, it appears that thousands of school children are still denied the right to a nonsegregated education. *1961 United States Commission on Civil Rights Report*, Book 2: *Education* (Washington, D.C.: U.S. Government Printing Office, 1961), p. 176.

4. A broad study of this subject is presented in Ernest W. Machen, Jr., *The Law of Arrest* (Chapel Hill: Institute of Government, University of North Carolina, 1950). For a discussion of the law of arrest in New Jersey, see Albert J. Klein, *Criminal Law*

in New Jersey (New Brunswick, N.J.: Rutgers University Press, 1953), pp. 185 ff., and *State* v. *Williams,* 29 N.J. 27, 148 A.2d 22 (1959).

5. The main reason for not asking prisoners about arrests on suspicion was that I felt they could provide little usable data on this practice, which sometimes involves a very delicate exercise of judgment by the police officer.

6. Federal Bureau of Investigation, *Uniform Crime Reports—1960* (Washington, D.C.: U.S. Government Printing Office, 1961), p. 90.

7. *Id.* at 31.

8. *Id.* at 90.

9. This is a study by Harold Norris entitled "Arrests Without Warrant," published in the October, 1958, issue of *The Crisis Magazine* and reproduced in *Hearings Before the United States Commission on Civil Rights, Detroit, Michigan, December 14–15, 1960* (Washington, D.C.: U.S. Government Printing Office, 1961), pp. 481, 484.

10. *Ibid.*

11. *Detroit Free Press,* December 29, 1960, p. 1.

12. *Ibid.*

13. *Norfolk* (Va.) *Journal and Guide,* May 20, 1961, p. 10.

14. *Report and Recommendations of the Commissioners' Committee On Police Arrests For Investigation* (District of Columbia, 1962), p. 34.

15. *Id.* at 69.

16. See Klein, *op. cit.*, p. 202.

17. This Board is described *infra*, pp. 218–219.

18. As quoted in *Commission Justice Report*, p. 23.

19. William Westley, "Violence and the Police," 59 *American Journal of Sociology* 34 (July, 1953).

20. *Commission Justice Report*, p. 25.

21. *Id.* at 6–12.

22. *Id.* at 14.

23. *Id.* at 12.

24. *Mapp* v. *Ohio*, 367 U.S. 643, 644 (1961).

25. *Ibid.*

26. *Id.* at 645.

27. *Barron* v. *Baltimore*, 32 U.S. (7 Pet.) 243 (1833); and see cases in note 28.

28. *Chambers* v. *Florida*, 309 U.S. 227 (1940); *Palko* v. *Connecticut*, 302 U.S. 319 (1937); *Brown* v. *Mississippi*, 297 U.S. 278 (1936); *Hurtado* v. *California*, 110 U.S. 516 (1884); *Davidson* v. *New Orleans*, 96 U.S. 97 (1878).

29. *Henry* v. *United States*, 361 U.S. 98, 100 (1959).

30. *Ibid.*

31. *Weeks* v. *United States,* 232 U.S. 383 (1914); *Boyd* v. *United States,* 116 U.S. 616 (1886).

32. *Weeks* v. *United States,* 232 U.S. at 393.

33. *Wolf* v. *Colorado,* 338 U.S. 25 (1949).

34. *Id.* at 29. The Supreme Court indicated two reasons for not wishing to impose the exclusionary rule on the states. First, it would mean that the contrary rules in the majority of the states, based on their own estimation of their needs, would have to be overridden. *Id.* at 31. Second, "other means of protection," such as criminal prosecutions against erring police officers, were available to protect the right to privacy. *Id.* at 30.

35. This is precisely what happened in the *Wolf* case, and in *Irvine* v. *California,* 347 U.S. 128 (1954), when the Supreme Court upheld a state conviction based on illegally procured wiretap evidence even though the Court was obviously outraged by the action of the Los Angeles Police Department. The Court said: "That officers of the law would break and enter a home, secrete such a device, even in a bedroom, and listen to the conversation of the occupants for over a month would be almost incredible if it were not admitted. Few police measures have come to our attention that more flagrantly, deliberately, and persistently violated the fundamental principle declared by the Fourth Amendment. . . ." *Id.* at 132.

36. See *Wolf* v. *Colorado,* 338 U.S. at 29, 33–38.

37. *Mapp* v. *Ohio,* 367 U.S. at 655.

38. *Id.* at 657.

39. *Olmstead* v. *United States,* 277 U.S. 438 (1928).

40. 47 U.S.C. 605.

41. This is extensively documented in Samuel Dash, Robert E. Knowlton and Richard F. Schwartz, *The Eavesdroppers* (New Brunswick, N.J.: Rutgers University Press, 1959).

42. Alan Barth, *The Price of Liberty* (New York: Viking Press, 1961), p. 132.

43. See, for example, *Nardone* v. *United States,* 308 U.S. 338 (1939); *Weiss* v. *United States,* 308 U.S. 321 (1939). In *Schwartz* v. *Texas,* 344 U.S. 199 (1952), the Supreme Court made it clear that while state officers violated section 605 when they tapped, the evidence was not excluded in a state trial—a holding consistent in spirit with its decision in the *Wolf* case. Now that the *Mapp* decision has overruled *Wolf,* it is probable that the Warren court would, in the same spirit but perhaps not on the same legal basis, overrule *Schwartz.*

44. One New Jersey prisoner, one Philadelphia prisoner, and three federal prisoners responded affirmatively to the wiretapping question—5 out of a total of 359.

45. See, for example, Dash, *et al., op. cit.,* pp. 65–66.

46. *Federal Rules of Criminal Procedure,* Rule 5.

47. *Revision of the Rules Governing the Courts of the State of New Jersey* (hereafter referred to as R.R.), Rule 8:3–3.

48. 354 U.S. 449 (1957).

49. *Upshaw* v. *United States,* 335 U.S. 410 (1948).

50. *State* v. *Mulvaney,* 21 N.J. Super 457, 460, 91 A.2d 359, 360 (App. Div. 1952).

51. *Stroble* v. *California*, 343 U.S. 181, 197 (1952).

52. See Appendix A, Item 23, C.

53. In *Commonwealth* v. *Shupp*, 365 Pa. 439, 75 A.2d 587 (1950), the Supreme Court of Pennsylvania stated that there was nothing legally improper in the fact that the defendant, when convicted of first degree murder and under sentence of death, was held by the police for fifteen days before a preliminary hearing—during which time he signed a confession.

54. *Commission Justice Report,* p. 240.

55. The Commission on Civil Rights described the facts in the 22 cases reversed by the Supreme Court on the basis of coerced confessions. Lengthy and incommunicado detention was an almost universal feature of these cases. *Id.* at 256–262.

56. See Appendix A, Item 9.

57. The responses from the federal prisoners are not completely indicative of the practices of federal civilian police agents. Many were originally detained by state or local police, or by military police. Therefore, even the small number of incommunicado detentions claimed by federal prisoners cannot be entirely laid at the door of the national civilian agencies.

58. *Cicenia* v. *La Gay*, 357 U.S. 504 (1958).

59. *Id.* at 505.

60. *Id.* at 512. The Newark policemen denied that they had been so blunt.

61. *Id.* at 508–509.

62. *Id.* at 509–510.

63. *Id.* at 508.

64. American Civil Liberties Union, Illinois Division, *Secret Detention by the Chicago Police* (Glencoe, Ill.: The Free Press, 1959), p. 13.

CHAPTER 2
The Police: Violence and Coercion

1. This account of the "Jones" case comes primarily from a private detective who investigated the case extensively.

2. *Brown* v. *Mississippi*, 297 U.S. 278 (1936).

3. *Commission Justice Report*, pp. 256–262.

4. See *State v. Murphy*, 87 N.J.L. 515, 94 Atl. 640 (1950) for the New Jersey rule.

5. See, for example, *State* v. *Pierce*, 4 N.J. 252, 258, 72 A.2d 305, 308 (1950). The privilege against self-incrimination contained in the Fifth Amendment to the United States Constitution applies only to federal trials. *Twining* v. *New Jersey*, 211 U.S. 78 (1908). No such explicit privilege is contained in the New Jersey Constitution.

6. See Appendix A, Item 10.

7. *Id.,* Item 15.

8. The position taken by the New Jersey Supreme Court, for example, is that "such cautionary instructions are not an essential step in the establishment of the fact that a confession is voluntary." *State* v. *Cole*, 136 N.J.L. 606, 612, 56 A.2d 898, 902 (E. and A. 1948); also see the cases noted on the page

cited in the opinion, and Lester B. Orfield, *Criminal Procedure from Arrest to Appeal* (New York: New York University Press, 1947), pp. 64–65.

9. See Appendix A, Item 12, A.

10. *Id.*, Item 12, B.

11. *Id.*, Item 13, A.

12. *Id.*, Item 13, B.

13. *Id.*, Item 14.

14. However, this was not the case with the military police. This study is not directly concerned with the military courts, but twelve prisoners convicted of serious offenses by military courts were included among the men who were interviewed at the federal prison. Their remarks can be dealt with only briefly.

These twelve men were easily more bitter than any group of prisoners interviewed during the course of this study. Most of these prisoners indicated that fear of violence by the military police was ever with them. One prisoner serving a fifteen-year sentence wrote on his questionnaire that, "I signed [a confession] because if I hadn't I do believe I would have been killed before going to court." This was in reference to the tactics of an unnamed military police unit in Germany. There is the possibility that these prisoners were exaggerating, but one fact cannot be denied. When their remarks are placed side by side with those made by hundreds of other prisoners, the picture presented is by comparison exceedingly unfavorable for military policemen.

15. The significance of the repetition by prisoners of identical stories claiming the third degree was also mentioned in William T. Root, Jr., *A Psychological and Educational Survey of 1,916*

Prisoners in the Western Penitentiary of Pennsylvania (Board of Trustees of Western Penitentiary), p. 208. [Place and date of publication not given; probably Pittsburgh, 1927.] Root stated:

"It is very difficult to determine to what extent the 'third degree' is practiced in our police stations and jails. It stands to reason that after [a prisoner signs] a written confession the claim of having been third degreed could easily be used to clear one's case with friends, relatives, and those unfamiliar with the conditions surrounding the conviction. On the other hand, there is no reason to suppose that prisoners, unacquainted with each other and often unacquainted with the district, could have any plan of collusion by which they would give us the same police station, the same police officers (or describe their appearance), and the same methods of third degreeing. In our smaller cities, there is no reason why certain ones have never been accused by any prisoner and other cities give us a continuous stream of men during a period of years all telling the same conditions of third degree brutality."

16. For example, 42 per cent of the New Jersey prisoners represented by assigned counsel and 40 by retained counsel claimed police violence or its threat in the course of the third degree.

17. See pp. 87–91, *infra*.

18. Among the New Jersey State Prison convicts who had allegedly been subjected to violence or its threat, 69 per cent of the whites and 62 per cent of the nonwhites claimed it was used in an attempt to coerce a confession. In the Bordentown Reformatory the responses were: white, 77 per cent; nonwhite, 68 per cent.

19. In this regard, however, see the material in the publication of the Greater Philadelphia Branch of the American Civil Liberties Union, *Civil Liberties Record* (June, 1960), p. 2.

20. See Appendix A, Item 8. It is significant that so many men admitted their guilt in these interviews. It is a standard joke among guards and other prison personnel that, "We've got nothing but innocent men in this prison. They are all in here on 'bum raps.'"

21. Forty-three of these prisoners claimed the threat of violence; 50, violence.

22. Sixty-six New Jersey prisoners and 6 Federal prisoners both admitted guilt and claimed the third degree.

23. *State* v. *Pierce*, 4 N.J. at 260, 72 A.2d at 309.

24. *Fikes* v. *Alabama*, 352 U.S. 191, 198 (1957).

25. *Ibid.*

26. *Blackburn* v. *Alabama*, 361 U.S. 199, 206 (1960).

27. Jerome and Barbara Frank, *Not Guilty* (New York: Doubleday, 1957), 180–181.

28. *In re Groban*, 352 U.S. 330, 349–350 (1957) (dissent).

29. See, for example, the case of "James Jones" earlier in this chapter. Other cases of confessions by innocent persons comparable to the one described there may be found in Frank and Frank, *op. cit.*, and in Edwin M. Borchard, *Convicting the Innocent* (New Haven, Conn.: Yale University Press, 1932). The Franks describe the case of Rudolph Sheeler, which occured in 1939 in Philadelphia. The basic facts, a confession forced by violence, are similar to the Jones case although the extent of wrongdoing by the police was more extensive in the Sheeler affair. Frank and Frank, *op. cit.*, p. 168. In the Borchard work, see the case of John A. Johnson, *op. cit.*, p. 112.

When a person confesses to his defense counsel, an investigation may reveal that for some reason that later comes to the surface the story is untrue. Ellery E. Cuff, the Public Defender of Los Angeles County, stated in this regard that "a Public Defender will soon have the experience in which the defendant has made a full confession of the crime to the officers—even to the Public Defender himself. But after a careful investigation into the details of the crime, the Public Defender learns the defendant's confession is not true. This happens often enough to warrant the exercise of care against accepting a confession too readily." Ellery E. Cuff, *The Public Defender and His Function in the Administration of Justice* (Los Angeles: Public Defender of Los Angeles County, 1950), p. 12. To illustrate this point, Public Defender Cuff told of a case where a young man had confessed a murder to the police and to defender attorneys. Upon investigation by the professional staff of investigators, the defense found that the man had seen the diamond ring, which he knew was the object in committing the crime, on a pendant around his mother's neck. Thinking she was somehow implicated, the son confessed to save her. The police accepted the confession. Only the investigation of the public defender's detectives saved the man from conviction and a probable trip to the gas chamber. *Id.* at 13–14.

30. Federal Bureau of Investigation, *Uniform Crime Reports—1960,* p. 105.

31. *Id.* at 1.

32. *Id.* at 106.

33. *Id.* at 105.

34. See Appendix A, Item 13, A.

CHAPTER 3
First Judicial Test

1. Analyses of the preliminary examination may be found in David Fellman, *The Defendant's Rights* (New York: Rinehart, 1958), p. 19 ff.; Orfield, *Criminal Procedure from Arrest to Appeal*, Chapter II; and in Ernst W. Puttkammer, *Administration of Criminal Law* (Chicago: The University of Chicago Press, 1953), pp. 88 ff.

2. *Thies* v. *State*, 178 Wis. 98, 103, 189 N.W. 539, 541 (1922).

3. R.R. 8:3–3(c).

4. *Lem Woon* v. *Oregon*, 229 U.S. 586 (1913).

5. See Appendix A, Item 23, C.

6. In Illinois it was found that in many municipal courts approximately half the cases brought into court for a preliminary examination were there dismissed. Illinois Association for Criminal Justice, *Illinois Crime Survey* (Chicago: Blakely Printing Company, 1929), pp. 36, 204–205, 297–298, 398–400. In Missouri the figures for dismissals were: 26.08 per cent for the state as a whole with 41.73 in the cities and 10.67 in country areas. Missouri Association for Criminal Justice, *Missouri Crime Survey* (New York: Macmillan, 1926), p. 275. And according to Raymond Moley, dismissals in the mid-1920's were found to be 58 per cent of all felony arrests in New York City, 55 per cent in Cincinnati, 49 per cent in Chicago, 41 per cent in Kansas City, 26 per cent in Cleveland, 22 per cent in Baltimore, 17 per cent in Milwaukee, and 17 per cent in St. Louis. Raymond Moley, *Politics and Criminal Prosecution* (New York: Minton, Balch, 1929), p. 28.

7. Missouri Association for Criminal Justice, *op. cit.*, p. 164.

8. R.R. 8:3–3(b).

9. See Appendix A, Item 17.

10. Only 15 per cent of the New Jersey prisoners said that they were informed of the assignment privilege by a municipal court judge. See legal discussion, *infra*, pp. 105–106.

11. The magistrates were asked, "What advice as to the right to counsel is offered by the magistrate to defendants (at preliminary examinations) as a matter of general procedure?" Only 11 magistrates, or 38 per cent of the total of 29 who answered, gave any indication that they informed defendants of the privilege of having counsel assigned if indigent. Eighteen indicated that they informed the defendant only of the right to retain counsel. One of the magistrates stated that advice in regard to counsel is never voluntarily given.

12. See Appendix A, Item 19, B.

13. See Appendix A, Item 19.

14. Bertram F. Willcox and Edward J. Bloustein, "Account of a Field Study in a Rural Area of the Representation of Indigents Accused of Crime," *Columbia Law Review*, 59 (April, 1959) 551, 559.

15. *Ibid.*

16. Special Committee of the Association of the Bar of the City of New York and the National Legal Aid and Defender Association, *Equal Justice for the Accused* (Garden City: Doubleday, 1959), p. 60. Hereafter, this book is cited as *Special Com-*

mittee to Study Defender Systems, as the group was known. To support its point the Committee mentioned the following words from the opinion in *Ex parte Sullivan,* 107 F. Supp. 514, 517–18 (D. Utah 1952): "Petitioners were entitled to have effective counsel *at the trial.* The question here is how they ever could have had effective counsel at the trial, no matter how skilled, in view of what went on before trial. They were denied effective counsel at the trial itself because of what went on before trial while the defendants were without counsel, and absolutely under the control of the prosecution.

"The time a defendant needs counsel most is immediately after his arrest and until trial. . . .

"Indeed, counsel was not appointed for them until after they had been arraigned and had entered their pleas of not guilty. By that time the evidence was all neatly tied up for delivery at the trial. . . . One can imagine a cynical prosecutor saying: 'Let them have the most illustrious counsel, now. They can't escape the noose. There is nothing that counsel can do for them at the trial.' "

17. *Report of the Commission on Legal Aid of the Bar Association of the District of Columbia* (Washington, D.C.: Commission on Legal Aid of the Bar Association of the District of Columbia, 1958), p. 92.

18. *New Jersey Stat. Ann.,* 2A:8–22 lists minor indictable crimes that may be disposed of by the municipal court when the defendant chooses to waive indictment and trial by jury; or, where the defendant so desires, they may be heard by the county court.

19. Kenneth R. Frankl and Arnold S. Trebach, *The Assigned Counsel System in Essex County, New Jersey,* Report to the Special Committee to Study Defender Systems (New York, 1956), Exhibit VIII. These sentences may be broken down as follows:

Sentences	Number of Defendants
6 months	45
9 months	7
12 months	10
15 months	1
18 months	1

20. The Chief Magistrate of the Newark Municipal Court estimated that 75 per cent of the people who appeared before his court, excluding minor traffic cases, were indigent. In the year ending August 31, 1956, this amounted to approximately 12,000 out of an estimated total of 16,000 defendants appearing in cases where the court could have imposed a jail or county penitentiary sentence. This information was contained in answers to the questionnaire mailed to the magistrate.

21. Address, Judge William B. Neely, Superior Court, Los Angeles, 34th Annual Legal Aid Conference, Denver, Colorado, October 11, 1956, *Defender Section—Collection of Papers* (Chicago: National Legal Aid Association, 1956).

22. Only five counsel were actually assigned to indigent defendants by the 32 municipal magistrates who answered the question that asked for "the approximate number of these defendants who were assigned counsel on the grounds of indigency from September 1, 1955, to August 31, 1956." The total number of indigent defendants in cases within the final jurisdiction of their courts was estimated by these magistrates to be 12,444.

23. *Special Committee To Study Defender Systems*, pp. 63–64.

24. *Id.* at 64.

CHAPTER 4
"Cop Out"

1. Frankl and Trebach, *The Assigned Counsel System in Essex County, New Jersey,* pp. 10–15.

2. *Id.* at 15. The statistics computed from the responses of the prisoners accord in general with these figures. Among each group, with the exception of the Philadelphia prisoners, the great majority did not go to trial. Appendix A, Item 7.

3. This was 242 out of the 354 prisoners in the sample.

4. In response to a question as to the highest grade of school completed, the breakdown for the entire prisoner sample was: grades 1–6, 12 per cent; grades 7–9, 38 per cent; grades 10–12, 39 per cent; and college, 6 per cent. Appendix A, Item 4.

5. Richard A. McGee, "The Administration of Justice: The Correctional Process," *National Probation and Parole Association Journal,* 5 (July, 1959) 225, 228.

6. The prisoners were asked, "Where were you treated better, in the jail where you waited around to enter your final plea (or for your trial) or in this prison?" The responses were: jail, 5 per cent; this prison, 60 per cent; the same, 6 per cent; did not answer, 29 per cent. Appendix A, Item 24.

7. See the challenging article by Professor Clarence Clyde Ferguson, Jr., "Formulation of Enforcement Policy: An Anatomy of the Prosecutor's Discretion Prior to Accusation," *Rutgers Law Review* 11 (Spring, 1957) 507, 524, n. 90, and cases cited therein. Professor Ferguson maintains that "The more recent

pronouncement of the New Jersey appellate courts as to the doctrinal content of multiple accusation has steadily increased the scope of the prosecutor's discretion to formulate charges and to time such charges. . . . [T]he extent to which the prosecutor may multiply charges measures in large part the strength of his bargaining position in the informal conviction process. And it is this process which receives the least judicial attention, and it is here that the exercise of discretion has its highest potential for abuse. The published results of the American Bar Association study appear to confirm critical speculations that the possibility or actuality of multiple charges on account of a single course of cognate behavior presents a situation in which there is a risk of coercing conviction by entry of guilty or non-contesting pleas."

8. See Appendix A, Item 22.

9. Donald J. Newman, "Pleading Guilty for Considerations: A Study of Bargain Justice," *Journal of Criminal Law, Criminology, and Police Science,* 46 (March-April, 1956) 780.

10. *Id.* at 788.

11. See Appendix A, Item 6.

12. *State* v. *Raicich,* 30 N.J. Super. 316, 104 A.2d 713 (App. Div. 1954).

13. See discussion of counsel law, *infra,* pp. 105–106.

14. For a discussion of the grand jury and its development, see Puttkammer, *Administration of Criminal Law,* Chapter VII; Orfield, *Criminal Procedure from Arrest to Appeal,* Chapter IV.

15. *Hurtado* v. *California,* 110 U.S. 516 (1884).

16. According to Fellman, *The Defendant's Rights*, p. 31, "The older states, and most states east of the Mississippi River, require grand jury action for all major offenses."

17. See, for example, Raymond Moley, "The Initiation of Criminal Prosecutions by Indictment or Information," *Michigan Law Review*, 29 (February, 1931) 403.

18. See, for example, *Missouri ex rel Hurwitz* v. *North*, 271 U.S. 40, 42 (1926). For an excellent discussion, see Fellman, *op. cit.*, Chapter 3.

19. Fellman, *op. cit.*, p. 30.

20. See p. 64, *supra*.

21. *United States* v. *Lattimore*, 127 F. Supp. 405, 406 (D.D.C.), *aff'd* 232 F. 2d 334. (D.C.Cir. 1955).

22. R.R., 3:4–2.

23. *Ibid.*

CHAPTER 5

The Indigent Defendant and the Law

1. See Appendix A, Item 20. Also see Emery A. Brownell, *Legal Aid in the United States* (Rochester, N.Y.: Lawyers Cooperative Publishing Co., 1951), p. 83; and *Report on the Assigned Counsel System in New Jersey* (Trenton, N.J.: Administrative Office of the Courts, 1955), p. 23. The latter report was based on a study I made under the auspices of the Administrative Office of the Courts of New Jersey. In the course of this study, a field trip was made to every county in the state.

2. Data from National Legal Aid and Defender Association.

3. *Powell* v. *Alabama*, 287 U.S. 45, 53–56 (1932). For an analysis of the historical development of the right to counsel in England and early America, see William M. Beaney, *The Right to Counsel in American Courts* (Ann Arbor, Mich.: University of Michigan Press, 1955), Chapter II.

4. *Powell* v. *Alabama*, 287 U.S. at 67.

5. *Id.* at 68.

6. *Id.* at 69.

7. *Id.* at 71.

8. 304 U.S. 458 (1938).

9. *Id.* at 463.

10. 316 U.S. 455 (1942).

11. *Id.* at 472.

12. *Id.* at 471.

13. *Id.* at 462.

14. *Id.* at 474.

15. *Id.* at 475.

16. *Id.* at 476.

17. R.R. 1:12–9 (a).

18. *State* v. *Terry*, 38 N.J. Super 31, 33, 118 A. 2d 106, 107 (App. Div. 1955).

19. See Justice Harlan's comment in *Gideon* v. *Wainwright*, 372 U.S. 335, 351 (1963).

20. *Id.* at 338.

21. Speech, Abe Krash, attorney, Washington, D.C., 41st Annual Legal Aid and Defender Conference, Miami Beach, Florida, October 23, 1963.

22. *Gideon* v. *Wainwright*, 372, U.S. at 345.

23. Speech, Abe Krash, *supra*, n. 21.

24. *Gideon* v. *Wainwright*, 372 U.S. at 344.

25. *Id.* at 351

26. 368 U.S. 52 (1961).

27. *Id.* at 53.

28. *Id.* at 55.

29. 83 S.Ct. 1050 (1963).

30. In this regard, see Justice Clark's comments on the distinction between capital and non-capital cases in *Gideon* v. *Wainwright*, 372 U.S. at 348.

31. *Johnson* v. *United States*, 352 U.S. 565 (1957).

32. 372 U.S. 353 (1963).

33. *Id.* at 357.

34. *Ibid.*

35. *Id.* at 356.

36. *Draper* v. *State of Washington,* 372 U.S. 487 (1963); *Lane* v. *Brown,* 372 U.S. 477 (1963). The procedures regarding the writ of habeas corpus were also broadened, thus facilitating a prisoner's collateral attack on his conviction, by two other cases issued on the same day as *Gideon—Fay* v. *Noia,* 372 U.S. 391 (1963), and *Townsend* v. *Sain,* 372 U.S. 293 (1963).

CHAPTER 6
The Defenders

1. Data from National Legal Aid and Defender Association.

2. *Special Committee to Study Defender Systems,* p. 48.

3. *Report of the Committee of County Judges on Counsel for Indigent Criminal Defendants,* as reproduced in Frankl and Trebach, *The Assigned Counsel System in Essex County, New Jersey,* Exhibit I.

4. *Id.* at 1.

5. R.R. 1:12–9(a).

6. R.R. 1:12–9(e).

7. R.R. 1:12–6.

8. R.R. 1:12–9(d).

9. Kenneth R. Frankl and Lionel N. Spring, *Analysis of Question-naire Submitted to Essex County Bar Association,* Report to the Special Committee to Study Defender Systems (New York, 1957), p. 6. Of the 653 attorneys who answered this question, 371 (56.6 per cent) reported some criminal experience; 282 (43.4 per cent) reported no criminal experience; and 62 (9.5 per cent) stated that their criminal court experience was extensive.

10. The two questions dealing with this point asked, "3. How are counsel selected for assignment in most cases?" "4. Are selection procedures for attorneys the same as in (3) for non-capital cases carrying a severe sentence? If not, how do they differ?" Only 3 of the 12 county judges stated that they took the seriousness of the charge into consideration when making assignments of attorneys, as the rule expressly directs. Two of these judges reported that they followed the practice of assigning an experienced criminal attorney in such cases.

11. See Appendix A, Item 16. The complete breakdown (which does not appear in Item 16) of the affirmative answers to the question on suggestions by police regarding hiring a particular attorney or bondsman were: New Jersey State Prison—18 per cent; New Jersey State Reformatory—13 per cent; Philadelphia prison—10 per cent; and federal prison—5 per cent.

12. See Appendix A, Item 23, A.

13. *Special Committee to Study Defender Systems,* p. 67.

14. *Ibid.* "The principal cause is that the Grand Jury meets only three times a year and counsel are assigned only after indictment." *Ibid.*

15. *Id.* at 71.

16. *Id.* at 74. The Special Committee also pointed out that for a variety of reasons, primarily financial, most other private and public defender agencies are not able to commence operation within such a short time after arrest.

17. See, for example, the statistics on Philadelphia in Appendix A, Item 23, A.

18. R.R. 1:12–9(a).

19. The responses of county judges to a questionnaire I sent to them in the summer of 1957 indicated the following: Nine judges stated that assignment of counsel was made at the arraignment; according to three judges, assignment was ordinarily made shortly before arraignment. Most prisoners I interviewed in 1957 also indicated clearly that assignment was made at the time of arraignment. During the 1959 interviews many New Jersey prisoners also told me they were assigned an attorney by the county judge at the time of the arraignment. But when the statistics from all of the New Jersey prisoners were compiled, they showed that, on the average, assignment took place weeks or even a full month before arraignment. (Appendix A, Item 23, A and B.) This is totally inconsistent with all the other evidence on this point. Yet, it does stand as an indication of a healthy trend. It is unfortunate that a detailed analysis of the responses to this query raises the question as to whether or not many prisoners unintentionally gave erroneous information on this point in the mass interviews. The question read, "How many days between arrest and the first time that you had a private interview with your lawyer?" It was orally explained that this question referred only to first contact with assigned counsel for those men who were indigent. But it seems likely that a number of prisoners indicated the time interval between arrest and first contact with a so-called jailhouse lawyer. During such interviews the main subject of inquiry is whether or not the prisoner can afford a fee. Upon determining that the pris-

oner is indigent, few of these attorneys provide legal advice. An experimental defender program instituted in Essex County in late 1963 provided counsel before arraignment—at the preliminary examination.

20. Sixty-seven per cent of all prisoners I interviewed were not released on bail.

21. Bail reform might well result in the constraint of certain prisoners who are not allowed to produce security, and in the release of others now incarcerated. More liberal requirements seem especially in order for those charged with minor crimes. For a brief but excellent discussion of the defects in bail procedure in the United States and suggested reforms, see Orfield, *Criminal Procedure from Arrest to Appeal*, pp. 129–134. The Vera Foundation is now engaged in a promising bail experiment in the courts of New York City.

22. Frank and Frank, *Not Guilty*, p. 88.

23. Rule 1:12–9(e) and *New Jersey Stat. Ann.*, 2A:163–1. The Special Committee to Study Defender Systems described the compensation situation in the 1950's: "No provision for the payment of counsel assigned in non-capital cases is found in twenty-seven states. Most of the remaining states provide only token payments which are grossly unremunerative for the services performed. Frequently the payments do not cover the expenses of counsel. Examples may be found in the provisions in South Dakota, Texas, and Virginia. The allowance in some states may be adequate depending, of course, on the amount of work required of the attorney and on the local fee scale. There is a trend in the new state legislation relating to the assignment of counsel toward leaving the amount of compensation to the trial court. In California, Colorado, Indiana, Maine, and Michigan, for example, the fee may be set by the court

with no statutory limit prescribed." *Special Committee to Study Defender Systems,* p. 120.

24. *Report on the Assigned Counsel System in New Jersey, op. cit.,* p. 29.

25. *New Jersey Law Journal,* 79 (June 14, 1956) 220.

26. Frankl and Spring, *op. cit.,* p. 5.

27. *Id.* at 7. Of the 572 attorneys who answered the question, 328 (57.3 per cent) replied that they questioned defendants as to their funds. Eighty-four attorneys found that defendants assigned to them had funds; but only 12 reported that they received a fee from a nominally indigent defendant. *Id.* at 7–8.

28. See note 23, *supra.*

29. *Ibid.*

30. R.R. 1:12–9(a).

31. The response breakdown of the prisoners who had been assigned counsel was:

	New Jersey	Philadelphia	Federal	Total
	PERCENTAGES			
Affidavit or written statement	58	43	3	45
Questioned about finances but not required to sign statement	36	57	71	45
Did not answer	6	0	26	10
TOTAL	100	100	100	100
Number of prisoners	(112)	(14)	(35)	(161)

32. See *Special Committee to Study Defender Systems*, p. 85.

33. James Stephen, *A History of the Criminal Law of England* (London: Macmillan, 1883), Vol. I, p. 397.

34. Beaney, *The Right to Counsel in American Courts*, pp. 8–10, and works there cited.

35. Roscoe Pound, *Criminal Justice in America* (New York: Henry Holt, 1930), p. 100.

36. Jerome Frank, *Courts on Trial* (Princeton, N.J.: Princeton University Press, 1949), p. 92.

37. *Id.* at 85.

38. *Ibid.*

39. *Id.*, Chapter VI, "The 'Fight' Theory versus the 'Truth' Theory."

40. *Supra*, pp. 80–81.

41. Newman, "Pleading Guilty for Considerations: A Study of Bargain Justice," p. 790.

42. For a comprehensive analysis of the treatment theory of the criminal law, see Hermann Mannheim, *Criminal Justice and Social Reconstruction* (London: K. Paul, Trench, Trubner, 1946).

43. Professor Jerome Hall observed that "the whole cause of the inadequacy of criminology for the criminal law (in addition to the limitations of criminology in itself) may be epitomized as follows: The criminologists are not lawyers, and the lawyers are not criminologists. More specifically, we do not have technologists who are equipped to apply criminology to the administra-

tion of the law." Jerome Hall, "Some Basic Problems in Criminology," *Annals of the American Academy of Social and Political Science,* 167 (May, 1933) 119, 133. Hall suggested that psychiatry may not only be used by parole boards "but also by judges
in helping to decide doubtful cases of application for probation,
and even farther back than that, by prosecutors in helping them
to decide whether to proceed or to *nolle prosequi* in doubtful
cases." *Id.* at 133, note 31.

44. See Newman, *op. cit.,* p. 789.

45. Nathaniel F. Cantor, *Crime and Society* (New York: Henry
Holt, 1939), p. 289.

CHAPTER 7
The Facts and the Plea

1. George Nye, *33rd Annual Report, Public Defender of Alameda
County, Oakland, California* [Reprinted, Chicago: National Legal Aid and Defender Association, 1959], p. 5.

2. The description of the Shephard case in the text is taken from
Frank and Frank, *Not Guilty,* pp. 74–78.

3. *Id.* at 75.

4. *Id.* at 76.

5. Nye, *op. cit.,* p. 7.

6. *Special Committee to Study Defender Systems,* p. 66.
     The Union County Bar Association explicitly recognized "the
hardship to the average lawyer for the time spent in such representation wherein his overhead expenses continue, and the
extended time spent away from his office results in neglect of
his regular practice." "Union Bar Endorses Assigned Counsel

System with Fees," *New Jersey Law Journal,* 80 (May 16, 1957) 237.

Judge William B. Neely of the Superior Court of the County of Los Angeles comments, "The expense of running a private law practice where the overhead can amount to about $20 an hour causes the average lawyer to be reluctant to contribute too much of his time to an assigned counsel system." Address, 34th Annual Legal Aid Conference, Denver, Colorado, October 11, 1956, *supra,* Chapter 3, n. 21.

See also the excellent discussion of this point in Sanford H. Kadish and Edward L. Kimball, "Legal Representation of the Indigent in Criminal Cases in Utah," *Utah Law Review* 4 (Spring, 1954) 198, 229–230. The authors wisely caution that the failure of unpaid attorneys ("men . . . deeply immersed in a material world") to live up to the ideal of public service in the defense of indigents should not be viewed "as moral failure, but rather as demonstrative of the fact that beyond certain limits society cannot expect the attorney to permit moral commitments to interfere with the material task of earning a livelihood." *Id.* at 230.

7. *Report on the Assigned Counsel System in New Jersey,* p. 39.

8. Frankl and Spring, *Analysis of Questionnaire Submitted to Essex County Bar Association,* pp. 5 and 8.

9. See Ellery E. Cuff, "Public Defender System: Los Angeles Story," *Minnesota Law Review* 45 (April, 1961) 715.

10. Address, Chief Investigator Edward Bliss, 34th Annual Legal Aid Conference, Denver, Colorado, October 11, 1956, *Defender Section—Collection of Papers* (Chicago: National Legal Aid Association, 1956).

11. Edward Bliss, *Defense Investigation* (Springfield, Illinois: Thomas, 1956), p. 41.

12. See Chapter 2, n. 29.

13. R.R. 3:5–11.

14. *State* v. *Rogers*, 30 N.J. Super 239, 104 A.2d 89 (Hudson County Law Div. 1954), *aff'd.*, 19 N.J. 218, 116 A.2d 37 (1955); *State* v. *Tune*, 13 N.J. 203, 98 A.2d 881 (1953).

15. *Id.*, 13 N.J. at 218–225, 98 A.2d at 888–893.

16. *Id.*, 13 N.J. at 210, 98 A.2d at 884.

17. Robert E. Knowlton, "Criminal Law and Procedure," *Rutgers Law Review* 11 (Fall, 1956) 72, 74.

18. Orfield, *Criminal Procedure from Arrest to Appeal*, p. 330.

19. Quoted in Orfield, *op. cit.*, p. 322.

20. Frank and Frank, *Not Guilty*, p. 243.

21. Edward Bennett Williams, *One Man's Freedom* (Atheneum: New York, 1962), p. 165.

22. *Ibid.*

23. *State* v. *Johnson*, 28 N.J. 133, 145 A.2d 313 (1958).

24. For an analysis of arraignment see Orfield, *op. cit.*, Chapter VI.

25. Under the 1963 counsel decisions, courts have a duty to assign counsel earlier than arraignment, in many cases. See discussion at end of Chapter 5.

26. See Appendix A, Item 6.

27. "The lawyer is bound by all fair and honorable means, to present every defense that the law of the land permits. . . ." American Bar Association, *The Canons of Ethics,* Canon Number 5.

28. For obvious reasons this is one of the most difficult statements to document in this entire study. The evidence referred to above is composed of interviews with attorneys, county prosecutors, county detectives, court officials, and prisoners.

29. See Appendix A, Item 21.

30. R.R. 3:7–10(b). See pp. 178–187, *infra,* for a discussion of the sentencing process.

31. *Supra,* pp. 84–87.

32. See Appendix A, Item 6.

33. *Ibid.*

34. *New Jersey Stat. Ann.,* 2A:113–3 prohibits a death sentence except after a jury trial, and prohibits a defendant charged with murder from pleading guilty; he must plead *non vult* or *nolo contendere.*

35. *New Jersey Stat. Ann.,* 2A:163–1 and R.R. 1:12–9(e).

CHAPTER 8

Trial and Sentence

1. See *Special Committee to Study Defender Systems,* Appendix, regarding provisions for the payments of fees in capital cases.

2. Nye, *33rd Annual Report, Public Defender of Alameda County, Oakland, California,* p. 8.

3. While this book does not deal with this point at length, it is clear that there are many prosecutors and policemen in this country who also are most concerned that the rights of the accused be protected. In particular, there are many prosecutors and policemen who would do everything in their power to secure the release of an innocent man.

4. See the discussion of the law regarding counsel in Chapter 5, *supra*.

5. Fellman, *The Defendant's Rights*, p. 40.

6. *Id.*, Chapter 4.

7. At common law the parties to suits were not allowed to testify because it was felt that there was a strong inducement for falsehood on their part. Orfield, *Criminal Procedure from Arrest to Appeal*, p. 459. When this disability was removed, the defendant, as Professor Puttkammer points out, was subject "to the same inquiry as any other witness as to whether he was a person whose testimony could be relied upon as truthful or, on the other hand, was one in whose word no trust could be placed—an inquiry which, of course, opened a possible door to many pieces of extremely unfavorable information about him." Puttkammer, *Administration of Criminal Law*, pp. 195–196.

8. *United States* v. *Grunewald*, 233 F.2d 556, n. 15 (2d Cir. 1956), *rev'd.* 353 U.S. 391 (1957). There are innumerable cases proving that defendants with a record, even a minor record, are at a serious disadvantage in the criminal courts. Such men are always prime suspects for unsolved crimes. It is frequently impossible for these men, once arrested, to obtain a fair trial. An example was the case of James W. Preston, who was convicted of assault with a deadly weapon in Los Angeles, California. The man whom the police were seeking had worn a mask covering the lower part of his face. Only his eyes were visible to the

victim as he wounded her while attempting to rob her of her jewels. Preston, with a minor criminal record, had been picked up by the police on a charge of illegally wearing a navy uniform. While in police custody, Preston was charged with the robbery and shooting. The victim identified him positively. Upon conviction by the jury of the lesser charge of assault with a deadly weapon, Preston received the sentence of from 11 years to life. After Preston served 18 months in prison, the real criminal was found. Borchard, *Convicting the Innocent,* pp. 190 ff. Professor Borchard maintained, that, "what doubtless weighed heavily against Preston was his previous record of delinquencies, though he had never committed a major offense." *Id.* at 195–196.

9. See *State* v. *Corby,* 28 N.J. 106, 136 A.2d 271 (1958).

10. R.R. 3:7–2(a).

11. R.R. 3:7–2(b) and (c). The charges on the trial of which 20 peremptory challenges are allowed are treason, murder, kidnapping, misprision of treason, manslaughter, sodomy, rape, arson, burglary, robbery, forgery, perjury, and subornation of perjury.

12. R.R. 3:7–2(c) provides that "in other cases each defendant shall be entitled to 10 peremptory challenges and the state shall have 10 peremptory challenges for each 10 challenges allowed to the defendant."

13. American Bar Foundation, *The Administration of Criminal Justice in the United States,* Vol. I: *Plan for Survey* (Chicago: American Bar Foundation, 1955), p. 161.

14. Letter from Ellery Cuff to Stephen J. Foley (Chairman of the Committee on Indigent Criminal Representation of the Junior Section of the New Jersey State Bar Association), December 27, 1956. In recent years the liberal attitude of the United

States Supreme Court regarding federal criminal procedure has had its effect on a number of state courts and has helped assigned counsel at the trial. For example, in *Jencks* v. *United States*, 353 U.S. 657 (1957), the Supreme Court held that a defendant was entitled to inspect relevant written reports by the FBI and other agents who testified at the trial. This case was decided in 1957. In 1958 the Supreme Court of New Jersey made it clear that a defendant's request to inspect the notes of a detective who appeared as a witness should ordinarily be granted by the trial court. *State* v. *Hunt*, 25 N.J. 514, 138 A.2d 1 (1958). Although this was a capital case, the language of the Court gave no hint that it intended the ruling to be restricted to such cases. Earlier, in *State* v. *Mucci*, 25 N.J. 423, 136 A.2d 761 (1957), the Court held that it was reversible error for the trial court to have refused defendant's motion to inspect statements that prosecution witnesses made to the grand jury two years before the trial. The prosecutor had called his witnesses into his office and allowed them to refresh their memories from the minutes of the grand jury on the morning of the trial. When the motion was made to inspect, the minutes were lying on a table within arm's reach of the prosecutor. Because of these peculiar circumstances, it is not entirely clear if the Court in the *Mucci* case meant that in future proceedings all requests to inspect the testimony of those witnesses before the grand jury who subsequently appear at the trial will be granted.

At any rate, it is clear that such liberal decisions make the task of the defense counsel at trial easier. Since they may be utilized by assigned counsel, they make up, in part, for the lack of investigatory facilities and the lack of an adequate discovery process. But whatever optimism is engendered by this development should be tempered by the realization that information from prosecution witnesses can never take the place of independent defense investigation.

15. Regarding criminal court experience of attorneys, see p. 114, *supra*.

16. Newman, "Pleading Guilty for Considerations: A Study of Bargain Justice," p. 789.

17. While some attorneys are quite satisfied with the results of pre-sentence investigations, others feel quite the contrary. One experienced New Jersey attorney wrote me: "It is the undersigned's sad experience, even in capital cases, that the probation department does little more than take a post-conviction statement from the defendant, rehash the prosecutor's files and then submit such 'data' to the sentencing judge. I find little significant effort to probe into the socioeconomic-familial background of the prisoner in most cases. For this reason, to the extent that the defense counsel can contribute to the pre-sentence report or file, by independent investigation and submission of data to the probation officer, his ultimate influence on the sentence may be appreciable."

18. R.R. 3:7–13.

19. Judges are reluctant to alter a sentence once it has been formally imposed in court. But it is not an infrequent occurrence—according to the records of the New Jersey State Prison, where 30 orders to alter inmate sentences may be received during the course of a month.

20. Accounts of this case were carried by the Newark *Evening News*, February 24, 1956, and March 15, 1956.

CHAPTER 9
The Convicted

1. New Jersey has an extensive system of civil legal aid. There is a legal aid society in all but one of New Jersey's 21 counties. See *Report on Legal Aid in New Jersey* (Trenton: Administrative Office of the Courts, 1955). However, most of the men

in prison are apparently not aware of the existence of these facilities—for many of them reported an urgent need for legal aid in civil cases regarding their family and property on the other side of the walls. This need is not being met.

2. Borchard, *Convicting the Innocent, supra,* Chapter 2, n. 29.

3. Frank and Frank, *Not Guilty, supra,* Chapter 2, n. 29. Several of the cases originally reported in Borchard, it should be noted, are repeated in the Frank volume. Professor Borchard stated that a remark, characteristic of the attitude of many lawyers and judges, made by a district attorney in Worcester County, Massachusetts, was a motivating force in the writing of his book. The district attorney was reported to have said, "Innocent men are never convicted. Don't worry about it, it never happens in the world. It is a physical impossibility." Professor Borchard replied, "The present collection of sixty-five cases, which have been selected from a much larger number, is a refutation of this supposition." Borchard, *op. cit.,* Preface.

4. According to one man I interviewed in prison during the summer of 1957, there were two men then in the death house, in part, because of perjured and coerced testimony. This prisoner had been the key witness in the state's case against these two men. The prisoner claimed that his testimony incriminating the men had been absolutely untrue and that he had been coerced by the prosecution into testifying. The prosecution had threatened to bring him to trial on another charge unless he testified. After he gave his perjured testimony, the charge against the prisoner-witness was dismissed by the county prosecutor. At the time he was interviewed, the witness was in the state prison because he had been convicted of another crime having nothing to do with the two men. Fortunately, the men in the death house were represented by two competent assigned counsel who were then preparing an appeal. I contacted these attorneys concerning the recanting witness, and his statement was used in

the appeal. The two men in the death house were eventually released from there, and their death sentences reduced to long prison terms.

5. New Jersey Stat. Ann., 2A:85–12.

6. The most complete discussion of this aspect of the right to counsel that I have yet encountered is Sanford H. Kadish, "The Advocate and the Expert—Counsel in the Peno-Correctional Process," Minnesota Law Review, 45 (April, 1961) 803.

7. R.R. 1:3–1(a). On March 18, 1963, the United States Supreme Court held that counsel must be assigned to the indigent defendant who wishes to take a first or direct appeal from his conviction. Douglas v. California, 372 U.S. 353 (1963). The decision did not deal with habeas corpus petitions.

8. The formal legal provisions regarding habeas corpus procedure in New Jersey are found in New Jersey Stat. Ann., 2A:67–13 through 2A:67–35. The cases dealing with appellate review of trials are discussed supra, pp. 00. An excellent analysis of post-conviction counsel problems in the federal courts—which suggests that the problems I found in New Jersey are widespread—is Bennett Boskey, "The Right to Counsel In Appellate Proceedings," Minnesota Law Review, 45 (April, 1961) 783.

9. R.R. 1:2–7.

10. R.R. 3:5–12.

11. New Jersey Stat. Ann., 2A:152–17.

12. 351 U.S. 12 (1956). Also see Burns v. Ohio, 360 U.S. 252 (1959); and Smith v. Bennett, 364 U.S. 708 (1961).

Two cases decided on the same day as Gideon v. Wainwright require that courts grant the cost of transcripts in some cases, even when not satisfied with the "sufficiency" of the appeal. *Lane v. Brown*, 372 U.S. 477 (1963); *Draper* v. *State of Washington*, 372 U.S. 487 (1963).

13. See William Rossmoore and Samuel Koenigsberg, "Habeas Corpus and the Indigent Prisoner," *Rutgers Law Review*, 11 (Spring, 1957) 611.

14. R.R. 1:12–9(b). By an amendment effective September 4, 1957, the old provision allowing the original counsel to continue after sentence was deleted.

15. Disagreement must be expressed, therefore, with a statement made by Rossmoore and Koenigsberg regarding "the question of what is to happen if the trial judge in the first instance decides that the application is not worthy of assignment to an attorney at all." They claimed that "the problem, if it really exists, is rare. . . ." Rossmoore and Koenigsberg, *op. cit.*, p. 613.

16. *State* v. *Almond*, 32 N.J. Super. at 465, 108 A.2d 494, 497 (App. Div. 1954).

17. Rossmoore and Koenigsberg, *op. cit.*, pp. 617–618. *Ex parte Sabongy*, 18 N.J. Super 334, 87 A.2d 59 (Mercer County Court Law Div. 1952) is an example of a case where after three unsuccessful applications, the prisoner's fourth petition for a writ of habeas corpus was successful. A habeas corpus application is never *res adjudicata*, i.e., prohibited by a previous unsuccessful application. *Ex parte Sabongy, ibid.*; *Price* v. *Johnston*, 334 U.S. 266 (1948); *Salinger* v. *Loisel*, 265 U.S. 224 (1924); *Leith* v. *Horgan*, 13 N.J. 467, 100 A.2d 175 (1953).

18. *State* v. *Bey*, 29 N.J. Super. 331, 332, 102 A.2d 684, 685 (App. Div. 1954).

19. *Commission Justice Report,* pp. 15–16.

20. *Id.* at 210–211.

21. *Id.* at 59 and 211.

22. *United States* v. *Johnson,* 238 F.2d 565, 571–572 (2d Cir. 1956) (dissent).

CHAPTER 10
The Institutions of Freedom

1. *Report on the Assigned Counsel System in New Jersey,* p. 36.

2. See discussion, *supra,* pp. 137–140.

3. For example, the *New Jersey Law Journal* editorialized in January, 1957, that the assigned counsel system "has been of some help in keeping the general bar in touch to some degree with practice in criminal causes and keeping alive professional responsibility for the administration of criminal justice." *New Jersey Law Journal,* 80 (January 10, 1957) 16.

4. As quoted in Robert Egerton, *Legal Aid* (New York: Oxford University Press, 1945), p. 21.

5. Gerald R. Moran, Professor of Criminal Law at Rutgers Law School, underscored the argument presented here in a comprehensive statement that appeared in an article entitled "The Future of the Criminal Law: Criminal Law in its Modern Public Law Context," *Rutgers Law Review,* 11 (Spring, 1957) 549, 581. "Our well-intentioned technique for providing for the defense of indigent defendants brings that desirably large segment of the bar into the criminal process which would appear to condition favorably the bar's performance of this responsibility

for . . . leadership [in reform]. However, among other serious deficiencies of our technique, attorneys are assigned too late, without appropriate funds, and too seldom for the bar to perform readily a leadership role. . . . Our specialists at criminal prosecution within the profession have manifested an ability and an unusually active predisposition to co-operate in fostering developments of our criminal law favorable to the state. The absence of a similar group of respected specialists at criminal defense deters the unfolding of legal developments . . . which would be favorable to persons suspected of, detained for, or first charged with, crime. *Ad hoc* professional attention comes too late, and continuing foresighted attention to the favorable development of the law pertaining to suspects, etc. tends, at best, to be only a part-time professional sideline or hobby of a limited few."

6. Data from National Legal Aid and Defender Association.

7. See Appendix D, Standards for Defender Services.

8. For a full description of existing defender systems, see *Special Committee to Study Defender Systems,* Chapter III.

9. Arnold S. Trebach, "A Modern Defender System for New Jersey," *Rutgers Law Review,* 12 (Winter, 1957) 289.

10. Ellery E. Cuff, "Public Defender System: Los Angeles Story," *Minnesota Law Review,* 45 (April, 1961) 715, 724, n. 22.

11. *Id.* at 729, n. 36.

12. *Id.* at 730, n. 39.
    When I visited the Los Angeles County Public Defender office in September, 1963, I found that both staff and budget had been increased in order to continue providing a high standard of service. During the 1962–63 fiscal year, a total of 30,382 criminal

cases were handled. At the time of my visit, there were 66 full-time attorneys and 12 investigators on the staff. The 1963–64 budget was $1,064,470.

13. Quoted in National Commission on Law Observance and Enforcement, *Report on Lawlessness in Law Enforcement*, p. 41.

14. *Commission Justice Report*, p. 82.

15. *Id.* at 83.

16. *Id.* at 84.

17. See, in this regard, *Commission Justice Report*, pp. 84–85.

18. *Ibid.*

19. *Id.* at 239–240, n. 59.

20. *Id.* at 85–86; 237, n. 40; and 241, n. 63.

21. *Id.* at 86.

22. *Id.* at 112.

23. *Id.* at 83.

24. *Ibid.*

25. See p. 21, *supra.*

26. *Ashcraft* v. *Tennessee*, 322 U.S. 143, 154 (1944).

27. *Brown* v. *Mississippi*, 297 U.S. 278 (1936).

28. *Supra*, pp. 12–18.

29. "Interrogations of arrested persons by the police are forbidden and confessions and admissions obtained in this way are inadmissible in evidence. . . . 'Police authorities are not permitted to examine him [the prisoner] without the protection of a magistrate.'" Edwin R. Keedy, "Criminal Procedure in Scotland," *Journal of Criminal Law* 3 (January, 1913) 738, 743 as quoted in Orfield, *Criminal Procedure from Arrest to Appeal,* p. 64, n. 57.

30. *Ibid.*

31. 42 U.S.C. 1983.

32. 18 U.S.C. 242.

33. *Commission Justice Report,* pp. 81, 111.

34. *Ibid.* In light of these facts, Recommendation 3 of the *Commission Justice Report* states (*id.* at 113):
    That Congress consider the advisability of amending section 1983 of title 42 of the United States Code to make any county government, city government, or other local governmental entity that employs officers who deprive persons of rights protected by that section, jointly liable with the officers to victims of such officers' misconduct.

35. 325 U.S. 91 (1945).

36. Both the legal and practical difficulties in the enforcement of the federal criminal Civil Rights Acts applicable to police misconduct are described in Chapter 4 of the *Commission Justice Report.*

37. Recommendation 2 of the *Commission Justice Report* states, at p. 112:
    That Congress consider the advisability of enacting a com-

panion provision to section 242 of the United States Criminal Code which would make the penalties of that statute applicable to those who maliciously perform, under color of law, certain described acts including the following:

   (1) subjecting any person to physical injury for an unlawful purpose;

   (2) subjecting any person to unnecessary force during the course of an arrest or while the person is being held in custody;

   (3) subjecting any person to violence or unlawful restraint in the course of eliciting a confession to a crime or any other information;

   (4) subjecting any person to violence or unlawful restraint for the purpose of obtaining anything of value;

   (5) refusing to provide protection to any person from unlawful violence at the hands of private persons, knowing that such violence was planned or was then taking place;

   (6) aiding or assisting private persons in any way to carry out acts of unlawful violence.

38. *Id.* at 269.

39. *Id.* at 79–80.

40. Much of my background information on the *Ombudsman* comes from an interview in April, 1962, with Dr. Johannes Klasment, an expert on Scandinavian law at the Library of Congress, and from an unpublished paper by Dr. Klasment entitled, "The *Ombudsman* and Related Systems of Governmental Supervision in Scandinavian and Other Countries."

41. Stephan Hurwitz, "Denmark's Ombudsman: The Parliamentary Commissioner for Civil and Military Government Administration," *Wisconsin Law Review* (March, 1961) 169.

42. *Id.* at 171.

43. *Id.* at 172.

44. *Ibid.*

45. *Ibid.*

46. *Id.* at 173.

47. *Ibid.*

48. *Ibid.*

49. *Ibid.*

50. *Ibid.*

51. *Id.* at 174.

52. *Id.* at 176.

53. *Ibid.*

54. *Id.* at 179.

55. *Id.* at 183.

56. *Id.* at 193–194.

Bibliography

BOOKS

Alexander, Franz, and Hugo Staub. *The Criminal, the Judge, and the Public,* rev. ed. Glencoe, Ill.: The Free Press, 1956.

American Bar Foundation. *The Administration of Criminal Justice in the United States,* Vol. I: *Plan for Survey.* Chicago: American Bar Foundation, 1955.

Barth, Alan. *The Price of Liberty.* New York: Viking Press, 1961.

Beaney, William M. *The Right to Counsel in American Courts.* Ann Arbor: University of Michigan Press, 1955.

Bliss, Edward. *Defense Investigation.* Springfield, Ill.: Thomas and Co., 1956.

Borchard, Edwin. *Convicting the Innocent.* Garden City, N.Y.: Garden City Publishing Co., 1932.

Brown, Esther Lucille. *Lawyers and the Promotion of Justice.* New York: Russell Sage Foundation, 1938.

Brownell, Emery A. *Legal Aid in the United States.* Rochester, N.Y.: Lawyers Cooperative Publishing Co., 1951.

Cantor, Nathaniel F. *Crime and Society.* New York: Henry Holt and Co., 1939.

Dash, Samuel, Robert E. Knowlton, and Richard F. Schwartz. *The Eavesdroppers.* New Brunswick: Rutgers University Press, 1959.

Donnelly, Richard C., Joseph Goldstein, and Richard D. Schwartz. *Criminal Law.* Glencoe, Ill.: The Free Press, 1962.

Fellman, David. *The Defendant's Rights.* New York: Rinehart, 1958.

Frank, Jerome. *Courts on Trial.* Princeton: Princeton University Press, 1949.

—— and Barbara Frank. *Not Guilty.* Garden City: Doubleday, 1957.

Goldman, Mayer C. *The Public Defender.* New York: G. P. Putnam's Sons, 1917.

Klein, Albert J. *Criminal Law in New Jersey.* New Brunswick: Rutgers University Press, 1953.

Mancuso, Edward T. *The Public Defender System in the State of California.* Chicago: National Legal Aid and Defender Association, 1959.

Orfield, Lester B. *Criminal Procedure from Arrest to Appeal.* New York: New York University Press, 1947.

Patterson, Haywood, and Earl Conrad. *Scottsboro Boy.* Garden City: Doubleday, Doran, 1950.

Puttkammer, Ernest W. *Administration of Criminal Law.* Chicago: University of Chicago Press, 1953.

Reynolds, Quentin. *Courtroom, The Story of Samuel S. Leibowitz.* New York: Farrar, Straus, 1950.

Schwartz, Murray L. *Cases and Materials on Professional Responsibility and the Administration of Criminal Justice.* Chicago: The National Council on Legal Clinics, 1961.

Smith, Reginald Heber. *Justice and the Poor.* New York: Carnegie Foundation for the Advancement of Teaching, 1919.

Stephen, Sir James F. *A History of the Criminal Law of England.* Vol. I. London: Macmillan Co., 1883.

Stone, Irving. *Clarence Darrow for the Defense.* Garden City: Doubleday, Doran, 1941.

Tweed, Harrison. *The Legal Aid Society, New York City.* New York: The Legal Aid Society, 1954.

Williams, Edward Bennett. *One Man's Freedom.* New York: Atheneum, 1962.

ARTICLES

Beaney, William M. "Right to Counsel before Arraignment," *Minnesota Law Review,* 45 (April, 1961) 771.

Bell, Robert K. "Legal Aid in New Jersey," *American Bar Association Journal*, 36 (May, 1950) 355.

Bennet, James V. "To Secure the Right to Counsel," *Journal of the American Judicature Society*, 32 (April, 1949) 177.

Boskey, Bennett. "The Right to Counsel in Appellate Proceedings," *Minnesota Law Review*, 45 (April, 1961) 783.

Bradway, John S. (ed.) "Law and Social Work," *Annals of the American Academy of Social and Political Science*, 145 (Sept., 1929).

—— and Reginald H. Smith. (eds.) "Legal Aid Work," *Annals of the American Academy of Social and Political Science*, 124 (March, 1926).

——. "Frontiers of Legal Aid Work," *Annals of the American Academy of Social and Political Science*, 205 (Sept., 1939).

Callagy, Martin V. "Legal Aid in Criminal Cases," *Journal of Criminal Law, Criminology, and Police Science*, 47 (Jan.-Feb., 1953) 587.

Celler, Emanuel. "Federal Legislative Proposals to Supply Paid Counsel to Indigent Persons Accused of Crime," *Minnesota Law Review*, 45 (April, 1961) 697.

Cuff, Ellery E. "Public Defender System: The Los Angeles Story," *Minnesota Law Review*, 45 (April, 1961) 715.

Fellman, David. "The Constitutional Right to Counsel in Federal Courts," *Nebraska Law Review*, 30 (May, 1951) 559.

——. "The Federal Right to Counsel in State Courts," *Nebraska Law Review*, 31 (Nov., 1951) 15.

——. "The Right to Counsel Under State Law," *Wisconsin Law Review* (March, 1955) 281.

Ferguson, Clarence Clyde, Jr. "Formulation of Enforcement Policy: An Anatomy of the Prosecutor's Discretion Prior to Accusation," *Rutgers Law Review*, 11 (Spring, 1957) 507.

Foote, Caleb. "Vagrancy Type Law and Its Administration," *University of Pennsylvania Law Review*, 104 (March, 1956) 603.

Goldman, Sidney. "The Rules of the Local Criminal Courts," *Rutgers Law Review*, 3 (June, 1949) 231.

Goldstein, Abraham S. "The State and the Accused: Balance of Advantage in Criminal Procedure," *Yale Law Journal*, 69 (June, 1960) 1149.

Hurwitz, Stephan. "Denmark's Ombudsman: The Parliamentary

Commissioner for Civil and Military Government Administration," *Wisconsin Law Review* (March, 1961) 169.

Kadish, Sanford H. "The Advocate and the Expert: Counsel in the Peno-Correctional Process," *Minnesota Law Review*, 45 (April, 1961) 803.

——— and Edward L. Kimball. "Legal Representation of the Indigent in Criminal Cases in Utah," *Utah Law Review*, 4 (Spring, 1954) 198.

Kamisar, Yale. "The Right to Counsel and the Fourteenth Amendment: A Dialogue on 'The Most Pervasive Right' of an Accused," *Chicago Law Reivew*, 30 (Autumn, 1962) 1.

Kaplan, Benjamin, and Warren J. Green. "The Legislature's Relation to Judicial Rule Making: An Appraisal of *Winberry* v. *Salisbury*," *Harvard Law Review*, 65 (Dec., 1951) 234.

Knowlton, Robert. "Criminal Law and Procedure," *Rutgers Law Review*, 11 (Fall, 1956) 72.

Monroe, Keith. "California's Dedicated Detective," *Harper's Magazine*, 214 (June, 1957) 57.

Moran, Gerald R. "The Future of the Criminal Law: Criminal Law in Its Modern Public Law Context," *Rutgers Law Review*, 11 (Spring, 1957) 549.

Newman, Donald J. "Pleading Guilty for Considerations: A Study of Bargain Justice," *Journal of Criminal Law, Criminology, and Police Science*, 56 (March-April, 1956) 780.

Pollock, Herman I. "The Voluntary Defender as Counsel for the Defense," *Journal of the American Judicature Society*, 32 (April, 1949) 174.

——— "Equal Justice in Practice," *Minnesota Law Review*, 45 (April, 1961) 737.

Rossmoore, William, and Samuel Koenigsberg. "Habeas Corpus and the Indigent Prisoner," *Rutgers Law Review*, 11 (Spring, 1957) 611.

Smith, Reginald Heber. "The English Legal Assistance Plan," *American Bar Association Journal*, 35 (June, 1949) 270.

Stewart, William Scott. "The Public Defender System Is Unsound in Principle," *Journal of the American Judicature Society*, 32 (Dec., 1948) 115.

Vanderbilt, Arthur T. "Our New Judicial Establishment: Record of First Year," *Rutgers Law Review*, 4 (Jan., 1950) 353.

————. "The First Five Years of the New Jersey Courts Under the Constitution of 1947," *Rutgers Law Review,* 8 (Spring, 1954) 289.

Willcox, Bertram F., and Edward J. Bloustein. "Account of a Field Study in a Rural Area of the Representation of Indigents Accused of Crime," *Columbia Law Review,* 59 (April, 1959) 551.

REPORTS

American Civil Liberties Union, Illinois Division. *Secret Detention by the Chicago Police.* Glencoe, Ill.: The Free Press, 1959.

Junior Section of the New Jersey Bar Association. "Report of Junior Section Committee on Indigent Criminal Representation," *New Jersey Law Journal,* 80 (May 16, 1957) 237.

National Commission on Law Observance and Enforcement. *Report on Lawlessness in Law Enforcement.* Washington: U.S. Government Printing Office, 1931.

Nye, George. *33rd Annual Report, Public Defender of Alameda County, Oakland, California.* [Reprinted, Chicago: National Legal Aid and Defender Association], 1959.

Onondaga County and the Public Defender System. Syracuse, N.Y. Onondaga County Department of Research and Development, 1955.

Report of the Attorney General's Committee on Poverty and the Administration of Federal Criminal Justice. Washington: U.S. Department of Justice, 1963.

Report of the Commission on Legal Aid of the Bar Association of the District of Columbia. Washington: Commission on Legal Aid of the Bar Association of the District of Columbia, 1958.

Report on the Assigned Counsel System in New Jersey. Trenton, N.J.: Administrative Office of the Courts, 1955.

Report on Legal Aid in New Jersey. Trenton, N.J.: Administrative Office of the Courts, 1955.

Special Committee of the Association of the Bar of the City of New York and the National Legal Aid and Defender Association (Special Committee to Study Defender Systems). *Equal Justice for the Accused.* Garden City: Doubleday, 1959.

U.S. Commission on Civil Rights. *Hearings in Detroit, Michigan Before the U.S. Commission on Civil Rights.* Washington: U.S. Government Printing Office, 1961.

U.S. Commission on Civil Rights. *Hearings in Los Angeles and San Francisco, California Before the U.S. Commission on Civil Rights.* Washington: U.S. Government Printing Office, 1961.

———. *1961 Commission on Civil Rights Report,* Book 5: *Justice.* Washington: U.S. Government Printing Office, 1961.

———. *The 50 States Report.* Washington: U.S. Government Printing Office, 1961.

UNPUBLISHED MATERIAL

Frankl, Kenneth R. *Philadelphia Voluntary Defender Association.* Report to the Special Committee to Study Defender Systems. New York, 1956.

———. *The Public Defender of the Rochester Court, Monroe County.* Report to the Special Committee to Study Defender Systems. New York, 1956.

———. *Representation of Indigent Defendants in the Criminal Courts of Chicago.* Report to the Special Committee to Study Defender Systems. New York, 1956.

———. *The Legal Aid Society of New York City With Particular Reference to New York County.* Report to the Special Committee to Study Defender Systems. New York, 1957.

———. *A Study in Contrast—The Public Defender Offices of Alameda and Marin Counties, California.* Report to the Special Committee to Study Defender Systems. New York, 1957.

——— and Lionel Spring. *Analysis of Questionnaire Submitted to Essex County Bar Association.* Report to the Special Committee to Study Defender Systems. New York, 1957.

——— and Arnold S. Trebach. *The Assigned Counsel System in Essex County, New Jersey.* Report to the Special Committee to Study Defender Systems. New York, 1956.

Trebach, Arnold S. *The Massachusetts Experience: Legal Aid in Criminal Cases.* Report to the Special Committee to Study Defender Systems. New York, 1957.

List of Cases Cited

Index

1